The Mozart Essays

The Mozart Essays

H.C. ROBBINS LANDON

with 21 illustrations

THAMES AND HUDSON

For
Eva Neurath
and
Thomas Neurath
with much love

© 1995 H.C. Robbins Landon

First published in the United States of America in 1995 by
Thames and Hudson Inc., 500 Fifth Avenue, New York,
New York 10110

Library of Congress Catalog Card Number 94-61396
ISBN 0-500-01653-4

Printed and bound in Slovenia

Contents

Preface

———————— ⟨∾⟩ ————————

IT SEEMS SCARCELY CREDIBLE THAT, TWO HUNDRED YEARS AFTER THE event, we should be uncovering at least one document of such importance as to render even more mysterious the final weeks preceding Mozart's death in December 1791. That document records the lawsuit brought by Prince Carl Lichnowsky, a rich aristocrat who has rightly gone down in history as Beethoven's long-suffering patron; it was registered at the Niederösterreichisches Landrecht (Lower Austrian Provincial Court) on 12 November 1791, but was never referred to in legal documents concerned with Mozart's death, nor was there any known record of the Prince's action to recover a substantial sum of money – which Mozart was ordered to pay. This absence makes the whole affair extremely curious, for the ramifications and conditions of the court's decision may have literally speeded Mozart to his early grave. And the effects of the composer's death on Lichnowsky should not be underestimated. The story as we now know it is recounted and illustrated here (pp. 213ff.).

Other recently discovered documents are perhaps less dramatic, but one is nonetheless surprised that they are now coming to light. One of these, which is also of considerable interest, is a sheet of paper bearing Mozart's handwriting which seems to list a summary of his income and expenses for one particular year (1786 or 1787) and which has already become the subject of some controversy among Mozart scholars (see pp. 206ff.). Other developments are discussed in the essay on 'Some Recently Discovered Documents Concerning Mozart's Last Year', since I felt that the documents in question would be unknown to many readers who do not study the specialist periodicals in which such finds are usually published.

In making a selection of topics on which I have published essays during the past twenty-five years, I was motivated by several factors. Often new research has rendered previous studies on a particular subject out of date. One of these concerns the prophetic incidental music to *Thamos, König in Ägypten* (K.345), which has only recently begun to gain the popularity it so richly deserves. Apart from citing documentary evidence and an analytical study of the paper and handwriting of the autograph scores, I have tried to apply the Berensonian principle of using a clear stylistic 'fingerprint' to support the other evidence in a quite revealing fashion. In another approach, a survey of Mozart's Masonic music seemed appropriate because there is increasing confusion as to what works are clearly Masonic (e.g. the *Masonic Funeral Music* [K.477], which however is now the subject of increasing speculation concerning its origins and precise chronology) and what is clearly not (e.g. the Adagio and Fugue in C minor for strings [K.546], a composition of supreme importance for its period, 1788, but which has nothing to do with Masonry).

A subject on which recent scholarly – and musical – interest has concentrated is the sacred vocal music – and not just the Requiem, which is the subject of a separate essay – with revealing differences in our perception of the chronology, purpose and content of these many and varied works. Here again, it is unlikely that the average English-speaking reader will have followed all the specialized publications – some of which appear in German only – in which this music is examined.

In 1990, Nimbus Records commissioned a new edition of the Requiem from me. Nowadays, we are presented with a variety of substitutes for the traditional text of those parts which were completed by Mozart's pupil, Franz Xaver Süssmayr, but in fact he was not the only pupil to work on the composer's unfinished score. A hitherto much neglected reconstruction of part of the MS. was entered on Mozart's actual autograph by his pupil Joseph Eybler, whose musical intuition and brilliance exceeded by far that of Süssmayr. And it was found that a third pupil, F. J. Freystädtler, had been involved in reconstructing the Kyrie fugue. My aim in reconstructing the Requiem differently was to use exclusively the work of Mozart's own pupils, in order to add as little as possible which would reflect my own personality. (This approach, I might add, is quite different from that found in some of the other reconstructions currently in vogue, which include *inter alia* a completely new Benedictus movement, i.e. written without recourse to any material from Süssmayr.) The new edition was first performed in 1990 at the Cheltenham Festival by the Hanover Chorus and Hanover Band conducted by Roy Goodman; their account of the work was issued on record by Nimbus. Next, the Requiem was performed at the Memorial Service held in St Stephen's Cathedral, Vienna, on 5 December 1991 for the Bicentenary of

Mozart's death; that performance, by the Vienna Philharmonic Orchestra conducted by Sir Georg Solti, was recorded live by Decca International and released in 1992 on CD and audio-visual disc. The score was published by Breitkopf & Härtel of Leipzig, the original publishers of the Requiem in 1800. In the foreword to my edition, which I have included here, I tried to provide all the authentic or at least contemporary documents concerning the work, not least the spectacular new information that part of the Requiem – probably the Introitus and Kyrie fugue – was first performed at a memorial service for Mozart held in St Michael's Church, Vienna, ten days after the composer's death. The details of this memorial service – an event not previously known to have occurred – were only published just as the bicentenary celebrations were getting under way.

A word concerning the illustrations: apart from a selection of portraits and manuscript material relating to the essays, I have included some little-known engravings from a series originally published in a three-volume work entitled *Bildergalerie katholischer Misbräuche* [*sic*], *Bildergalerie klösterlicher Misbräuche* [*sic*] and *Bildergalerie weltlicher Misbräuche* [*sic*], Frankfurt and Leipzig, 1784 (vols. 1 and 2) and 1785 (vol. 3). Although these volumes were supposedly published in Germany, the contents and the illustrations seem rather to be placed in Austria and in particular in Vienna. Frequently, the engravings depict everyday events of the kind Mozart would have known and witnessed in the 1780s, often in an uncanny way (see pp. 71ff.). When I purchased this set from a Viennese antiquarian bookseller, I felt sure that readers would appreciate the topicality of the subject matter in connection with Mozart and that a selection of these scenes would enhance the present collection of essays. A list of the essays which have appeared previously is given on p. 237.

I hope, therefore, that English-speaking readers will find in this book much material that is new to them. The range of subject matter included in the essays perhaps reflects the inescapable fact that Mozart has now become one of the most thoroughly investigated of all composers – a consummate and versatile genius whose creative *œuvre* is also the most popular in the history of Western music.

Château de Foncoussières   H.C.R.L.
November 1994

Mozart

Mozart c'est l'art sensible, instinctif, enchanteur.
Il a si bien traduit la cosmique harmonie.
Il écoutait l'espace et c'est là son génie
D'avoir senti passer le souffle créateur.

Il captait tous les sons, l'esprit divinateur,
En inventait le rhythme et la grâce infinie.
Une pensée aimable, à l'élegance unie,
Inspirait ses motifs au style évocateur.

Soupirs, appels, échos, mouvements de tendresse,
Pérennité d'accents transparents de jeunesse,
De beauté, d'idéal et d'amour si touchant,

Musique instrumentale, ineffable lyrisme
où fondent en vibrant tous les éclats du prisme:
Mozart! C'est bien la danse éclose avec le chant.

Alphonsine Binda

Alphonsine Binda, now living in retirement in Vichy, has published over two hundred poems and has been awarded prizes by a number of French city authorities, including Nice, Marseilles, Pau and Annecy, as well as by the Association Belgo-Hispanique.

The Essays

Salzburg in 1756:
the world into which Mozart was born

W OLFGANG AMADEUS MOZART WAS BORN ON A BITTERLY COLD
day in January 1756 – 'a miracle which God caused to be
wrought in Salzburg', wrote his father Leopold. Salzburg is a
beautiful Baroque city and the basis of its economic prosperity, dating back
to Roman times, was also the origin of its name: the exportation of salt (*Salz*
= salt, *Burg* = castle, stronghold). It stood at a great crossroads between east
and west, north and south, a fact which in many ways made it much less
provincial than its size would suggest (nowadays it is the thriving capital of
the Austrian *Land* Salzburg with a population of well over 100,000). The
city was the seat of a prince-archbishop and belonged to that curious phenomenon called the Holy Roman Empire of German Nations (i.e. quite different from the Roman Empire under which the city later known as
Salzburg had begun to flourish), a loose federation founded by Charlemagne
in 800, which included two kingdoms, duchies, principalities, counties and
independent imperial cities. The empire's ruler had almost always been a
member of the Habsburg family. In 1756 the Emperor ruling this vast terri-
tory, which stretched from the Baltic and North Seas to the Alps and
included most of the present-day Czech Republic and Slovakia, Romania,
Poland, the former Yugoslavia and part of Russia, was Francis Stephen of
Lorraine (reigned 1740–65). He was the consort of Empress Maria Theresa
(reigned 1740–80), herself the mother of sixteen children and as joint sovereign a *Landesmutter* (literally, mother of the nation) as well. On a visit to
Vienna in 1762, the boy Mozart was to sit on her lap and kiss her: he knew a
good motherly soul when he saw one.

Austria formed a large and vital part of the Holy Roman Empire. Within
and under it Salzburg was both a secular and an ecclesiastical seat of government: the Archbishop held sway over not only the Church but also *Land*
Salzburg; he was elected by the cathedral chapter. When Mozart was born,

the incumbent was Siegmund, Count von Schrattenbach (reigned 1753–71), who was to become a sympathetic and tolerant patron of the Mozart family, allowing them extended leaves of absence when they travelled all over Europe to present to an astonished series of courts the two greatest *Wunderkinder* of their age, Wolfgang and his elder sister Maria Anna ('Nannerl', as she was known in the family).

There existed in Austria a large and powerful aristocracy, which was usually considered to have three sections: namely, the 'high' nobility, the counts and the barons. The 'high' nobility, princes of the Holy Roman Empire such as the Esterházys, the Liechtensteins, the Schwarzenbergs or the Colloredos, were fabulously wealthy and owned vast estates. Such a family lived in a large town palace, usually in Vienna, but perhaps also in Prague or other, smaller cities, which they inhabited in the winter months; they also owned beautiful summer estates, often in Hungary or Bohemia. They had hundreds of servants and often employed a private orchestra or even, like the Esterházys, an entire opera company. Most if not all of the male members of the family pursued governmental careers – they staffed the principal positions of the *corps diplomatique* and were often heads of government departments – or army careers. They tended to intermarry with other families of their own class or form liaisons with members of foreign aristocracy. Although many of the marriages were arranged, one notable exception was Prince Paul Anton Esterházy, who enjoyed a brilliant military as well as diplomatic career, and married the Italian lady of his love, a Marchesa di Lunati-Visconti (a member of the highest Italian nobility).

The members of the second class of the nobility, the counts, were often as old in lineage as the princes or dukes, and in some cases equally rich. They too were expected to be members of the government and filled key positions all over the monarchy. They mostly married others within this same class, but often their pretty ladies would marry into the highest nobility.

The third class consisted of the barons, and they too were often very ancient families. They filled many army posts as well as positions of relative importance within the Imperial government, whether central (= Vienna) or provincial (e.g. = Salzburg). Worthy civil servants were rewarded by being ennobled into this class.

The middle class, less numerous and powerful than in northern countries, was beginning to spread its wings in Austria when Mozart arrived on the scene. They were the shopkeepers, the factory owners, the developers, the businessmen, the 'do-ers' in society. They were soon to rival the nobility in their passion for, and support of, music: by the time Mozart arrived in Vienna in 1781, every self-respecting lady and gentleman sang, played the piano or another instrument, and to a standard which was often nearly professional. In this they were certainly influenced by the Habsburg court, where all the archdukes and archduchesses were accomplished, even brilliant, musicians: Emperor Joseph II, who was to engage Mozart as his *Kammermusicus* (chamber composer), could read a full score at sight and his brother, Leopold II, for whose coronation as King of Bohemia Mozart would write *La clemenza di Tito* in 1791, could conduct an orchestra from the harpsichord. Music was an elemental force in Austrian life, from the very top to the very bottom of society.

Naturally, most of the population were peasants, farming the rich soil of Hungary, cultivating vineyards along the Danube, and giving the enormous monarchy its cattle, sheep, its clothing and wood (there were then vast forests in Bohemia and Poland), and building its ships in northern Italy and Trieste (both part of the monarchy in those days). Their living conditions were better than those of the industrial proletariat in the nineteenth century; but in Hungary, for example, a contemporary reported that 'the people live like animals in underground caves ...'. Yet on the whole, food was cheap and plentiful in Mozart's Austria, and when he journeyed from Vienna to the Bohemian capital, Prague, he would have seen rich harvests and contented farmers along the way.

The nobility and, very soon, the middle classes followed French fashions. Those who could afford to went to Paris and bought their clothes where European fashion had its centre. Prince Paul Anton Esterházy and his wife, *née* Marchesa di Lunati-Visconti, spent 11,384 *livres*, or 4,552 florins in Austrian currency, on their Parisian clothes in 1759, which sum was more than ten times the salary of Joseph Haydn when he was engaged by the Esterházy family in 1761, and more than one-third of the total budget of its *Herrschaft* (estate) Eisenstadt for the year 1763. Leopold Mozart's salary when he was engaged as violinist in the Salzburg orchestra in 1747 was a mere 240 florins *per annum*.

In 1756 Austria was at war for the fourth time with Prussia: this was the Seven Years' War, which had had its origins in 1740, when Prussia had annexed the province of Silesia (now in Poland) from Austria, and Maria Theresa had, naturally, resisted. The French-Indian Wars in America, which were part of the 1756–63 conflict, were far more devastating in their effect than anyone could have imagined. The Seven Years' War started when Frederick II 'The Great' invaded Saxony, an Austrian ally, with 66,000 men on 29 August 1756. The new constellation of allies included Austria, the unlikely bed-fellow France (otherwise a traditional enemy), Russia, Sweden and most of the German princes; ranged against them were England, Prussia, the Princes of Hanover, Brunswick, Hesse-Cassel and Gotha.

In Austria, young men had no taste for the war and, in a royal decree of 24 July 1758, the churches were ordered

> to announce to the people that one has remarked with displeasure that many of the young unmarried men in the country, for fear of being draft-ed as soldiers, have inflicted bodily injuries to their limbs or even muti-lated themselves. It must be explained to them how irresponsible this is.

Austria was never a warlike nation: it is one of its most endearing charac-teristics. And if the war imposed a great financial drain on the monarchy, it is unlikely that its effects were much felt in faraway Salzburg, for whose citi-zens the capture of Quebec by General Wolfe must have been of only very remote interest.

Travel in those days was difficult and slow. Considering that until 1781, when Wolfgang settled in Vienna, he would spend significant periods trav-elling by stagecoach or *diligence*, one ought to realize the extent of the dis-comfort, boredom and even danger associated with travel. Carriages broke down, and in remote parts of Europe there were robbers and brigands ready to steal cash and jewels. In 1765 an official train of carriages took nine hours to travel from Mantua to Cremona, 8½ hours from Cremona to Milan, 7½ hours from Milan to Tortona and 9¾ hours from Tortona to Genoa – four days to make a journey that we could make easily in one day on the Italian *autostrade* – with a good lunch included.

In this highly organized and structured society, it was difficult to progress upwards socially. Musicians were still largely considered as servants and wore *livrée*; they were treated in noble households (like those of the Schwarzenbergs and the Esterházys) as 'house officers', which was a consid-erable step above. But even Mozart kissed his archbishop's hand at *levées* and was used to being addressed, like servants, in the third person. It was against this system that Mozart revolted, with little success financially, if with start-ling musical effect.

The Catholic Church was the state religion in Austria, and it dominated people's lives to an extraordinary extent. Each individual existed first in a church record, and ceased to exist in a similar document: you were baptized and confirmed into the Church and it was there that you married. Divorce began to be possible when Mozart lived in Vienna, but it was an extremely difficult process and socially amounted to a catastrophe. The Austrians have to this day an expression on that subject: 'Scheidung nie, Mord vielleicht' (Divorce never, murder perhaps). Music in church played a dominant role, too, and was Wolfgang's principal occupation in Salzburg.

One of the seminal philosophical forces of the Enlightenment, into which Mozart was born, was Freemasonry, which became increasingly more powerful as the century progressed. It is often said that Mozart became a Freemason because he could not find in the Church the spiritual strength that his questing intellect required; but that is to be doubted. On the evidence of Mozart's letters, and of many statements made by his wife Constanze, it is clear that the composer regarded the Church and its music as a central part of his life; and certainly his church music, now much better known in Anglo-Saxon countries than even fifty years ago, is a major aspect of his total *œuvre*. Leopold Mozart, Wolfgang's father, shared Joseph Haydn's concept of God as the centre of the universe, believing that it is He who has provided mankind with order, rationality, goodness and forgiveness. Haydn felt himself to be a small cog in God's mighty system. Mozart may have approached the problem from another viewpoint, but certainly his scores show order, rationality, goodness and, in his operas, a loving forgiveness which should serve as a model for everyone in any century.

1 Tobias Philipp, Freiherr von Gebler (1726–88), author of the play
Thamos, König in Ägypten, for which Mozart composed incidental
music in the 1770s (see pp. 38ff.); engraving by J.E. Mansfeld.
Private collection.

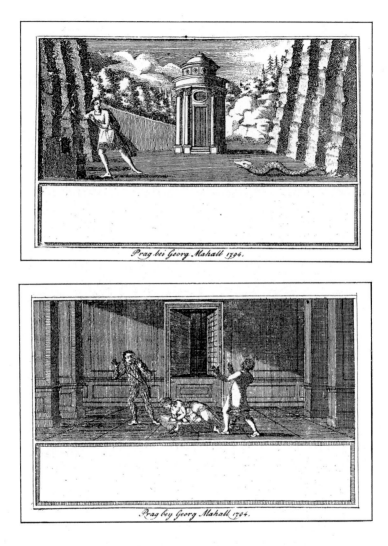

Prag bei Georg Mahall 1794.

Prag bey Georg Mahall 1794.

2, 3 Two scenes from *Die Zauberflöte*: Tamino and the snake, and Papageno and
Monostatos with Pamina. Engravings by Georg Mahall, Prague, 1794.
Österreichische Nationalbibliothek, Vienna.

4 The 'Paris' Symphony (K.297 [300a]): first page of the score showing the
string parts in a copyist's hand and the woodwind, brass and timpani parts
written by Mozart himself. See pp. 95ff.
Mozarteum, Salzburg.

Sinfonie von W. A. Mozart.
pag 1
Violini
Viola
Flauti
oboe
Corni
Basso
MOZARTEUM
1881

5 The 'Coronation' Mass (K.317): first page of the Oboe I part from Haydn's set
of MS. parts prepared by an Esterházy copyist. See pp. 180f.
Esterházy Archives, Eisenstadt.

6 The fragmentary Kyrie in C major (K.323 [Anh.15]), consisting of 37 bars: first
page of the autograph score. See p. 184.
Mozarteum, Salzburg.

7 The Motet 'Ave, verum corpus' (K.618): first page of the autograph, signed
and dated 'di Wolfgango Amadeo Mozart mpria: Baaden, li 17 di giugnio 1791'.
Österreichisches Staatsarchiv, Vienna.

Von Mozart und seiner Handschrift
MOZARTEUM
1881

di Wolfgango Amadeo Mozart
Baden. li 17 di giunio 1791
Ave verum Corpus
Adagio
sotto voce
Violini
Viola
Canto
Alto
Tenore
Basso
Organo e Basso
Ave ave verum Corpus natum de Maria virgine, vere passum immolatum in
Joseph Schellhamer

8–10 Two pages from the court record (now in the Hofkammerarchiv, Vienna) listing under entry no. 4384 (bottom left and top right) a summary of the judgment against Mozart in November 1791 in the lawsuit brought by Prince Carl Lichnowsky (seen, above left, in an anonymous portrait in oils) claiming repayment of debts totalling 1435 fl. 32 xr.; for details and a translation of the entry see pp. 213f.
The Prince's wife, Christiane (*née* Thun, one of the 'Three Graces'– see pl. 11), is portrayed opposite in an anonymous oil painting.
Both portraits Beethoven Society, Hradec u. Opavy, Czech Republic.

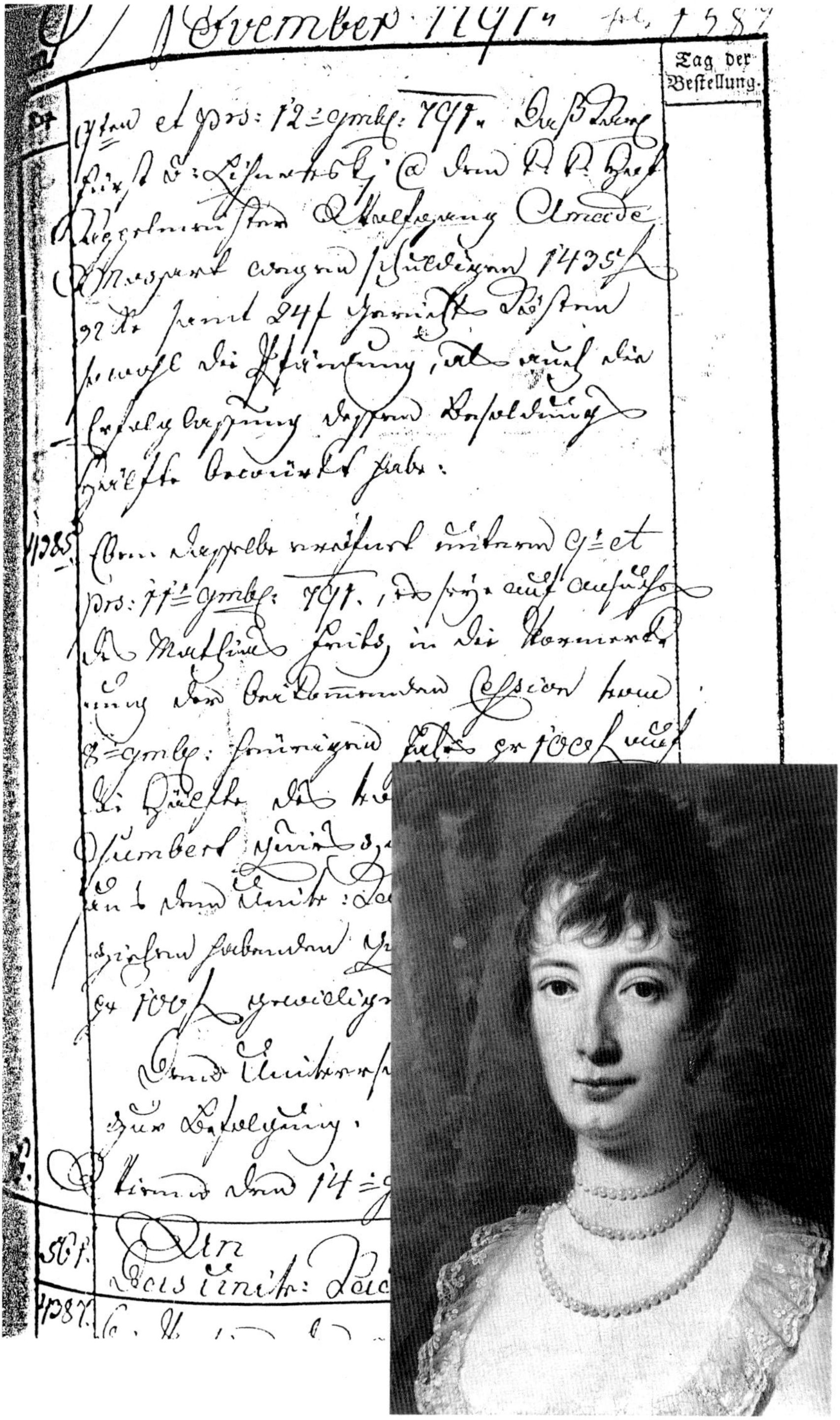
November 1791.
Tag der Bestellung.
1585
1587

11 The Countesses Thun: the sisters Elisabeth, Maria Christine
(Christiane, who married Prince Carl Lichnowsky – see pl. 8), and
Maria Carolina, known as the 'Three Graces' (see p. 215); group
portrait in oils by F.H. Füger.
Collection of Prince Razumovsky, Vienna.

Idomeneo, rè di Creta (K.366)

WHEN MOZART WAS COMMISSIONED IN 1780 TO WRITE *IDOMENEO* for the court of the Elector Palatine of Bavaria, Karl Theodor (recently removed from Mannheim to Munich), the young composer began work on the opera before setting out from Salzburg for the Bavarian capital – a journey of some 175 km (110 miles) – on 6 November. He left behind not only his father Leopold and his sister Nannerl, but also *Idomeneo*'s translator/librettist, the Court Chaplain Abbate Giambattista Varesco, and the ensuing correspondence between Wolfgang and Leopold (involving Varesco) gives us a uniquely detailed description of Wolfgang's methods of preparing and rehearsing a major operatic project. It also reveals Mozart's unerring sense of the essence of operatic timing: if a scene interrupted the flow of the action, it must be cut; if a whole magnificent aria – such as Elettra's exit scene in Act III – was too long, then it must be sacrificed. Mozart had opera in his blood and for the young composer this commission represented the chance of a lifetime.

The Munich cast was not, perhaps, ideal: Mozart could have had access to better singers in Milan, Naples or Vienna, but Munich now had one advantage which was quite simply overwhelming – the former Mannheim orchestra, always regarded as Germany's first, which had moved with the Elector. Its precision, the fine quality of its woodwind players, its sonority and brilliance were justly celebrated; and Mozart rose to the challenge. *Idomeneo* is the greatest score ever written for this orchestra.

On his arrival, Wolfgang went at once to call on the *Intendant* of the Munich Opera, Joseph Anton, Count Seeau, who had held that position under the late Elector Maximilian III Joseph, and had been responsible for Mozart's previous Munich opera, *La finta giardiniera* (1774–5). Seeau was well disposed towards the young composer, and recently influential members of the orchestra had been singing his praises – not least Kapellmeister Christian Cannabich. Seeau told Mozart that it had been decided to print Varesco's libretto in Munich for the performance.

'Some slight alterations will have to be made here and there,' wrote Wolfgang in his first Munich letter, dated 8 November 1780, 'and the recitatives will have to be shortened a bit. But *everything will be printed*. I have just one request to make of the Abbate. Ilia's aria in Act II, Scene 2, should be altered slightly to suit what I require. "Se il padre perdei, in te lo ritrovo", this verse could not be better.

'But now comes what has always seemed unnatural to me – I mean, in an aria – and that is, *a spoken aside*. In a dialogue all these things are quite natural, for a few words can be spoken aside hurriedly; but in an aria where the words have to be repeated, it has a bad effect ... we have agreed to introduce here an aria andantino with obbligatos for four wind instruments, that is, a flute, oboe, horn and bassoon. I beg you therefore to let me have the [newly written] text as soon as possible ...' Mozart then goes on to complain of his castrato, Vincenzo dal Prato, who was to sing the part of Idamante. But Dorothea Wendling, who was to sing Ilia, was enchanted with her beautiful opening scene and 'insisted on having it played three times in succession.'[1] Wolfgang went to the theatre, and listened to a performance of a new overture by Christian Cannabich; '... if you had heard it,' he told his father, 'you would have been as much pleased and excited as I was ... Do come soon, and hear and admire the orchestra ...'. Leopold answered and enclosed Varesco's revised version of Ilia's aria, 'which is, I think, quite suitable. If not, let me know at once.'[2]

In his second letter, dated 13 November, Wolfgang relates that 'As translations are so badly done here, Count Seeau would like to have the opera translated [from Varesco's Italian adaptation into German] in Salzburg. Only the arias need be in verse.' This was for the projected two-language libretto, and in fact the German version was prepared by a family friend, J.A. Schachtner. Mozart then adds, 'To Act I, Scene 8, Quaglio [the stage designer] has made the same objection that we made originally – I mean, that it is not fitting that the king should be quite alone in the ship. If the Abbé thinks that he can be reasonably represented in the terrible storm, forsaken by everyone, without a ship, quite alone and exposed to the greatest peril, then let it stand; but please cut out the ship, for he cannot be alone in one ... The second duet is to be omitted altogether – and indeed with more profit than loss to the opera. For, when you read through the scene, you will see that it obviously becomes limp and cold by the addition of an aria or duet, and very *gênant* for other actors who have to stand by doing nothing;

and besides, the noble struggle between Ilia and Idamante would be too long and thus lose its whole force.'[3]

In his next letter (15 November) Wolfgang describes how the tenor Anton Raaff, now aged sixty-six and destined for the title role, wanted some changes in his first aria, and no aria in Act III. 'In the 1st scene of Act II, Idomeneo has an aria or rather a sort of cavatina between the choruses. Here it will be *better* to have a mere recitative, well supported by the instruments. For in this scene, which will be the finest in the whole opera (on account of the action and the grouping which were settled recently with [the stage director and choreographer, Pierre] le Grand), there will be so much noise and confusion on the stage that an aria at this particular point would cut a poor figure – and moreover there is a thunderstorm, which is not likely to subside during Herr Raaff's aria, is it? ... But to my molto amato castrato dal Prato I shall have to teach the whole opera. He has no notion of how to sing a cadenza effectively, and his voice is so uneven.'[4] In that same letter Mozart relates that Count Seeau had presented him to the Elector after lunch on Sunday, and that the Elector was 'very gracious' and said: 'I am glad to see you here again.' Mozart courteously answered that he would do his best to retain the Elector's good opinion of him, whereupon he clapped Mozart on the shoulder and said: 'Oh, I have no doubt whatever that all will go well.'

Leopold wrote on 18 November, enclosing more alterations made by the unwilling Varesco after being firmly coerced by Leopold, who had some good ideas of his own to contribute. 'Idamante must not say (as Varesco makes him do) that he has witnessed the glory of his father; he must say the exact opposite, that is, that *he regrets not having been able to witness the great deeds and the glory of his father*. You must note all these points in your copy immediately, so that when you are composing the music, none of them may be overlooked.' Raaff was promised a new aria and 'His former one, between the choruses, will now be altered to a spirited recitative, which can be accompanied, if necessary, by thunder and lightning ...'[5] 'One more important point. If there is anything else to be added,' concludes the ever prudent Leopold, 'you must let me know by the next post, for Varesco cannot go on copying the text for the printer as he has been doing and then have to throw it aside and start afresh. So you must consider carefully whether it can now stand as it is, particularly as the German translation ought to be done in Salzburg ...'

Wolfgang reassures his father in a letter of 24 November: 'Do not worry, dearest father, about my opera. I trust that all will go well. No doubt it will be attacked by a small cabal, who in all probability will be covered with ridicule; for the most distinguished and influential families of the nobility are on my side, and the leading musicians are one and all for me. I cannot tell you what a good friend Cannabich is – how active and successful! ... Do try to come to Munich soon. If only the [in code: Archbishop] were not so ...Why, we can all live together. I have a large alcove in my bedroom, which has two beds. These would do capitally for you and me. As for my sister, all we need do is get a stove put in the other room, [the cost of] which will only be a matter of four or five gulden; for, even if we were to heat the stove in my room until it is red-hot and leave the doors open into the bargain – still the other room would not be endurable, for it is bitterly cold here.

'Do ask Abbate Varesco if we may not break off at the chorus in Act II, "Placido è il mar", after Elettra's first verse when the chorus has been repeated ... for it is really far too long.'[6] Mozart made this vital and dramatic change, of course, though Varesco's new aria for Raaff pleased neither the composer nor the singer, who quoted an aria from Metastasio's libretto for *Achille in Sciro* as a model. Then Wolfgang continues: 'Tell me, don't you think that the speech by the subterranean voice [the Oracle, Act III, Scene 10] is too long? Consider it carefully. Picture to yourself the theatre, and remember that the voice must be terrifying – must penetrate – that the audience must believe that it really exists. Well, how can this effect be produced if the speech is too long, for in this case the listeners will become more and more convinced that it means nothing. If the speech of the Ghost in *Hamlet* were not so long, it would be far more effective ...' Mozart made several drafts of this ghostly number, in which he was soon involved with Count Seeau himself. He had a further practical request to put to his father: 'For the march in Act II, which is heard in the distance, I require mutes for the trumpets and horns, which are unobtainable here. Will you send me one of each by the next mail, so that I may have copies made?'[7]

Leopold evidently thought that the strain of Munich might be too great for Wolfgang. 'Should you fall ill, *which God forbid,*' he wrote on 30 November, 'do not hide it from me, so that I may come at once and look after you. If I had been with your mother during her illness [in Paris in 1778], she might still be alive; but no doubt her hour had come, and so I had to be absent. Here we see the hand of God, which, however, we recognize only in our hours of need and lose sight of at other times …' Leopold now begins to resort to strategy when dealing with the cuts in *Idomeneo*. '… As for the chorus "Placido è il mar", you may stop where you like; but remember that everything must be printed in the libretto.'[8]

Wolfgang now held his first orchestral rehearsal which, he reported, 'went off extremely well. There were only six violins in all, but we had the requisite wind instruments … This day week, we are to have another rehearsal, when we shall have twelve fiddlers for the first act … I cannot tell you how delighted and surprised they all were. Count Senheim said to me: *"I assure you that though I expected a great deal from you, I really did not expect that".* Mozart also quotes a remark by the oboist Ramm, another of his admirers, who said: ' *"I must honestly confess that no music has ever made such an impression on me …"'* He further states that 'Yesterday morning, Mr Raaff came to see me again in order to hear the aria in Act II ['Fuor del mar']. The fellow is as infatuated with it as a young and ardent lover might be with his fair one …"[9]

Leopold, acting as go-between for the composer and his librettist, writes on 4 December, 'All that you have pointed out shall be done. You know that *I too thought the subterranean speech too long.* I have given Varesco my candid opinion and it will now be made as short as possible …' Speaking of his son's style, Leopold says, '… when your music is performed by a mediocre orchestra it will always be the loser, because it is composed with so much discernment for the various instruments and is far from being commonplace, as, on the whole, Italian music is …'[10]

The Empress Maria Theresa had died and in many parts of the Austro-Hungarian monarchy the theatres were closed during the period of official mourning, but Wolfgang reports happily on 5 December that 'the death of the Empress does not affect my opera in the least, for none of the theatres [here] have been closed and plays are being performed as usual. The entire mourning is not to last longer than six weeks … I beg you to have my *black suit* thoroughly brushed, shaken out, done up as well as possible and sent to me by the next mail coach – for next week everyone will be in mourning …' There were requests for still more changes to be made by poor Varesco. Domenico de' Panzacchi wanted his recitative in Act III lengthened by a couple of lines, 'which owing to the *chiaro e oscuro* and his being a good actor will have a capital effect …'[11]

Leopold had meanwhile found the trumpet mutes and despatched them on 7 December, noting that 'the horn mutes belong to the two watchman's apprentices, who at the moment are not in Salzburg … I enclose Varesco's whole text with the exception of the last aria for Raaff …'[12] Two days later, he writes again, 'Here is the suit, such as it is. I had to have it patched quickly, for the whole taffeta lining of the waistcoat was in rags …'[13]

A few days thereafter, he sends a note from Varesco and also the aria for Raaff in Act III, 'Torna la pace', which, in the event and after all the trouble it caused, was cut. 'Act I with the translation and possibly Act II will arrive in Munich next week by mail coach … I advise you when composing to consider not only the musical but also the *unmusical public*. You need to remember that for every *ten real connoisseurs* there are a *hundred ignoramuses*. So do not neglect the so-called *popular* style …'[14]

Meanwhile, Leopold was hearing glowing reports of his son's new opera. On 15 December, he mentions that Johann Baptist Beecke, the flautist in the Munich court orchestra, had written to a friend in Salzburg telling him that *'tears of joy and delight came into his eyes when he heard it* [Act I], *and that all the performers maintained that this was the most beautiful music they had ever heard, that it was all new and strange.'* To this Leopold added, *'Knowing your work as I do,* I am perfectly certain that these statements are not empty compliments …'[15]

Wolfgang reports on 19 December to Salzburg: 'I have received safely the last aria for Raaff (who sends greetings to you), the two trumpet mutes, your letter of the 15th, and the pair of socks. The second rehearsal went off as well as the first. The orchestra and the whole audience discovered to their delight that the second act was actually more expressive and original than the first … the work is almost finished. Only three arias, the final chorus of Act III, the overture and the ballet are still lacking – and then – adieu partie! …'

Even at this stage Mozart was still pruning text (and music), reporting to his father that 'The scene between father and son in Act I and the first scene in Act II between Idomeneo and Arbace are both too long. They would certainly bore audiences, particularly as in the first scene both the actors are bad, and in the second, one of them is … Those scenes are being printed as they stand. But I should like the Abbate to indicate how they may be shortened – and as drastically as possible – for otherwise I shall have to shorten them myself. These two scenes cannot remain as they are – I mean, when set to music …'[16]

This time, Leopold sided with Varesco, explaining their arguments in a long letter to Wolfgang, who replied two days after Christmas: '... In regard to the two scenes which are to be shortened, it was not my suggestion, but one to which I have consented – my reason being that Raaff and dal Prato spoil the recitative by singing it without any spirit or fire, and so monotonously. They are the most wretched actors ever to have walked on a stage. I had a desperate row the other day with Seeau about the inexpediency, inconvenience and the practical impossibility of omitting anything. However, everything is to be printed as it is, to which he at first refused *absolument* to agree ... The last rehearsal was splendid. It took place in a spacious room at Court. The Elector was there too. This time we rehearsed with the whole orchestra (I mean, of course, with as many players as can be accommodated in the opera house). After the first act the Elector called out to me quite loudly, Bravo! When I went to kiss his hand, he said " *This opera will be charming and cannot fail to do you honour.*" And later the Elector said with a laugh: " *Who would believe that such great things could be hidden in so small a head?*" Mozart was having a certain amount of trouble with Raaff, who was unhappy at the idea of a quartet in the last act, 'Andrò ramingo e solo'. 'The more I think of this quartet, as it will be performed on stage, the more effective I consider it; and it has pleased all those who have heard it played on the clavier. Raaff alone thinks it will be completely ineffective. He said to me when we were alone together: "Non c'è da spianer la voce" [You can't let yourself go in it]. As if in a quartet the words should not be spoken much more than sung. That kind of thing he does not understand at all. I simply said: "My very dear friend, if I knew of one single note which ought to be altered in this quartet, I would alter it at once. But so far there is nothing in my opera with which I am as pleased as this quartet; and when you have once heard it sung in concert, you will talk differently. I have taken great pains to serve you well in your two arias; I shall do the same with your third one – and shall hope to succeed. But as far as trios and quartets are concerned, the composer must have a free hand." Whereupon he said he was satisfied.' Mozart notes that 'I have had my black suit turned, for it was really very shabby. Now it looks quite presentable.'[7]

Leopold, by now thoroughly alarmed at the amount of suppression to which Wolfgang was subjecting the libretto, wrote on 29 December: 'A Happy New Year! *I absolutely insist* that everything Varesco has written *shall* be printed. The omissions amount to only a few lines [little did he know!] ... I wish we could correct the proofs together in Salzburg. There is nothing more objectionable than to find in a book a number of misprints, which often make the meaning quite unintelligible. It would be a good thing if you yourself were to undertake to read through the revised proofs before the final printing ... I assume that you will choose very deep wind instruments to accompany the subterranean voice. How would it be if, after the slight subterranean rumble, the instruments *sustained, or rather began to sustain, their notes piano and then made a crescendo such as might almost inspire terror, while after this and during the decrescendo the voice would begin to sing?* Owing to the rumble, which must be short, and rather like the shock of a thunderbolt, which sends up the figure of Neptune, the attention of the audience is aroused; and this attention is intensified by the introduction of a quiet, prolonged and then swelling and very alarming wind-instrument passage, and finally becomes strained to the utmost when, behold! *a voice* is heard. Why, I seem to see and hear it ..."[18]

Wolfgang was obviously very impressed by his father's depiction of the scene and followed his advice to the letter, using an orchestra with three trombones and two horns. This first version, the length of which obviously bothered him, consisted of seventy bars in Adagio. We shall hear more of this oracle scene anon.

In his letter of 30 December, Wolfgang tells his father 'I have not quite finished the third act, and, as there is no extra ballet, but only an appropriate divertissement, in the opera, I have the honour of composing music for that as well; but I am glad of it, for now all the music is by the same composer ...' Then he reports that the Elector said at court in the evening after rehearsal: 'I was quite surprised. No music has ever made such an impression on me. It is magnificent music.' Next the quartet is discussed, and the difficulty of getting dal Prato to sing it properly. 'Raaff is delighted that he was mistaken about the quartet and no longer doubts its effectiveness.' There was still great discussion about the last aria for Raaff, who now put forward a hair-raising scheme to substitute an aria from Metastasio's libretto for *Natal di Giove*. 'No one knows the words,' said Raaff, 'and we can keep quiet about it.' Mozart then adds: 'He fully realizes we cannot expect the Abbate to alter this aria a third time, and he will not sing it as it stands ..."[19]

On 3 January 1781, he writes to his father, '... My head and my hands are so full of Act III that it would be no wonder if I were to turn into a third act myself ...' He acknowledges receipt of Varesco's revised aria for Raaff, which meant that it would not be necessary to print one version and sing another. But by this time Varesco was – with a good deal of justification – very annoyed. Leopold reports that on New Year's Day, after church, he paid his calls and 'then went to see Varesco at half-past ten. He was horribly angry and said the most foolish things, as Italians or half-Italians do …'[20]

By 18 January Wolfgang was able to report that 'the rehearsal of Act III went off splendidly. It was considered much superior to the first two acts. But the libretto is too long and consequently the music also (an opinion which I have always held). Therefore Idamante's aria, *"No, la morte io non pavento"* is to be omitted; in any case it is out of place there … The omission of Raaff's last aria too is even more regretted; but we must make a virtue of necessity. The speech by the oracle is still far too long and I have therefore shortened it; but Varesco need not know anything of this, because it will be printed just as he wrote it …'[21]

Leopold and Nannerl left Salzburg on 25 January to be present at Wolfgang's *Idomeneo*, produced at Munich on 29 January with the following cast:

Idomeneo	Anton Raaff
Idamante	Vincenzo dal Prato
Ilia	Dorothea Wendling
Elettra	Elisabeth Wendling
Arbace	Domenico de' Panzacchi

The libretto by Varesco had been adapted from Antoine Danchet's French-language *tragédie lyrique*, first produced in Paris in 1712 with music by André Campra. Mozart was, of course, quite right in thinking it too long, but in the end the situation had become so out of hand that, having printed a two-language libretto with parallel German and Italian texts that included virtually the whole of the opera, Count Seeau was now obliged to print an entire new Italian libretto with the text as it was actually performed in Mozart's final version. Even at the last minute there were problems. Mozart required trombones only in the oracle scene in Act III, and Count Seeau seems to have objected to the unnecessary costs. Mozart wrote that he had forced Seeau to allow the trombones, but in the final printed libretto the oracle scene's text agrees only with a musical version for two clarinets, two bassoons and two horns (this was the fourth version of this music).

The actual performance was probably directed by the leader Christian Cannabich, with Mozart at the harpsichord. The sole extant review, in the

Munich *Staats-, gelehrten und vermischten Nachrichten* of 1 February 1781, mentions only that the première took place on the 29th ult., and that the 'composition, text and translation are all products of Salzburg. The decorations, of which the view of the harbour and Neptune's temple were executed in capital fashion, are masterpieces of our famous theatrical designer ... Lorenz Quaglio, which excited everyone's attention.'[22]

From 7 to 10 March 1781 Leopold, Nannerl and Wolfgang Mozart paid a visit to Augsburg (Leopold's birthplace), staying at the Holy Cross Abbey. There Wolfgang and Nannerl played four-hand duets on the fortepiano. When they returned to Munich, it was time to go their respective ways – Leopold and Nannerl to Salzburg and Wolfgang to Vienna, where the Archbishop of Salzburg, Hieronymus Colloredo, awaited him.

Idomeneo seems to have been a success in Munich, but after the final performance (probably on 26 February 1781) the work disappeared and, except for a private performance in Vienna in 1786, it was never heard again in Mozart's lifetime. It was a curious and cruel fate for a masterpiece over which the composer and his associates in Salzburg and Munich had laboured so well and so successfully.

This work is unique among Mozart's mature operas in many ways. In it there are more crowd scenes and 'action' choruses than in any of his other mature stage-works. Mozart shows that he was acutely aware of the practical problems, musical and dramatic, that such large-scale crowd scenes bring with them; and he solves them with consummate mastery, from the amazing storm chorus in Act I, 'Pietà! Numi, pietà', to the ravishingly beautiful E major chorus of Act II, 'Placido è il mar, andiamo', and the frightening final chorus in this act, 'Corriamo, fuggiamo', and, most tellingly perhaps, in the fateful 'Oh voto tremendo' (Act III), with its sinister muted trumpets.

Idomeneo was the first of Mozart's operas to make full use of a large and superbly trained opera orchestra, with its pairs of flutes, oboes, clarinets, bassoons, horns (later increased to four), trumpets, kettledrums and the usual strings. To have the ex-Mannheim orchestra was obviously a source of constant inspiration to him while writing the score. Particularly the woodwinds are used with panache and daring – one thinks at once of Ilia's Aria in Act II, 'Se il padre perdei', with its quartet of wind instruments used in the manner of a Mannheim sinfonia concertante (flute, oboe, bassoon and horn, the latter using the new 'stopped note' technique, whereby the note may be lowered by placing the right hand in the bell of the instrument, thus enabling the player to provide notes not otherwise available to him).[23]

There is another aspect of *Idomeneo* which is unique. Although it is a 'number opera', that is with the usual division of recitative (either *secco* or accompanied by the orchestra), aria, duet, etc., the ongoing action suggested to Mozart to blur these divisions. Many numbers lead on to the next without a break. The E major chorus when Elettra is supposed to sail away ('Placido è il mar') breaks off into a *recitativo secco* and then into the trio 'Pria di partir'. This in turn leads into the storm chorus with four horns, 'Qual nuovo terrore!'. That chorus stops abruptly to move at once into Idomeneo's grand accompanied recitative, 'Io solo errai', while this then takes us straight into the final chorus of the act, 'Corriamo, fuggiamo', again with four horns, trumpets and drums. It is thus tightly integrated music of a kind which is only comparable to the quite different finale writing of the later Vienna operas (*Le nozze di Figaro, Don Giovanni*, etc.). Altogether, in operatic terms *Idomeneo* displays a sense of unity, a dramatic cohesiveness, which Mozart rivalled only in *Così fan tutte*, composed eight years later.

It was seen that Mozart himself thought highly of the Quartet in Act III. Many years after his death, Constanze talked of *Idomeneo* to two British visitors, Vincent and Mary Novello, who had arrived in Salzburg in 1829 to present a gift of money from the London Philharmonic Society to Nannerl, who was by then ill and blind. Both Vincent and Mary Novello kept diaries, in which they recorded two interesting statements made by Constanze about the opera.

[Vincent Novello's Diary]

Question. Which were the greatest favourites with him of his *own* compositions?

She said he was fond of 'Don Giovanni', 'Figaro' and perhaps most of all 'Idomeneo', as he had some delightful associations with the time and circumstances under which it was composed.

[Mary Novello's Diary]

She told us that after their marriage they paid a visit to Salzburg and were singing the Quartet of 'Andrò ramingo' when he was so overcome that he burst into tears and quitted the chamber and that it was some time before she should console him.[24]

As the editor of the Novello Diaries (Rosemary Hughes) writes, singing the quartet, 'in which the young Idamante faces exile and disaster, had brought upon him a wave of overwhelming and unaccountable emotion, like a presage of woe.'

Mozart's style had undergone a profound change when he returned to Salzburg after his frustrating and costly journey to France in 1778. In 1779 and 1780, he returned to his native town with a musical vocabulary which had doubled in size. There was a dark richness to many of the works of these two last brilliant years in Salzburg – such as the slow movement of the Sinfonia Concertante (K.364) or the C major church music ('Coronation' Mass, K.317, *Missa Solemnis*, K.337, and the two Vespers settings, K.321, 339) or the final Salzburg Symphony (in C, K.334), with its ominous development section in the first movement. Mozart goes a step further in the music for *Thamos, König in Ägypten* (K.345), the final version of which was completed in 1779/80 in Salzburg – here for the first time we find music which is sometimes of frightening violence, with sinister overtones which are quite new in Mozart ('Ihr Kinder des Staubes'): this is the real precursor of *Idomeneo*, with its relentless pace and its dark-hued grandeur (see the separate essay on *Thamos*, pp. 38ff.).

*   *   *

In 1786, Mozart, after several other failed attempts, persuaded Prince Carl Auersperg to put on a concert version of *Idomeneo* during Lent (13 March) – in concert because, although the Prince had his own private theatre, opera performances on a public stage were not permitted during Lent. Amateurs and talented aristocrats took part, hence Vienna's cast was (as far as it is known) as follows:

Idomeneo	Giuseppe Antonio Bridi
Idamante	Baron Pulini
Ilia	Anna von Pufendorf
Elettra	Maria Anna Hortensia, Countess Hatzfeld

Count Hatzfeld, a brilliant violin player and the pupil of Pierre Vachon (whose quartets, published in Paris, were admired), assisted: Elettra was his step-brother's wife, who had sung in Gluck's *Alceste* two months earlier under the composer's direction.

The role of Idamante was now sung by a tenor, Baron Pulini, for whom Mozart wrote a new beginning to Act II, the Recitative and Aria, 'Non più' and 'Non temer, amato bene' (K.490), with a movingly beautiful violin solo for Count Hatzfeld. Mozart also wrote a new version of the love duet between Ilia and Idamante in Act II, 'Spiegarti non poss'io' (K.489). Unfortunately, the complete score of this Vienna version does not exist, so that details of the performance remain obscure. It is, however, interesting that Mozart, in the middle of his work on *Le nozze di Figaro* (Vienna, 1 May 1786), was able once again to steep himself in the quite different world of *Idomeneo*, for the two new scenes and the extant revisions of other numbers accord well with the dramatic organization of the original Munich score. Figaro does not usurp Idomeneo.

To sum up, we quote the conclusion that David Cairns draws in his admirable article on the subject:[25]

Humanity may need, as never before, the sanity, the life-renewing laughter of Mozart's comedies, but it needs too that handful of special masterpieces whose qualities of courage, hope, compassion and honesty of vision make them its natural parables and sacred texts. *Idomeneo* is one of those works. Perhaps Edward Dent was right: it should never be taken for granted, but always 'attended in a spirit of pilgrimage'. It is a secular Passion, with power to chasten and uplift a distracted age.

Mozart's Incidental Music to

Thamos, König in Ägypten (K.345 [336a])

I N RECENT YEARS THIS EXTRAORDINARY MUSIC, COMPOSED FOR A FIVE-
act play by Tobias Philipp, Freiherr von Gebler (1726–86), and partly
reworked in 1773, 1775–6 and 1779–80, yet far ahead of its time, has been
receiving a great deal of long-overdue attention. The chronology of the choruses and other pieces has proved to be one of the most difficult problems of
Mozart research, involving a study of eighteenth-century theatrical practice,
as well as detailed examination of the paper, handwriting and watermarks of
the autographs. Much of the information included here does not appear
even in the revised 6th edition of the Köchel Catalogue (1984). I therefore
felt that in view of the work's new-found popularity, readers might find a
summary of the latest research useful.

The contemporary documentary sources concerning *Thamos*, as far as
they are known at present, are:

1 Letter from the play's author, Tobias Philipp, Freiherr von Gebler, to the
literary critic and author Christoph Friedrich Nicolai in Berlin, dated
Vienna, 31 May 1773:

> … If I should be so honoured as to have my Thamos performed there [in
> Berlin], I can provide music for the choruses which is not badly written
> and has been thoroughly revised by Herr Ritter Gluck.

The choruses were composed by Johann Tobias Sattler, who died in
Vienna on 19 December 1774. The original textbook, of which the first four
pages are reproduced in facsimile in the *NMA*, Series II, Werkgruppe 6,
Band I (edited by Harald Heckmann), is entitled 'Thamos, / König in
Egypten / Ein heroisches Drama / in fünf Aufzügen / [design with three
putti] / [lines] / Prag und Dresden, 1773. / In der Waltherischen
Hofbuchhandlung'. The copy reproduced, formerly in Leopold Mozart's
library, is now in the Mozarteum, Salzburg. The Foreword reads as follows:

The names Menes, Ramesses, Thetmos (here, because of the easier pro-
nunciation, Thamos) do not follow each other directly in any dynasty of
Egyptian kings. But one is aware of the uncertainty and darkness which
prevail in the oldest history of this kingdom and how variously, according to Julius Africanus, Eusebius, Josephus, Eratosthenes and other histo-
rians, the succession of Egyptian kings has been treated. In most of their
chronicles we find only the names, and in more than one dynasty not
even that has come down to us. The poet thus enjoys an open field, on
which to place at will names and dates. He placed them, according to his
plan, in the further point of past history. In those times when supersti-
tion had not yet debased reason to the point where crocodiles, cats and
even squills were the object of worship by entire populations, but where
idolatry, closer to its origins and to a certain extent purer, was limited to
favourable constellations or paganism. He [the present author] could
therefore present priests without [their customary] shaven heads and eye-
brows, which create a very odd impression on stage. He could invent
sacred vows and whole groups of consecrated virgins; he could have
hymns sung in the temples: although he has read that Egyptian priests
comported themselves in such an extraordinary fashion apparently only
in later periods,[1] and that during their religious services there was no
music. If this were the place, he could, especially concerning this last
point, express not unfounded doubts. But he is content to some extent to
rebuff criticisms levelled against his abuse of the costumes worn. Who
has demanded a strict observance of such things during theatrical performances? In like fashion one may be indulgent regarding the *place where
the action occurs*, about which Syncellus tells us that a line of kings had
their residence at Heliopolis: although other writers only record the
Tanites, Memphians, Dispolites, or the Thebans and Sahidicians.

Otherwise, may the present attempt, in which sundry new devices
were risked, be received by the public with indulgence.

A word concerning the choruses of the first and fifth acts. If one miss-
es in them the high flight of ideas, the accuracy and beauty of poetic
expression which the circumstances might have demanded, the author
may take leave to suggest that poets who enjoy a close relationship with
the Antique might be minded to deliver a more successful attempt themselves rather than act as stern judges.

Further editions of the textbook are: Vienna 1774, 'beim Logenmeister', i.e. for the Court theatres; *Theater der Deutschen*, 18. Theil, 1776, Königsberg and Leipzig, 1776, J.J. Kanter; and *Tamos Rè d'Egitto Dramma eroico* ... da Gio. Luigi Baroni [*sic*] de Berghof Secretario di S.A. il Principe di Colloredo, Vienna 1780, J.J. Jahn (a copy is attached to Mozart's autograph MS.).

Although no copy of Sattler's choruses is known to have survived, we may in fact have his music thanks to two spurious editions of two of the choruses to *Thamos* published in Bonn under Mozart's name by Simrock (publisher's number 2727, *c.* 1829) and by the Musikalisches Magazin auf der Höhe, Braunschweig (Brunswick), Spehr, 3 Gesänge, Lieferung 3, XII No. 1, together with K.Anh.246 (C 8.06) and K.Anh.247 (C 8.07). The choruses are: No. 1, 'Schon weichet Dir, Sonne!', E flat, *Andante molto con gravitate*; and No. 2, 'Gottheit, über Alle mächtig', C major, *Langsam* – see Köchel Catalogue, 6th edition, Anh. 243 (C 7.02), for the incipits. These are the choruses for the first and fifth acts that Mozart was also to set, initially in 1773. Deutsch, *Dokumente*, p. 130.

2 Performance of *Thamos* in Preßburg on 11 December 1773. Report in the *Preßburger Zeitung*:

> On the 11th inst. their royal highnesses Archduchess Christine and her high consort Duke Albrecht of Sachsen-Teschen, together with their court and many members of the high nobility, again attended our theatre, where the Wahr Company gave the new heroic drama by Freyherr von Gebler, Imperial Royal Court Councillor, entitled 'Thamos, König in Egypten'. It was mounted with all the required splendour, insofar as the small size of the stage allowed. The sets required for this piece, the costumes suitable for the actors and actresses, the most harmonious music executed by many instruments in a very large orchestra, delighted the eye and the ear of the public. The playhouse was so exceptionally full that many could not take part in this delightful spectacle and had to be turned away.
>
> *Haydn Yearbook* VIII (1971), p. 169.

Nowhere is there any mention of which music was performed, but the large orchestra suggests that it might have been the new music by Mozart, which certainly existed by this time. The Wahr Troupe later (1774) went to Eszterháza for the summer, but there is no complete record of their repertoire; presumably, however, Wahr would have performed the same pieces as in Preßburg, for which see the list in Landon, *Haydn, Chronicle and Works: Haydn at Eszterháza 1766–1790*, p. 185.

3 Letter from Gebler to Nicolai, dated Vienna, 13 December 1773:

> ... I ... enclose in any case the music for Thamos, which was recently composed by a certain Sigr. Mozzart [*sic*]. It is his original concept and the first chorus is very fine.
>
> Deutsch, Dokumente, p. 131.

It seems, then, that the Preßburg performance could well have been the first in which the two new Mozart choruses, for the first and fifth acts, were performed. These choruses are now printed as No. 1a, 'Schon weichet Dir, Sonne!' (pp. 166ff.), and 6a, 'Gottheit, über Alle mächtig' (pp. 202ff.) in *NMA*. They are scored for four-part choir (SATB), 2 oboes, 2 bassoons, 2 horns, 2 trumpets, 3 trombones, timpani and strings.

4 Report in the *Historisch-Kritische Theaterchronik von Wien*, Vienna, 24 March 1774:

> On Easter Monday the German Theatre will be opened with the new tragedy by the writer of *The Minister* (Freyherr von Gebler) entitled: Thamos König in Egypten, with choruses composed by Herr Starzer. I await with pleasure the opportunity of devoting more time to this beautiful piece.

[The same, 13 April 1774:]

> The *Theaterchronik* made a serious mistake in its issue No. 1, where under miscellaneous notices it was stated that Herr Starzer wrote the choruses to Thamos. It was not Herr Starzer but Herr Mozart who wrote the music.
>
> On 4 April the German Theatre was opened with Thamos König von Egypten [*sic*] with a ballet by Herr Angiolini ... Thamos, a heroic drama in five acts is by the well-known and popular poet of [the plays] *The Minister* and *Klementine*. As in all the other pieces by this author, in Thamos his decent [*tugendhaftes*] heart speaks to us. The whole tragedy is full of warmth, full of the dignity of heroic poetry, and it does not have the excessive length of other tragedies produced here; for that reason alone, and especially considering our local poets, it is to be praised, and not least because of its sound dialogue, rich in thought.
>
> It consists of only five-and-a-half *Bogen* [*Bogen* = sheets, each making 4 pages].

Straight away in the Preface the author faces all objections with his own particular modesty – objections which some clever critics might wish to raise if they insist on judging everything in a false light. –

The caveat concerning the choruses in the first and fifth acts is no less praiseworthy, although in my opinion not necessary. They created their effect – for the music by Herr Karl Mozzart [*sic*] is finely and artistically composed – and more than that, I think, the author did not want. – Pity though that they were not better sung ....

[The same, 8 May 1774:]

Our German players will have the honour of appearing before the all-highest Court this year, and four times weekly. They began last Wednesday [4 May] with Thamos. The company usually receives a fee of 50 ducats for each performance [at the Theatre in the royal residence, Laxenburg Castle].

Deutsch, Dokumente, pp. 133f.

5   Letter from Gebler to Nicolai, dated Vienna, 14 February 1775:

… The good Magister Sattler, who composed the first music (I think, however, that I sent to Your Noble Self the better music by Mozzart [*sic*]) has meanwhile died of consumption.

Deutsch, Dokumente, p. 136.

6   *Theaterwochenblatt für Salzburg*, 17 January 1776:

On 3 January *Thamos*, a tragedy in five acts by Freyherr von *Gebler* … Following Klopstock, he made the experiment of putting the choruses of the Ancients into a heroic tragedy, and to connect the two in such a fashion that interest in the action is not thereby weakened. The composer of the choruses caused the fifth act to be over-long through repetitions. The choruses should be sung straight through and would be better if they were more varied. They could also be left out altogether without harming the piece, as happened in Vienna.

Deutsch, Dokumente, pp. 139f.

Despite the rather negative tone of this review, it is probable that it provides evidence of the second, 1775–6, version of Mozart's incidental music. Here we must consider recent studies of paper and handwriting, the results of which in relation to *Thamos* have been brilliantly summed up thanks to the combined efforts of Wolfgang Plath (one of *NMA*'s general editors) and

Alan Tyson, the former analyzing with the changing aspects of Mozart's handwriting (*Schriftchronologie*) and the latter examining paper and watermark types.[2]

Close study of the paper and watermarks of the autograph for *Thamos* yielded two results, the first of which led to the dating 1775–6 for the work's second version. Tyson writes as follows:

> The autograph sources are in Berlin (Staatsbibliothek Preussischer Kulturbesitz); they consist of the entr'actes on oblong-format paper and the choruses on upright-format paper. Most of the entr'actes are on a paper found also in K.243, the *Litaniae de venerabili altaris sacramento*, the autograph of which is dated 'March 1776', and in K.102, the finale that Mozart wrote at some undetermined time in order to make a symphony out of the overture to his April 1775 opera *Il Rè pastore*, K.208 (Köchel gives this the number K.213c and offers a tentative dating of August 1775). Only the entr'acte No. 7a is on a different paper: this is found elsewhere, folded differently to produce an upright-format shape, in the divertimento K.251, dated 'July 1776'. Thus the paper of the entr'actes is matched in other Mozart autographs from the year 1776. Plath dates them by the handwriting to '*c.* 1777'; there seems no doubt that they were written before the *grand voyage* of the years 1777–1779 to Paris and other places.

It follows, then, that the entr'actes were composed in 1775 or 1776 and *apparently* first performed in Salzburg in January 1776. As will be seen, the revised choruses cannot date from 1775–6, so this leaves us with the first version of the first act and fifth act choruses of 1773, which Mozart could have had performed for the 1776 version. In other words, the 1776 version probably consisted of the two choruses of the Vienna version of 1773 in addition to five pieces of instrumental music (*NMA*, nos. 2, 3, 4, 5 and 7a). Concerning the review in the Salzburg paper, if – as we have surmised – the fifth act included at the beginning the 1773 chorus (No. 6a), 'Gottheit, über Alle mächtig!' (a hymn, sung alternately by both choruses [*Sonnenjungfrauen*, Virgins dedicated to the Sun, and Priests]), it will have concluded with No. 7a, later discarded when Mozart added the chorus 'Ihr Kinder des Staubes' (No. 7) for the third version of 1779–80. The autograph MS. of this chilling D minor entr'acte (No. 7a) bears a number of stage remarks in Leopold Mozart's hand, e.g. 'Pherons Verzweifelung.

Gotteslästerung und Tod' – 'Pheron's Desperation. Blasphemy and Death'
–; or, at bar 18, 'Anfang des Donnerwetters' ('Beginning of the thunderstorm'). This number appeared in the play at the very end, after a few
exchanges of dialogue in Act V, Scene 3. The cue lines are the High Priest's
'So strafen die Götter, wenn man sich gegen sie empört. Merkt es,
Sterbliche! Und reizt nicht ihren Zorn!' ('Thus do the Gods punish when
one pits oneself against them. Mark that, mortal! And call not forth their
anger!'). It may be that the anonymous Salzburg critic considered two numbers – the opening chorus (No. 6a) and the closing *Schlußmusik* – too much
for Act V. It is also possible that chorus No. 6a was performed twice, perhaps at the end of the work.

7 The appearance of Johann Böhm and his theatrical Troupe in Salzburg
during the 1779–80 season. Köchel, 6th edition, p. 353; Deutsch,
Dokumente, p. 165.

Böhm's Troupe included actors and actor-singers. As it happens, a complete list of the members of the Troupe for 1780 survives; it was compiled
after they had left Salzburg and were playing in Augsburg, and it appeared
in the *Theater=Kalender auf das Jahr 1781* (Gotha bey Carl Wilhelm
Ettinger), pp. CXXXV–VII. A much less complete list is found in the preceding Gotha *Theater=Kalender* (1780, where the Troupe is listed as being in
Augsburg and Salzburg, p. 231). It reads in translation as follows:

I. German Theatre
The Böhm Troupe
Residence: Augsburg: in the Winter Maynz. Principal: H. Böhm. Music
director: H. Mayer. *Korrepetitor* [rehearsal manager]: H. Geiger.
Bassoonist: H. Kraus. Theatrical Painter and Machinist: H. Hornung.
Soufleur [prompter]: H. Giegler. Actresses: Mad. Ams: comic mothers,
confidantes. Mslle Ballo: young roles in Singspiele. Mad. Bellomo: leading heroines in Singspiele. Mad. Böhm: leading young heroines, gentle-
women in tragedies and comedies. Leading naive and comic roles in
Singspiel[e]. Mad. Brandt: leading gentle roles in tragedies and comedies.
Mad. Müller: soubrettes, peasant girls. Mad. Smitt: leading and secondary lovers in Singspiel[e]. Mad. Vogt: very young gentle and naive
roles: she sings. Mad. Zimmerl: leading soubrettes in comedies and
Singspiele. Actors: H. Amor: minor roles. H. Ams: fathers, officers, con-
fidants. H. Bellomo: lovers in comedies and Singspiele. H. Bilau: leading

young heros, lovers in tragedies and comedies. H. Böhm: leading servant roles, peasants and caricature roles in comedies and Singspiele. H. Brandl: leading comic fathers, Jews and comic roles in comedy and Singspiele. H. Kerscher: secondary fathers, confidantes, servants in tragedies, comedies and Singspiele. H. Müller: noblemen, traitors in tragedies and comedies. H. Murschauser: leading bravura singers in Singspiele. H. von Voltnau: secondary roles. H. Smitt: lovers, officers and noble roles in tragedies, comedies and Singspiele. H. Stierle: leading nagging, serious old men, tyrants, fathers in tragedies, comedies and Singspiele. H. Zimmerl: first lovers in Singspiele. Secondary roles in tragedies and comedies. Ballet: H. Vogt: ballet-master and leading serious dancer. H. Peter Vogt: leading comic dancer. H. Storchinfeld: solo dancer. Mad. Zimmerl: serious dancer. Mad. Storchinfeld: comic dancer. Mad. Müller: solo dancer. Mselle Weinert, Mad. Stierle: alternatively solo dancers, apart from 4 pairs of *corps de ballet* dancers [*Figuranten*]. Note: The troupe, to maintain discipline and to improve steadily, has accepted the Vienna Rules [prevailing in the Court Theatres] and has established a fund to which each member contributes a small amount, and out of which medicines for those who are ill are paid for.

Although the evidence for Mozart's association with the Böhm Troupe is circumstantial, it is nevertheless substantial. First we have the entries in his sister Maria Anna's (Nannerl's) Diary (including many in Wolfgang's hand) for the year 1779.[3] In April and May (and on two days in June) – the Böhm Troupe played at Salzburg during April and May 1779 and between September 1779 and March 1780 – the following entries are pertinent:

6 April: '… papa, I and my brother to the comedie'.
8 April: '… catherl [Gilowsky] with us to the operette …'.
11 April: '… afterwards to the comedie'.
12 April: '… ceccarelli came to us and went with us to the comedie'.
14 April: '… afterwards to the comedie'.
18 April: '… afterwards to the comedie'.
22 April: '… at 4 [p.m.] came home, afterwards at the ballet rehearsal in the theatre …'.
23 April: '… catherl with us to the comedie, a windy day'.
24 April: '… mitzerl taken with us to the comedie, we were in the gallery'.

26 April: '... afterwards to the comedie'.

2 May: '... afterwards the whole company to the comedie'.

3 May: '... my brother went to the comedie'.

4 May: '... afterwards to the comedie'.

9 May: '... afterwards all of us to the comedie: after the comedie a walk'.

13 May: '... afterwards to the comedie'.

19 May: '... we went to the comedie, when I returned I got a headache from having wept so much in the comedie'.

24 May: '... to the comedie at 6 o'clock'.

25 May: '... at 8 o'clock to church, afterwards I met neither *la* lodron nor Fräulein Mayer: beforehand I was at the rehearsal in the theatre ... at 6 o'clock to the comedie'.

28 May: '... afterwards with catherl to the comedie'.

30 May: '... wolfgang went to the comedie'.

31 May: '... afterwards catherl went with us to the comedie'.

1 June: '... we to the comedie'.

2 June: '... afterwards to the comedie'.

In September the Böhm Troupe returned, but the Nannerl-Wolfgang Diary is incomplete and theatrical entries start only on 2 December, where Wolfgang writes:

'... on the 2nd the theatre was opened for the 51st time after the overture was finished by a bell ringing ... Finally Böhm entered the orchestra pit – and everyone woke up – an introduction was played – and – kling kling! – the curtain was raised – and the monologue [solo] ballet started – Diano [*sic*] und Endimion ...'.

4 December (Nannerl's hand): '... the theatre was opened for the 52nd time with a rather bad comedy in 3 acts [entitled] der unglückliche bräutigamm. The ballet Themire und Thirsis.

5 December: '...·the theatre was opened for the 53rd time with a comedy [entitled] die wirtschafterin, the ballet diana und endimion.'

6 December: '... the theatre was opened for the 54th time with a comedy in 5 acts [entitled] die frau wie man sie selten findet, the ballet der ungarische zwifelkrämmer.'

9 December: '... the theatre was opened for the 55th time with an operette in 3 acts, verses and music by Böhm, [entitled] die verkapte braut, the ballet caliope, the operette very bad.'

We may abbreviate further entries:

10 December: Comedy in one act: *Der Edelknab.* Ballet *Horazier und Curazier.*

12 December: Comedy *Die Insel der gesunden Vernunft* with ballet attached.

13 December: Operette *La Frascatana* (Paisiello), Ballet *Der betrunkene Bauer.*

14 December: Goldoni's play *Der Lügner.* 'Der Zwifelkrämmer was the last play before the holidays.'

Nannerl's Diary again breaks off, but is resumed in Mozart's hand on 18 March 1780, in the entry for which a concert is listed, including Madame Böhm, who sang in a Salieri Trio as well as performing a Grétry Aria with obbligato oboe and harp.[4]

This impressive list of theatre-going is simply evidence of typical entertainment in eighteenth-century society; unfortunately, vital sections of Nannerl's Diary which might have identified when *Thamos* was first performed in its third version are missing. There is, however, one interesting entry in the above list, when Nannerl notes that she attended a *rehearsal* in the theatre on 25 May 1779. Could this refer to a rehearsal (dress rehearsal?) for *Thamos*? Significantly, it is the only entry in which she mentions attending a rehearsal.

There is one more piece of evidence that ought to be added to the chronicle, and that is the story of Karl Martin Plümicke's play *Lanassa*, which soon featured in Böhm's repertoire with music from *Thamos* and with a Mozart Symphony in E flat (K.184) as Overture. This seems to indicate that Böhm had some kind of rights allowing him to use *Thamos* music as well as the symphony. (Mozart himself could have heard *Lanassa* when he was in Frankfurt in 1790 for the coronation festivities of Leopold II; on 17 September, Böhm announced the piece, saying clearly on the theatre programme that 'the music for the entr'actes and the choruses is by the celebrated Mozart, composer of *Die Entführung aus dem Serail*'.)[5]

There is, however, no concrete evidence for Mozart's having composed this third version of *Thamos* in 1779–80 except for one revealing fact: the appearance of the autograph manuscript. Again we turn to the analyses by Wolfgang Plath and Alan Tyson. The following passage from Tyson's account continues directly from that quoted above:

The paper of the choruses in Thamos can also be matched in other dated scores from the same time. For it too is found in the divertimento K.251 of July 1776, and also in two church sonatas, K.244 and K.245, dated 'April 1776'. It is found as well in several undated scores, *all* of which have been assigned to the years 1776 or 1777. Thus it would seem plausible to assign the choruses in *Thamos* to the same time as the surviving entr'actes – to 1776 or 1777.

But *Schriftchronologie* gives a different message: according to Plath the surviving autograph of the choruses dates from 1779 or even later. Yet no other autograph from these years is on paper of this type, with upright format: in the years 1779 and 1780, to judge from the dated scores of K.317–321 and K.336–339, Mozart was using quite different papers.

There is no doubt that Plath is right: the writing in the choruses is different from that in the entr'actes. Perhaps the most plausible explanation is that, for an unknown reason, though possibly after some revision, Mozart decided to recopy the choruses, and concluded that his task would be easier if he used paper of the same size and shape as before; so he purchased a small stock of the paper he had been using three or four years earlier. (This would not have been difficult, for the paper came from a mill in Salzburg itself.)

The problem we come up against, then, is the obscure stage-history of the play – the times that it was played at Salzburg, and its various revivals. It would seem that we have entr'actes from 1776 or 1777, and choruses from 1779 or 1780. Here paper-studies can easily be reconciled with *Schriftchronologie*.

The three choruses added for the Böhm Troupe are as follows:

a No. 1 (*NMA* listing) 'Schon weichet Dir, Sonne!'. Scoring: 2 flutes, 2 oboes, 2 bassoons, 2 horns, 2 trumpets, 3 trombones, timpani, strings, chorus (Sonnenjungfrauen, Priests). If we compare the first, 1773, version of this music with the version supposedly composed in 1779 or 1780, a stylistic 'fingerprint' comes to our aid. It will be recalled that one of the new rhythms – or rather old French rhythms – which Mozart adopted in France during his stay in 1778 was the characteristic ♩. ♫♩ ♩ . This does *not* appear in the old version of the chorus (No. 1a) where at bars 10 and 12 we notice, in the trumpets, the rhythm ♩ ♬♬ , which also turns up again in the recapitulation at bars 149 and 151. Now if we examine the music of the Böhm version, we find at the same places the post-Parisian ♩. ♫♩ ♩ , not only in the trumpets but also in the timpani. Here, then, is an interesting method for reinforcing the supposition that this music must have been composed after Mozart's sojourn in Paris.

b No. 6 'Gottheit, über Alle mächtig'. Scoring as in No. 1. Here the differences between the 1773 version (No. 6a) and this one are even more striking. Apart from the omnipresent Mozartian fingerprint ♩ ♫♩ ♩ which greets us in bar 3 of the 1779–80 music – but not in No. 6a of 1773 – the most startling addition is the French ♩. ♫♫♫ in trumpets and timpani at bar 4, which thrusts through the string texture: the strings play the very French 'ouverture' chain dotted notes ♩. ♫♫. ♫♫. ♫♫. ♫ which fill the entire bar. The other rhythm of the trumpets and drums appears again at bar 11, while the Parisian phrase ♩. ♫♩ ♩ appears *only* in the 1779–80 text, also at bars 25 (trumpets), 26 (kettledrums), 33 (kettledrums), 41 and 43 (trumpets and drums), 62 (trumpets and drums), 66/7 (drums only), 197 (trumpets and drums), 198 (kettledrums), 204 (kettledrums), 247 (trumpets and drums). It is in fact almost a textbook case of establishing chronology through a simple stylistic criterion.

c No. 7 'Ihr Kinder des Staubes'. Scoring as in No. 1. Here there is a long timpani roll which is marked 'con sordini' on the autograph. This instruction does not mean 'with mutes', as it would today, but simply indicates the use of felt-covered sticks, or rather hard wooden sticks with a piece of material wrapped around them. This information, which seems to be little known nowadays, comes from Grétry's *Richard Cœur-de-lion* (1784): the French practice seems to have been to employ 'baguetes garnies'. Thus, during the crusader's song, the trumpets and horns are muted, 'while the timpani have "two pieces of cloth tied to the sticks"'.[6]

The text of this chorus is not contained in Gebler's *Thamos*, and it has always been assumed, ever since Jahn's biography (published in 1856),[7] that Mozart's friend Johann Andreas Schachtner, a local Salzburg poet, had fashioned the words for this new Finale, which was to replace the instrumental music No. 7a, mentioned above. The editor of *NMA*, Harald Heckmann, writes:

> The position of this Chorus (No. 7) as the conclusion of the entire work is to a certain extent in conflict with the remark in Mozart's hand on No.

7a ...: 'After the 5th and last Act'. One might think that both pieces were played at the end of the drama one after the other, that the instrumental piece was heard not at the end of [see above, p. 44, for the relevant cue lines], but during, the last act, at the end of the Second Scene. This possibility is suggested by two remarks in Leopold Mozart's hand on the autograph of this instrumental piece [see above, p. 44]. There is no doubt that they refer to the above-mentioned scene in the last act. But apart from Mozart's handwritten indication that the piece is to be played *after* the last act, a study of the autograph suggests yet another solution. From the carefully crossed-out section of the page in question – see the facsimile in *NMA* – it may be seen that the rest of the piece was removed from the main body of the score. Only the first page remained with the score, diagonally crossed out by Mozart, who apparently wanted to replace the instrumental piece with the newly composed, effective final chorus, and therefore removed it [No. 7a] from the score. Since, however, the beginning [of No. 7a] was on the reverse side of the last page of No. 5, the page could not be removed. Instead, he crossed it out. For these reasons the piece, characteristically, has no number in the [autograph] score ... .

The *NMA* offers several pages of facsimile which may be analyzed, in the light of all the recent research, as follows:

Pages 1 and 2 of Chorus No. 1 in the 1779–80 version. 4° with the very unusual number of sixteen staves per page. This is a characteristic specimen of Mozart's extremely neat, legible handwriting.

Pages 1 and 2 of the instrumental piece No. 7a, the first page crossed out, the second (like the first) containing remarks in Leopold Mozart's hand. This was the conclusion of the 1776 version.

We may now proceed to the final sections of this documentation:

8 Wolfgang to his father Leopold, letter from Vienna dated 15 February 1783:[8]

Mon trés cher Père!
I thank you from my heart for the musique you sent! – I am very sorry that I can not use the musique for Thamos! – This piece is here, because it was not successful, under the cast-off pieces; which are no longer performed. – It ought to be performed just because of the music, – and that will surely not happen; – certainly that is a pity! – ... .

9   The arrangements of some of the *Thamos* choruses as Latin Motets. It is not known exactly when these arrangements were made, certainly before the coronation ceremonies for Leopold II as Emperor in Frankfurt in 1790 and as King of Bohemia in Prague in 1791, when the first of these Latin arrangements, 'Splendete te, Deus', is known to have been performed. There were also versions with different, religious texts in German, and one of these was in Mozart's possession at the time of his death.[9] There was also in his library the Latin arrangement of No. 6 as 'Jesu, Jesu, Rex tremendae'. All this suggests that not only did these arrangements have Mozart's sanction, but that he was perhaps responsible for attempting to salvage at least these three magnificent choruses by having the arrangements made, thus enabling them to be played in church and in the concert hall. The sources may be examined in Köchel, 6th edition.

No. 1 Latin version: 'Splendete te, Deus'. German alternative text: 'Preis dir! Gottheit'. MS. parts, Esterházy Archives, Eisenstadt, as *Motetto* with Latin text. See Landon, *Haydn, Chronicle and Works: Haydn at Eszterháza 1766–1790*, p. 557n.

No. 6 Latin version: 'Jesu, Rex tremendae Majestatis'. German alternative texts: (1) 'Gottheit, über Alle mächtig'; and (2) 'Gottheit, dir sei Preiß und Ehre!'. MS. parts, Esterházy Archives, Eisenstadt, as *Motetto* with Latin text.

No. 7 Latin version: 'Ne pulvis et cinis'. German alternative text: 'Ob fürchterlich tobend sich Stürme erheben'. MS. parts, Esterházy Archives, Eisenstadt, as *Motetto* with Latin text.

We need not be encumbered by these vexed questions of versions and chronology as far as performances and recordings of this uniquely valuable music are concerned. Indeed, the medium of the compact disc has proved ideal for presenting the different versions of *Thamos*, as has been done in a recording conducted by John Eliot Gardiner,[10] featuring the whole of the 1776 version (including Nos. 1a and 6a), followed by Nos. 1, 6 and 7 of the 1779–80 version, all played on original instruments.

*   *   *

Before considering some aspects of the music for *Thamos*, I thought it would be helpful to provide a synopsis of the plot and to position Mozart's various numbers in the context of Gebler's drama.

The cast, as listed by Gebler, is:

Thamos,	King of Egypt
Pheron,	a Prince of the Royal House
Mirza,	Leader of the Sun Virgins
Sethos,	High Priest of the Temple of the Sun (bass)

Sais	Noble Egyptians, who are being
Myris	educated by Sun Virgins

Phanes,	a Soldier
Mammon,	a Priest of the Sun Cult

Chorus of Priests, Chorus of Sun Virgins
Lords of the Kingdom and other Egyptians, Warriors

The action is set in the Sun City (Heliopolis). The stage depicts, in the first, third, fourth and fifth acts, the Temple of the Sun, and in the second a gallery of the residence of the Sun Virgins. The poet places the Sun Temple in the middle, behind it are the dwellings of the priests; on the one side is the house of the Sun Virgins, on the other is the royal castle, which two buildings are linked to the Temple of the Sun. The action lasts from morning until evening.

First Act

The scene shows the interior of the Temple of the Sun in Heliopolis. In the background one sees a golden effigy of the sun. Lamps placed behind illuminate it. On the altar in front of the sun's effigy burns the sacrificial flame, into which the High Priest, flanked by two other priests, casts incense. On the right-hand side of the altar stands the chorus of the Sun Virgins, and opposite them the chorus of priests. All are clad in white. On the veils of the Sun Virgins are embroidered effigies of the sun. When the curtain is raised, a hymn in praise of the god is sung alternately by the two choirs.

It will not have escaped the astute reader that there are many elements which look forward to *Die Zauberflöte* (1791) – the Egyptian setting, the chorus of priests, the presence of a high priest, the rituals and a certain air of secrecy, not to say conspiracy, as we shall shortly see. In the first chorus (No. 1) the ambience of *Die Zauberflöte* is at once evoked in the opening words:

'Night, light's enemy, gives way to the sun'. In this majestic C major movement, Thamos is crowned king and prayers are offered to bring 'joyful days'
to his people. A chorus of priests with solo tenor and solo bass invokes the
gods to render 'happy youth obedient and virtuous, and [to] give the men
courage'. After another statement from both choirs, the Sun Virgins pray
that 'Egypt's daughters be a credit to their sex and the pride of their hus-
bands. May they be content to fulfil their still duty, in the bloom of their
youth and in maturity'. These interjections, in G major for the priests and F
major for the Sun Virgins, look forward to a similar structure in the D
major finale to Act I of *Idomeneo* (*NMA*, No. 9), where two-part solo writing for soprano and alto 'Da lunge eimira' is set off by tenor and bass solo
'Dall' onde fuore', and by the principal chorus on the other; there is even a
kind of insert in G major and in a slower tempo for soprano and alto soli,
'Su conca d'oro' which leads back to the chorus and its previous music. To
suggest these returns in a more formal way, the movement is entitled
'Ciaconna'.

Now the plot begins to unfold. Traitors plan to depose Thamos. The
usurper is Pheron, whom Thamos considers to be one of his close friends
and advisers. Act I concludes with a piece of incidental music (*NMA*, No. 2)
describing this treachery, identified in Leopold Mozart's hand on the autograph as '… the decision taken between Pheron and Mirza to put Pheron on
the throne'. The music that follows is in Mozart's most severe C minor,
again amazingly prophetic of his use of that tonality in such works as the
Piano Concerto (K.491) – unsettling, yet dramatic in a straightforward,
manly way. The syncopations that dominate much of the texture underline
the drama's situation.

In Act II, Mirza and Myris discuss Thamos's beloved fiancée Sais, whom
they would like to separate from him. At the end of Act II there is an
Andante in E flat in which, according to Leopold Mozart's description:
'Thamos's good character shows itself … The Third Act with Thamos and
the traitor Pheron'. The entr'acte reveals in the music, first, 'Thamos's honesty' (Leopold Mozart) at bar 11, with oboe solo and bassoons in thirds, but
preceding this – again in Leopold Mozart's words, – 'Pheron's false character' is portrayed with jagged syncopations: these two elements are juxta-
posed throughout this unusual instrumental number.

Act III begins with a confrontation between Thamos and Pheron. Later,
Pheron, alone, cries 'Weakling! How little you [Thamos] know the value of

ruling! A throne, won by the sword or built by the hands of the people, remains a throne'. Meanwhile, the traitors tell Sais that Thamos loves not her but Myris, while Thamos has chosen Pheron to be Sais's bride – all 'disinformation', of course.

Act IV begins with a so-called 'melodrama', a form perfected by the Bohemian composer Georg Benda, whose work Mozart is known to have studied and admired: here the music is like a recitative, but instead of being sung, the lines are spoken – in this case by Sais. (Often these spoken lines are omitted when the work is given in a concert peformance, and this is a pity.) Sais refuses to become the 'tool of faithless traitors' and resolves to become a priestess – 'Sun, as priestess I dedicate myself to thy service'. It is one of the most original movements in this original work: beginning in G minor, with rough off-beat accents and rushing tremolo strings, it ends serenely in B flat as she takes her vows. Thamos has meanwhile overheard all this and realizes that they have both been betrayed. Pheron makes his *Götterdämmerung*-like decision: 'If Pheron falls, thousands fall with him'. There follows a potent *Sturm und Drang* movement in D minor (No. 5, Allegro vivace assai). At this point Leopold Mozart noted on the autograph: 'The fourth act closes in general confusion.' This truculent movement is again curiously prophetic: it looks forward to the D minor Piano Concerto (K.466) and to the whole violent world of Mozart's writing in minor keys. It ends in a defiant D major and leads to the opening chorus of Act V, where a hymn is sung by the assembled nobles, warriors and all the principal actors and actresses. A slow introduction in Mozart's most sumptuous D major style, with horns, trumpets, trombones blazing, leads to a vivid quick section marked Allegro vivace. There is a slower middle section in A major, first with the soli (tenor, bass) of the priests, then with the Sun Virgins – again in the best *Idomeneo* style – with the uncannily prophetic words, 'sanfter Flöten Zauberklang' ('gentle flutes' magical sound') and 'so mengt sich, Osiris Söhne, unser Lied in eure Töne' ('thus mingles, O sons of Osiris, our song with yours'). The first swift section returns, builds to a brilliant climax to which a thunderous kettledrum roll contributes. There is a pause (*fermata*) and the tempo slows to Moderato and a conclusion of mild orchestral beauty, dying away ('calando') to *pp*.

Nowadays, conductors frequently choose to play No. 7a first and to conclude *Thamos* with the later choral (vocal) version of No. 7. This scheme makes musical sense and also salvages No. 7a, which is the terrifying D minor piece discussed above, describing Pheron's death and a thunderstorm. The 1779–80 Chorus No. 7 is perhaps the most astonishing movement in the whole work. It is a description of terror and fear such as we know from *Don Giovanni*, also using the same key, D minor, composed in 1787. The High Priest sings 'Children of dust, tremble and quake, before you again rise up against the gods. Avenging thunder defend them against the blasphemer's vain deceits!' In a continuation of sinister power, the strings sink down, almost as if to anticipate the terrified people, who sing, 'We children of the dust tremble and quake, and bow our heads to the earth'. There is a long-held chord, and then the music shifts very quietly to D major, as hope is touchingly reborn and the score seems to unfold like some exotic plant – all *pp* – and even the kettledrums change from their muted sound back to their customary hard sticks. With a dash the final Allegro begins and the prayers of the faithful rise to the Temple of the Sun.

Thamos is a great *tour de force*, opening vistas far into the future. In its final 1779–80 version, it is one of the group of great works that Mozart created in heady profusion, on his return from Paris, during those two prolific years at Salzburg. Of course, music such as *Thamos* transcended the bounds of the archbishopric in which Mozart was court organist, but he was soon to be liberated from that confining atmosphere, first by going to the welcoming city of Munich for *Idomeneo*, and from there to his mercurial rise and fall in the Imperial capital, Vienna.

Die Zauberflöte (K.620)

W̲ E HAVE NO PRECISE DATE WHEN MOZART'S *DIE ZAUBERFLÖTE* was commissioned by Emanuel Schikaneder, impresario of the Freyhaustheater or the Theater auf der Wieden, located in a suburb of Vienna (now the fourth district). Schikaneder was a successful playwright, actor and (of sorts) a singer; Mozart had known this clever impresario since he had 'played' Salzburg with his troupe during the season 1780–1. In 1780 Mozart had even written an aria (alas, lost) for a member of the troupe. By March 1791 Mozart was composing a vocal piece for two members of the Schikaneder company in Vienna; this was the amusing concert aria, 'Per questa bella mano' (K.612), written for Franz Xaver Gerl (who would soon create the role of Sarastro in *Die Zauberflöte*), featuring a virtuoso part for the first double-bass player of the Freyhaus orchestra, Friedrich Pischlberger. This suggests that Mozart was by then already in close contact with this successful troupe, which gave performances of German plays and German operas (*Singspiele*) and sometimes presented Italian operas too in their theatre.

However, there was another reason why Mozart had decided to turn his immense talents to German opera. Apart from the fact that his *Entführung aus dem Serail (Il Seraglio)*, composed in 1782, had been the most successful opera of his career and was being performed all over Germany, Mozart had every reason to doubt whether, under the new Emperor Leopold II, he would receive any commissions for Italian operas. Mozart's highly successful rival, Antonio Salieri, held sway over the Italian company in the Burgtheater, Vienna's most prestigious theatre. So long as the previous Emperor, Joseph II, had reigned, Mozart was sure of operatic commissions for the Italian troupe: Joseph II had seen to it that Mozart had been asked to write *Le nozze di Figaro* and *Così fan tutte*, and in 1788 he had promoted (though not witnessed) the Viennese première of *Don Giovanni* (composed the year before for Prague). But Joseph II had died in 1790, shortly after the première of *Così fan tutte*, and Mozart had been lucky that his position with

Joseph II as 'Chamber Composer' with a salary of 800 florins had been confirmed by his successor. Leopold II, and especially his wife, were passionately fond of Italian opera, and one of the monarch's first operatic commissions was for Domenico Cimarosa, who arrived late in 1791 to compose what was to prove his masterpiece for the Vienna Burgtheater, *Il matrimonio segreto* (1792), the greatest success of Austrian theatrical history. (When the Bohemian Estates in Prague commissioned the coronation opera for Leopold II, who was to be crowned King of Bohemia in September 1791, they turned first to Antonio Salieri, and it was only after he refused that they approached Mozart, who at once began to compose *La clemenza di Tito*.)

I believe that Schikaneder had probably suggested the idea of composing a German opera to Mozart in the autumn of 1790, and that his proposal was the reason why Mozart felt obliged to turn down two offers to go to London late in 1790, one via Nancy Storace for the King's Theatre in the Pantheon (where he was to be the principal composer for a season), and the other via the impresario Johann Peter Salomon to come to London to write symphonies for his famous subscription concert series. In the event Haydn, whose employer Prince Nicolaus Esterházy had died in September 1790 and who was now free to travel, went with Salomon to London, where he made a fortune in the course of two extended visits.

*   *   *

Schikaneder had opened the Freyhaus Theater on 12 July 1789 with a German comic opera entitled *Der dumme Gärtner aus dem Gebirge, oder die zween Anton* (The Foolish Gardener from the Mountains, or the Two Antons), with text by Schikaneder and music by two members of his troupe, the tenor Benedikt Schack and the bass singer Franz Xaver Gerl. The opera was an instant success and was given no less than thirty-two times in 1789. Its arias were sung all over the city, and in 1791 Mozart wrote a set of piano variations on one of them, 'Ein Weib ist das herrlichste Ding auf der Welt' ('A wife is the most marvellous thing in the world').

All his life, Mozart had never quite achieved the sensational popular successes of Joseph Haydn, whose style brilliantly combined artful learning with tunes that anyone could whistle. Haydn had been the first composer in music history whose compositions had achieved international popularity, being equally loved and admired in Britain, France, Spain, Russia, Germany and Hungary. The only success of this kind in Mozart's career had been *Entführung*, but that work's popularity was, of course, limited to German-speaking countries: no one in Paris, London, Madrid or Rome had ever seen it performed. Now, Mozart and Schikaneder calculated, they would write the kind of opera that would become an instantaneous success: and they were quite right in their calculations, as we shall see.

The forces over which Schikaneder presided were of exceptional quality. Some of his singers were Burgtheater material, such as Mozart's sister-in-law Josepha Hofer, for whom he composed the brilliant but demanding role of the Queen of the Night. The orchestra of the Freyhaustheater was also highly professional and included some thirty-five players, with five first violins, four second violins, four violas, three cellos, three double basses, pairs of flutes, oboes, clarinets, bassoons, horns and trumpets, three trombones and a kettledrummer.

Schikaneder was a man of the theatre with an unerring eye for what the public liked – 'machine' effects, with which *Die Zauberflöte* abounds (trap-doors through which the three ladies arrived on stage, fire, gondolas appearing from above and carrying three boys, etc.), and simple Haydnesque arias that Schikaneder actually sang himself; in those days, almost all actors were expected to sing in such companies. But both Mozart and Schikaneder had a different and astonishing idea of what *Die Zauberflöte* should seek to represent: the glorification of Freemasonry.

The Ancient and Venerable Order of Freemasons, established earlier in the century in London, had spread throughout Europe and to North America (Jefferson, Washington and Franklin were all Masons). In Austria the Craft flourished under Joseph II, and Haydn, Mozart and most of the intellectual élite were members, along with many members of the government and the nobility (for example, Haydn's Prince Nicolaus Esterházy, who was Master of Ceremonies in Mozart's Lodge, Crowned Hope, *Zur gekrönten Hoffnung*). But recently it had come under deep suspicion for harbouring the ideas of the French Revolution – liberty, equality, fraternity – which indeed was to a certain extent true. Evidence of a supposed conspiracy of the Freemasons in 1791 came to light recently in the Austrian Archives: the affair was investigated at the time and the man ultimately responsible for Mozart's *La clemenza di Tito*, Count Heinrich Rottenhan, persuaded Emperor Leopold II that most of the men under suspicion were harmless crackpots or eccentrics. Nevertheless, the Craft was under a cloud when

Schikaneder (who had been initiated in Regensburg) and Mozart decided to glorify it with their new opera.

Die Zauberflöte is replete with Masonic symbols: in the middle of the Overture, the music stops and the rhythmic sign for the second degree of Freemasonry, that of the Fellow Craft, is presented in the winds and the brass: the reason for this reference to the second degree, as will become apparent, is that Tamino, the Prince, has yet to undergo his final ritual and become, *mutatis mutandis*, a Master Mason (the third degree). The symbolic figure three dominates, in fact, the entire work: there are three flats in the key-signature of E flat, three boys, three ladies. In other multiples of three, we find that there are eighteen priests, and that Sarastro, the High Priest, first appears in Act I, Scene 18, which in the so-called Scottish Rite is the degree of the Sovereign Cross, or Rose-Croix. In the orchestral introduction to the crucial scene with the armed men which precedes Tamino's initiation, Scene 28 of Act II, there are precisely eighteen groups of notes before the *fugato* (bar 7) begins.

In a booklet printed in London in 1725 entitled *The Grand Mystery of the Free Masons discovered*, we read in the ritual 'Examination Upon Entrance in the Lodge':

Q. How many precious Jewels?
A. Three; a square Asher [Ashet? i.e., dish or platter],
    a Diamond, and a Square.
Q. How many Lights?
A. Three; a Right East, South and West.
Q. What do they represent?
A. The Three Persons, Father, Son and Holy Ghost. …

Q. How many steps belong to a Right Mason?
A. Three. …

Q. How many particular Points pertain to a Free-Mason?
A. Brotherly Love, Relief, and Truth, among all Right Masons; for
    which all Masons were ordain'd at the Building of the Tower of
    Babel, and at the Temple of *Jerusalem*.

In 1723, another print revealed

   If a Master-Mason you would be,
   Observe you well the *Rule of Three* …

By the time any Mason attending the Freyhaustheater auf der Wieden had finished listening to *Die Zauberflöte*, he would have realized that he had heard the first Masonic opera. Naturally, the exact ritual was not presented in detail on stage, but there was enough of it, shown obliquely and heavily illustrated by numerology, for there to be no doubt about the work's Masonic content. But how was this possible? In the 1725 publication referred to above, we read:

Q. In the name of, &c., are you a Mason?
   What is a Mason?
A. A Man begot of a Man, born of a Woman, Brother to a King.
Q. What is a Fellow?
A. A Companion of a Prince.
Q. How shall I know you are a Free Mason?
A. By Signs, Tokens, and Points of my Entry.
Q. Which is the Point of your Entry?
A. I Heal and Conceal, under the Penalty of having my Throat cut, or my Tongue pull'd out of my head.

It has often been questioned how it was possible for Mozart and Schikaneder to reveal all these secrets of the Craft without 'having their Throats cut, or their Tongues pull'd out of their Heads'. Obviously, they must have taken steps to 'clear' the whole operatic text with the Grand Lodge of Austria before putting it on the stage. In any event, after Mozart's death his fellow Masons accorded him a grand 'Lodge of Sorrows', of which the oration was printed; they also published his final Masonic Cantata, composed and performed shortly before his death, for the benefit of his penniless widow Constanze.

But there is one extraordinary point about the Masonic content of this opera which must be stressed here. When the time comes for Tamino's initiation, to which we have referred above, he is not alone. Now in a normal Lodge, the Masons enter two by two (but in the rite of initiation the individual Mason is alone, of course). Tamino, however, enters not with another man but with his lady, Pamina. Women had no role in Freemasonry except in France where, characteristically, female Lodges existed then and still exist today. Sarastro, the *soi-disant* Worshipful Master in *Die Zauberflöte*, is distinctly anti-feminine. So what is Pamina doing in this crucial scene? There can be no doubt that this is a purely Mozartian concept. In all his mature operas, women play a vital role, and Mozart was the first operatic composer to investigate the hopes, loves and tragedies of the female sex, to interpret lovingly their motivations and reactions. In all his stage works of the last decade of his life, loving forgiveness plays a central part, e.g. at the end of *Figaro*, when the Countess touchingly forgives her cynical, philandering husband, Count Almaviva; or even more dramatically, in *La clemenza di Tito*, when the Emperor Titus forgives his would-be assassins at the end of the work. Here, in *Die Zauberflöte*, Mozart seeks to reform the St John Masonry to which he belonged by asking that the women be included in the Craft's membership. We have no idea whether the Viennese Masons reacted to this innovation in any way. But in any case it was too late: four years after the opera's première, Masonry was forbidden in Austria and the ban remained in force until 1918, when it was lifted after World War I.

*   *   *

The late Egon Komorzynski's classic description of the Freyhaus and its theatre is cited below in translation. The whole complex included not only the theatre but also the inn which Mozart frequented with the theatrical personnel, and

> consisted of a monstrous complex of houses connected to each other with six large courtyards, thirty-two stairways and 225 apartments; it had its own church, dedicated to St Rosalia, workshops for almost every kind of handicraft, an oil press belonging to the Marsano family, an apothecary and a mill, the wheel of which was driven by a stream diverted from the river Wien. It was called 'Freihaus' because – thanks to the owners – it was freed of all taxes. In the great courtyard there was a garden with allées, flower-beds and a wooden pavilion …: that was where Schikaneder's people gathered after the rehearsals and after performances, making a great racket well into the night, under the leadership of the jovial director, who called the actors and actresses 'his children' and who presided with good humour. The one, lengthwise side of the courtyard was taken up by the theatre, an impressive building of stone with a tile roof, which Schikaneder enlarged and raised. It accommodated 1,000 people, was 30 metres long and 15 metres wide, the stage was 12 metres deep and was equipped with all the necessary requisites – safety, comfort and stage machinery; it had a double row of boxes, an orchestra [*parterre*]

of two parts and, in Mozart's time, two galleries (Schikaneder later added a third).

Since, in this enormous place, there was no lack of apartments, the director and most of the members of the company lived in the Freihaus …

The wooden pavilion referred to above is now in the garden of the Mozarteum in Salzburg, while the furniture is in the family castle of the Counts (later Princes) von Starhemberg, the owners of the land on which the Freyhaus stood, at Eferding in Upper Austria. Mozart is supposed to have written parts of *Die Zauberflöte* in this little pavilion, and also to have used it for rehearsal purposes (a more likely operation if one imagines a clavichord, or spinet, as having been the small instrument used to accompany the singers).

The poet Ignaz Franz Castelli, who grew up in the Viennese district of Mariahilf, used to attend the theatre in its final days. He was there for the first time in 1798 and paid 7 kreuzer. He described the theatre as a large, rectangular building of box-like structure. The interior was simply decorated; to the side of the door where one entered was the stage, in front of which were two life-size statues, on the right a knight with a poniard, on the left a half-nude woman. Tickets in the pit cost 17 kreuzer and in the top gallery a 7 kreuzer coin.

In order to secure one of the cheap seats, Castelli had to arrive there at three in the afternoon. He recalled that

> After the theatre opened … I had to sit for three hours, bathed in heat and sweat and impregnated by the garlicky fumes of the smoked meats being consumed … . Finally the lamps were dimmed and my sun started to rise. The musicians came into the pit one by one, those lucky ones, who can sit there every day …

The opera proved to be the greatest success of Mozart's – and Schikaneder's – career. The theatre was sold out night after night. There was something in this work for everyone: for the connoisseur; for the man or woman 'on the street'; even for children, who loved the animal scenes. Its solemn message of 'beauty and wisdom' – the last lines of the text – touched the hearts of men and women alike. People roared with laughter over Papageno's jokes; they trembled at the wicked Queen of the Night, whose second aria with its dizzy coloratura astonished every vocal connoisseur in the house; they felt curiosity and slight fear at the sight of Sarastro and his Priests, solemnly assembled like the members of a Masonic Lodge. *Die Zauberflöte* had the same kind of instantaneous and lasting success that only Haydn had previously achieved (and was just then achieving on a massive scale in London).

On his deathbed, Mozart used to follow the performance in his mind's eye, with his watch in hand. 'Now they've finished the first act – now is the passage "Dir, große Königin der Nacht"' (Scene 30 of Act II, just before the end). On 5 December 1791, at fifty-five minutes past midnight, in that silent hour when a man's strength is at its ebb, Mozart's great spirit left his frail body. Within a year his music had become the talk of Germany, mainly because of *Die Zauberflöte*; two hundred years later he has become the most famous and best-loved composer of all time. He deserves no less.

Mozart and Paris

— ❧ —

M OZART TRAVELLED TO PARIS IN 1778 WITH GREAT EXPECTATIONS.
The French capital boasted numerous musical organizations, of
which the most famous were the Opéra and the Concert Spirituel, with its very large orchestra and chorus (a total of 100 musicians,
including a string corpus of forty-three). Paris was also the centre of the
music-publishing world: Joseph Haydn's first string quartets and symphonies had been issued there in 1764, the very year in which the eight-year-
old Mozart's violin sonatas (K.6–9) were published at the time of his first
visit to Paris.[1] All of the leading German and Italian composers published
their music in Paris, and these editions were circulated all over Europe, even
finding their way to remote Austrian and Bohemian monasteries and castles.
Christoph Willibald Gluck had achieved triumphs with his French operas,
and recently his music had been pitted in Paris against that of the successful
Italian operatic composer, Niccolò Piccinni; that famous conflict, into
which were drawn the leading intellectuals of Parisian life, was at its height
when Wolfgang and his mother settled into quarters belonging to Herr
Mayer, agent of the Augsburg merchant Joseph Felix Arbauer, on the Rue
Bourg l'Abbé (now Paris 3ᵉ, beginning at 205 Rue Saint-Martin and ending
at 66 Boulevard de Sébastopol) on 23 March 1778.

The first thing that struck Mozart and his mother was that Paris was
exceedingly expensive, both as to their rent and to everyday needs.
'Everything here is twice as dear as it was twelve years ago when we were
here the last time', writes Maria Anna Mozart on 5 April 1778. Mozart
would leave his mother alone in their dark quarters and make the rounds of
the city, looking up old friends and acquaintances such as Baron Friedrich
Melchior Grimm, whose literary and political bulletins (*Correspondance
Littéraire*) from the Seine were read all over civilized Europe; or the
Mannheim flautist Johann Baptist Wendling; and the Palatine Envoy to the
French court, Carl Heinrich Joseph, Count von Sickingen, at whose house
Wolfgang would later play his 'Paris' Symphony (K.297) for the first time.

Maria Anna Mozart had to have meals brought in from a *traiteur*, and the food was both expensive and of poor quality. Their money was disappearing at an alarming rate. 'Wolfgang and I – when he eats at home – spend 15 sols for lunch and only 4 sols for supper', she writes on 12 June, having already listed with some horror, on 29 May, a catalogue of some of the food prices then prevailing in the French capital:

a pound of good butter costs 30 to 40 sols, the bad (which is inedible) 24 sols, a pound of beef is 10 sols, veal 12 to 14 sols, a leg of lamb 3 livres, a young chicken 3 livres, the wine is dear and bad, all ruined by the innkeepers, it's even more expensive here than it was in England when we were there [in 1764 and 1765] …

Finally, they moved to larger and more airy quarters, organized by an old Parisian friend, the Marquise d'Épinay, and on 10 April – in the letter quoted above which Maria Anna began on the 5th – Wolfgang gives the new address as 'Rue gros chenet, vis à vis celle du Croissant à l'hôtel des 4 fils emont' (now Rue du Sentier, Paris 2e).

Leopold Mozart began, rightly, to be very worried about his wife's and son's financial situation; but Wolfgang, in that letter of 5–10 April 1778, adds a note telling his father not to be concerned about their life in the French capital, 'for I am in a place where one can quite certainly make money'. Realizing that it will not be easy, Wolfgang adds,

… the French gentlemen have improved their taste only to the extent that they can now hear good music too, and that they moreover admit that their music is bad, or at least they can tell the difference … but – when they sing! – *oimè* – if only French girls wouldn't sing Italian arias. I can pardon their French yelling, but to ruin good music! That's not to be tolerated …

This kind of severe criticism was soon augmented. Wolfgang had to wait in cold *antichambres* and to play on out-of-tune pianos while the hostess and their friends continued to draw. He wrote to his father on 1 May,

They ask for me on this or that day. I play and then they say, *O c'est une Prodige, c'est inconcevable, c'est étonnant* – and that's it … Altogether Paris is very changed. The French are not nearly as polite as they were 15 years ago, they now strongly incline to rudeness …

Furthermore, Wolfgang finds that, as far as the musical taste of the French is concerned, he 'is among real animals and beasts … but how could it be different when all their actions, loves and passions are like that in real life …'. For his part, Leopold continually exhorts his son to be reasonable. He knows that in Paris one has to pay 100 visits in vain, that the French get rid of one with compliments, and that 'you will have your enemies everywhere, that is inevitable with all persons blessed with great talents …' (11 May). Wolfgang must not allow his enemies to get him down and disturb his equilibrium; Leopold reminds his son of the earlier events in Italy, notably the intrigues connected with his first opera in Milan, also with his third opera there [*Lucio Silla*]. 'You must fight your way through.' But Wolfgang was deeply frustrated in Paris; he raged against the French in a letter to his father of 18 July. He found it difficult to have any kind of pleasant and honest relationship with them, 'especially with women – most of them are whores and the rest have no manners …'.

But Mozart was also his own worst enemy. He was arrogant, difficult, impatient, intolerant and smug. Baron Grimm was in despair and on 27 July wrote to Leopold Mozart accordingly, informing him that his son was

not very active, easily distracted, too little concerned with the means that lead to fortune. Here, in order to be successful, you have to be cunning, enterprising, audacious. For his happiness I would wish him half the talent that he has and double the enterprising spirit, and I would not be embarrassed. By the way, here he can choose one of two ways to earn a living. The first is to give harpsichord lessons; but he cannot count on having students unless he works very hard at it and even has recourse to charlatanerie. I do not know how he will have enough strength to keep up this profession, because it is very tiring to run around all four corners of Paris and to work yourself to the bone, just to please. And moreover, this business will not suit him because it will keep him from composing, and *that* he loves beyond everything else. Without teaching he could dedicate his time entirely to composing, but in this country most of the public is not very knowledgable as far as music is concerned. You are acclaimed for your name, and the artistic value of the work can often only be judged by a very small number of people. The public, at this moment, is so ridiculously torn between Piccinni and Gluck, and all the explanations you hear about music are pitiful. For your son, it will be very difficult to succeed between these two parties.[2]

While this was perhaps a realistic picture of Wolfgang's weaknesses, Baron Grimm's views also amounted to a severe condemnation of Parisian musical knowledge and taste – in other words, he provides oblique support for the objections Wolfgang had been constantly voicing. On 13 August Leopold reacted to the content of Baron Grimm's letter, quoting his opinions and telling his son that he was too candid ('*treuherzig*').

All was not lost, however; and although 1778 was not one of Mozart's most productive years, the music that he did compose proved to be in many respects remarkable, indeed decisive for his later development as a composer. As early as Easter week, he had performed his first substantial work in Paris, eight additional movements to Ignaz Holzbauer's *Miserere* (K.Anh.1), now unfortunately lost; they were part of a programme put on by the Concert Spirituel. Two months later, Mozart's music was played at the Opéra: it was part of a Ballet entitled *Les petits riens* (K.Anh.10 [299b]) which followed Piccinni's *Le finte gemelle* under the composer's direction. The first performance was on 3 June and the Ballet was repeated several times; apart from the remarkable Overture, it is not absolutely certain which of the extant pieces are Mozart's and which by other hand(s). Grimm's famous *Correspondance Littéraire* mentions the event but not Mozart's music, nor was he listed in the rather extensive review in the *Journal de Paris*, where the choreographer Jean Georges Noverre's action is described and the music praised ('*très agréable*'). Wolfgang, however, had a personal crisis on his hands: on 9 June, his mother was so ill that she was cupped, and on the 10th she went out for the last time. On 3 July she died, aged 57, and next day was buried in the cemetery of Saint-Eustache. In a now famous letter addressed to their Salzburg friend, the Abbé Bullinger, Wolfgang tried to prepare Leopold for news of the tragedy, but when it did arrive, both father and daughter were devastated. It had been an exceptionally happy marriage.

Life had to go on, however, and Wolfgang had finished his most famous composition for the French capital, the 'Paris' Symphony in D major (K.297 [300a]), performed at the Concert Spirituel, with its large orchestral forces, on Corpus Christi Day, 18 June. The director of the Concert Spirituel, Joseph Legros, suggested to Mozart that he should write another slow movement, which the composer did (there has been much discussion recently as to which of the two slow movements is the original); he also made substantial revisions to the orchestration of the flanking movements, and it was in this new guise that the 'Paris' Symphony was performed on 15 August (Ascension Day) at the Concert Spirituel and repeated on 8 September. Legros retained the right to publish the work, but this did not happen until ten years later, after Mozart's name was again beginning to circulate in Paris.

Mozart's frustration was not diminished when not he but Johann Christian Bach received the commission ('*scrittura*' as Mozart referred to it, in Italian) to write an opera for the 1779 season; its title was *Amadis des Gaules*. Wolfgang writes to his father from St Germain on 27 August:

> Mr Bach from London has been here for the last 14 days, he is to write a French opera – he's only here to listen to the singers, then he returns to London, writes it and comes back to stage it: – you can imagine his joy and my joy when we saw each other again [after 1765 in London] – perhaps his joy is not so sincere – but it has to be said that he's an honest man and deals correctly with people; I love him (as you well know) with my whole heart – and respect him; and he – it is quite certain that to my face as well as with other persons – and not exaggeratedly, but seriously – truthfully praised me ...

In the summer of 1778, Mozart composed what might be regarded as his finest Parisian work – the Piano Sonata in A minor (K.310 [300d]) which is dated on the autograph manuscript (on loan at the Pierpont Morgan Library, New York). If the 'Paris' Symphony and *Les petits riens*, as well as the Concerto for Flute and Harp (K.299) for the Duc de Guines, were to some extent public works written to secure the plaudits of the Parisian salons and general public, the Sonata in A minor is obviously a highly personal work, written out of inner conviction and perhaps out of some desperate necessity. Stern, resolute, impassioned – this, we feel, is the real Parisian Mozart, the man behind the masque. The same applies to another exceptional work in a minor key, the Violin Sonata in E minor (K.304 [300a]), which was probably begun in Mannheim but finished in Paris and, with five other violin sonatas, engraved there; Sieber published them in November 1778 as Opus I. Of them all, that in E minor is as exceptional as the Piano Sonata in A minor, a strikingly original creation of great inner strength and a curiously impersonal sorrow.

By September, and after a last unsatisfactory meeting with Baron Grimm, Wolfgang recognized that he had failed in his attempt to secure a suitable position in Paris. It is true that he had been offered the post of organist at Versailles at 2,000 livres *per annum*, but although Leopold thought his son should accept the appointment, Wolfgang considered that he would be too isolated from the real musical world of Paris, and, moreover, he reckoned that the post of organist at Versailles was not really in keeping with his ambitions. Parisian society was preoccupied with other things, for example Gluck, Piccinni, young composers on the spot like Grétry and Gossec, the deaths of Voltaire and Rousseau; the young man from Salzburg was decidedly not in the forefront of everybody's mind that spring and summer of 1778 in Paris.

With hindsight we can say that the best thing Mozart ever did was to leave Paris and return to Austria. His career, already brilliant as far as the quality of the music he composed at Salzburg in 1779 and 1780 was concerned, took on an entirely new dimension when he moved to, and settled in, Vienna. And it was the Austrian capital, not the beautiful city on the Seine, which would prove the ideal place for him to live and to develop his unique gifts – the piano concertos and the Italian operas would have been unthinkable in Paris, to name the two categories in which Mozart was to reign absolutely supreme in Vienna. And it is unlikely that Paris would have been the ideal place to foster Mozart's great string quartets and quintets: nor was there a sympathetic fatherly colleague like Joseph Haydn in Paris.

Despite all this, it would be a great mistake to dismiss Paris and its role in Mozart's life out of hand. There is no question but that he became a truly great composer only after he had experienced frustrations and bitternesses, as well as the personal tragedy of his mother's death, during his six months' stay in the French capital. There had been flashes of brilliance in his earlier music – such as the violin concertos or Symphony no. 29 in A (K.201); and we have seen that Paris brought to fruition two extraordinary works in the minor-key sonatas. When he returned to Salzburg, however, greatness descended on him like some magnificent cloak. Nor were his musical experiences in Paris as negative as his letters might suggest. On a personal level, he had, with youthful bravado, resolved to dislike the French and all their works; but his musical mind was not so prejudiced, and it is clear that he was impressed not only by Gluck's operas, but also by the great tradition of French stage works, and in particular the music of Rameau. When it came to composing *Idomeneo* in 1780 and 1781, Mozart had clearly assimilated brilliantly not only the French technique of opera construction and ballet scenes, but also Rameau's scintillating orchestration. Some of the boldest instrumental effects in *Idomeneo* are inspired by that great precursor – and of course the very libretto comes from France and another fine French composer, Campra.

Even in the field of church music, Mozart found that he could learn from the great Baroque tradition of France – in 1778 it was still very much alive at Versailles, and in other great churches of Paris as well. Consider that typically French kettledrum rhythm which is familiar from the music of Lully and Charpentier, in both sacred and secular works: ♩. ♫♩ ♩ .

One looks in vain for this rhythm in the kettledrum parts of Mozart's music prior to the Paris experience, but it would be featured prominently in the symphonies, serenades and church music that he composed after he returned to Salzburg: one may consult the first movement of the 'Posthorn' Serenade or the end of the first movement of Symphony no. 34 in C (K.338), where this rhythm dominates the texture in both trumpets and timpani for bar after bar. There are many other examples, too numerous to mention. And if one may permit oneself to offer a speculative suggestion, it is that after 1778 Mozart's music takes on one typically French characteristic in even greater quantity and quality than before – that of elegance. No artist could have lived for months in Paris without observing that all-pervading French '*qualité de vie*', and if Mozart profited from one French trait, it was that. And surely no music is more elegant than Mozart's mature works, composed from 1779 to 1791. They are the essence of good taste, and even France's most hostile critics could hardly gainsay that good taste has always been an essential aspect of life for French men and women, for their houses and furnishings, for their clothes and chic, for their prose, poetry, drama, and – not least – their music. Always the consummate innovator, Mozart was also unrivalled as an assimilator.

Picture Essay: Aspects of Life in
Austria in Mozart's Time

THERE FOLLOWS A SELECTION OF ENGRAVINGS BY J.E. MANSFELD, AN artist who was well known in Austria in the late eighteenth century for his visual reportage, as well as for his portraits of leading figures in the arts and society. The engravings illustrated here are taken from a three-volume work published in Frankfurt and Leipzig (vols. 1 and 2 in 1784, vol. 3 in 1785), entitled *Bildergalerie katholischer Misbräuche* [*sic*], *Bildergalerie klösterliche Misbräuche* and *Bildergalerie weltlicher Misbräuche* respectively; their content is – as the titles suggest – partly satirical (German *Mißbräuche* = abuses), reflecting contemporary patterns of human behaviour in the context of the Church, monastic life and everyday secular situations. The subject matter is, however, also an invaluable visual record of the prevailing social scene in the 1780s, especially in Vienna, such as Mozart would have known it.

The individual captions to the engravings reproduced provide a brief description of the topical aspects of each scene.

12 In the theatre. Possibly the Burgtheater, Vienna. The small
orchestra is in the front row (pit) – the neck of a double bass is
visible – and in this production the size of the band suggests that it
was probably intended for entr'actes and incidental music
(the original caption indicates that a play is being given).

13 The card game. Mozart loved playing cards, but it is to be
doubted if he ever gambled seriously or for large sums of money, as
has sometimes been suggested. Card playing was an extremely
popular pastime in Vienna in the 1780s. Notice the cleric playing at
the table on the left.

14 A concert of dilettanti during a period of Court mourning.
In a large room the players as well as the group of onlookers are
shown in mourning attire. The daughter of the house
is seen playing a solo on the piano and the
audience applauds.

15 The ballroom. Mozart was passionately fond of dancing and was apparently extremely accomplished. The scene depicted would have been typical of Carnival time preceding Lent. The orchestra can be seen on the balcony at the back (visible: a horn-player and strings).

16 A Prelate's banquet in a palace. Such a lavish scene might have
been witnessed by Mozart at any of the grand abbeys with which he
and his father had associations. Notice the orchestra of monks
in the right foreground.

17 The marriage feast. A room in an inn, with high-spirited guests
around the table. The cook (standing, foreground) offers a plate to
the guests and collects tips, while the innkeeper collects the hats and
canes to hold in case the bill is not paid, and a band of street
musicians enters the room (after Mozart's own wedding in 1782, the
Serenade for Thirteen Instruments (K.361) is said
to have been performed).

18 The monastery theatre. One such theatre, in Lambach Abbey
(Upper Austria), still exists. Wolfgang and his father visited
Lambach in 1769, when each presented a signed MS. copy of a
symphony as a gift for the monks.

19 A ceremonial funeral procession, a Cross-bearer and children
from the Bürgerspital ('mostly hunchbacked'), then representatives
of other hospitals. The clerics include Franciscans, Minorites,
Paulites, Carmelites, etc. As the members of the funeral party
earnestly read their prayer-books, the procession passes through a
large square. Mozart will have witnessed such funeral processions
many times in Vienna.

The Symphonies: a survey

I N 1764, WHEN MOZART WROTE HIS FIRST SYMPHONY IN LONDON, THE form was flourishing all over Europe. In those days, Paris was the centre of music publishing, and it was from there that many works of German and Austrian origin, as well as those by French and Italian composers, were distributed throughout the Continent. In Germany and Austria it was cheaper to have a symphony copied and sell it in manuscript form, usually as a set of parts (full scores were very rarely copied). In Vienna, there existed numerous *scriptoria* which did a flourishing trade in manuscript parts of the latest symphonies, selling them all over the Austrian monarchy. Many symphonies by composers of the Austrian school survive only in such MS. copies prepared by Viennese music firms. This situation continued to obtain until *c.* 1780, when several publishers in Vienna, such as Torricella, Artaria and Huberty, began to print sets of parts of symphonies. For the next twenty years, the copyists continued to produce manuscript copies of symphonies for sale in parallel with the published editions, which were still considerably more expensive.

From its origins as a three-movement overture to an Italian opera, the form had moved north and become a concert piece (one Italian composer, G.B. Sammartini, did, however, specialize in non-operatic symphonies, largely composed in Milan). By the 1750s composers like Wagenseil and Georg Reutter Jr. were composing concert symphonies in Vienna. The standard number of movements remained three: fast, slow, very fast – or (something of a Viennese speciality) fast, slow, tempo di minuetto. By *c.* 1760, Viennese composers like Leopold Hofmann, who was Kapellmeister at St Stephen's Cathedral in Vienna, and Joseph Haydn, then at the court of Count Morzin in Bohemia, were composing four-movement symphonies with a minuet in second or, more usually, third place. This too had been an Austrian speciality since 1740, when Mathias Georg Monn had written a symphony with a very Austrian-sounding minuet. At this crucial date of 1760, yet another kind of four-movement symphony had entered the

Austrian musical vocabulary, one that had its origins in the old-Italian church sonata (*sonata da chiesa*), where there was an entire opening slow movement. Joseph Haydn took over this idea and adapted it to the Austrian symphony. Sometimes he would compose such a work in three movements, ending with a tempo di minuetto (as in Symphony no. 18), sometimes there are four movements: slow, fast, minuet and trio, very fast. Three such symphonies of the late 1750s (nos. 5, 11, 17) were written for Count Morzin, and one of the curious specialities of this type of church sonata symphony was that all four (or three) movements were in the same key.

Thus, in his formative years in Salzburg, Mozart will have had many models upon which to base a symphony but, as matters turned out, he actually started to compose symphonies while on the Grand Tour. The Mozart family had journeyed through Germany to France, where in 1764 Wolfgang published his first music (four violin sonatas, issued as opp. 1 and 2). After five months in Paris, the family moved to London, arriving there at the end of April 1764. Leopold Mozart contracted a throat ailment and became dangerously ill, and while he was recovering, the family rented a house in Ebury Street, Chelsea (which still exists). Many years later, Wolfgang's sister Nannerl recalled that 'in order to occupy himself, Mozart composed his first symphony with all the instruments of the orchestra, especially trumpets and kettledrums.' He also told his sister, 'Remind me to give the horn something worthwhile to do!' It appears that this symphony is lost, but fortunately at least one work in autograph and dated 'Sinfonia di Sig. Wolfgang Mozart a London 1764' has survived, though the date is not in Mozart's hand. This is K.16 in E flat, composed when Wolfgang was eight, and first played, together with other symphonies, at a concert originally announced for 15 February 1765 but postponed until the 21st.

HAYMARKET. Little Theatre.

The Concert for the Benefit of Miss and Master MOZART will be certainly performed on Thursday the 21st instant, which will begin exactly at six, which will not hinder the Nobility and Gentry from meeting in other Assemblies on the same Evening.

Tickets to be had of Mr Mozart, at Mr Williamson's in Thrift-street, Soho, and at the said Theatre.

Tickets delivered for the 15th will be admitted.

A Box Ticket admits two into the Gallery.

To prevent Mistakes, the Ladies and Gentlemen are desired to send their Servants to keep Places for the Boxes, and give their Names to the Boxkeepers on Thursday the 21st in the Afternoon.

In a letter Leopold informed his friend and landlord in Salzburg, Lorenz Hagenauer, that 'all the symphonies at the concert will be by Wolfgang Mozart. I have to copy them myself, unless I am willing to pay one shilling for each sheet.' Later in the season, a benefit concert for the two Mozart children was announced:

For the Benefit of Miss MOZART of Thirteen, and Master MOZART of eight years of Age, Prodigies of Nature.

HICKFORD'S Great Room in Brewer Street, this Day, May 13, will be A CONCERT of VOCAL and INSTRUMENTAL MUSIC.

With all the OVERTURES [i.e. symphonies] of the little Boy's own Composition.

The Vocal Part by Sig. Cremonini; Concerto on the Violin Mr Barthelemon; Solo on the Violoncello, Sig. Cirii; Concerto on the Harpsichord by the little Composer and his Sister, each single and both together, &c.

Tickets at 5s each, to be had of Mr Mozart, at Mr Williamson's, in Thrift-street, Soho.[1]

There is also a recently discovered symphony, in F major (K.Anh.223 [19a]), now in the music collection of the Bayerische Staatsbibliothek, Munich; the source is a set of MS. parts largely copied on French paper by Leopold Mozart. There are two possibilities: either this was paper acquired and taken with them from France in April 1764, or the work was composed (or revised?) after the Mozarts left London. On the title page Leopold Mozart wrote 'di Wolfgango Mozart / compositore de 9 Anj'. Since Wolfgang had turned nine on 27 January 1765, there is the distinct possibility that this work was among the symphonies given at the two public concerts listed above.

On their arrival in London, the Mozart family found a flourishing symphonic life, in which the two principal protagonists were both German *émigrés*, Johann Christian Bach (youngest son of Johann Sebastian) and Carl Friedrich Abel. These two prodigiously talented musicians had banded together to establish a subscription concert series called the Bach-Abel Concerts. Their symphonies were supple, sophisticated and immaculately orchestrated; together, they created an intoxicatingly attractive orchestral style and it was only natural for the young Wolfgang to fall under their spell. He sat on Christian Bach's knee and they improvised music together, with Bach playing a phrase on the harpsichord and Mozart continuing it. Wolfgang was equally impressed by Abel and copied out an entire E flat symphony (on British paper, such as he also used for his own Symphony, K.16), using clarinets, and as a result this was at first thought to be a genuine Mozart work (K.18 [Anh. 109i]).

The Mozarts left hospitable Britain for Holland, where they stayed as guests of the Princess of Weilburg, sister of the Prince of Orange. They gave concerts in Ghent, Antwerp, The Hague and Leiden. At The Hague, on 30 September 1765, there was an orchestral concert, previously announced in *'s-Gravenhaegse Vrijdagse Courant*:

> By permission, Mr MOZART, Kapellmeister to the Prince-Archbishop of Salzburg, will have the honour of giving, on Monday, 30 September 1765, a GRAND CONCERT in the hall of the Oude Doelen at the Hague, at which his son, only 8 [*sic*] years and 8 months old, and his daughter, 14 years of age, will play concertos on the harpsichord. All the overtures will be from the hand of this young composer, who, never having found his like, has had the approbation of the Courts of Vienna, Versailles, and London. Music-lovers may confront him with any music at will, and he will play everything at sight. Tickets cost 3 florins per person, for a gentleman with a lady 5.50 fl. Admission cards will be issued at Mr Mozart's present lodgings, at the corner of Burgwal, just by [the inn called] the City of Paris, as well as at the Oude Doelen.

And there soon followed another, similarly worded announcement of a concert to be given on 22 January 1766:

> By permission, the children of Mr Mozart, Kapellmeister of the orchestra of the Prince-Archbishop of Salzburg, will have the honour of giving a grand concert on Wednesday, 22 January 1766, at the Oude Doelen at The Hague ... The price of admission is 3 gulden per person, for a gentleman with a lady 1 ducat. Tickets are issued at Mr Mozart's lodgings at the house of Monsr. Eskes, master watchmaker, on the Hof-Spuy, the Hague, where the Court of Utrecht is situated, and also at the Oude Doelen.[2]

Again, there is a symphony which has survived only in a copy written in Leopold Mozart's hand, K.19 in D, the cover of which shows that, apart from K.16 in E flat, there were at least three other works in the genre in circulation by 1765–6: the above-mentioned symphony in F major (now K.19a), the lost one in C (with trumpets and drums?; an *incipit* of a symphony in C, which appears as K.Anh.222 [=19b], has a very J.C. Bach-like beginning) and K.19 in D. As for the second concert in The Hague, we have yet another symphony, this time in B flat (K.22), again copied – but in this case in full score – by Leopold and dated by him 'Synfonia / di Wolfg. Mozart a la Haye nel mese Decembre 765'. A final work composed in Holland for the installation of the eighteen-year-old William V, Prince of Orange, as Regent of the Netherlands, was entitled 'Galimathias Musicum' (K.32), a kind of burlesque miniature symphony featuring popular folk melodies, including a Christmas carol set in the style of a 'pastorella' or pastoral substitution for the minuet and trio. There is a kind of draft version, partly in Leopold's hand and partly in Wolfgang's, which is today housed in two libraries: the Gemeentemuseum, The Hague; and the Bibliothèque Nationale, Paris. However, there also exists a more complete, 'authorized' manuscript, prepared by a professional scribe, for a performance at the princely Fürstenberg court in Donaueschingen Castle, and this version was used in the authoritative *Neue Mozart-Ausgabe* (edited by Wolfgang Plath).

While in Holland, both Wolfgang and his sister suffered serious illnesses, and these may have forced the family to stay there longer than originally planned. From January to April 1766 they gave a whole series of concerts, many with orchestra, in Amsterdam and elsewhere, at which Wolfgang introduced his new symphonies. One of the new works he wrote for performance in The Hague was a G major Symphony (now known, because an authentic copy was discovered in the Benedictine Monastery at Lambach in Upper Austria, as the 'Old Lambach' Symphony); this work (K.Anh. 221 [45a]) was possibly also composed for the investiture of William V, along with 'Galimathias Musicum'. The Bayerische Staatsbibliothek owns a set of parts of K.45a which appear to represent the original performance material. The first and second violin parts are in the hand of an unknown scribe, the *Basso* part is in Nannerl's hand and the rest are in Leopold Mozart's highly professional hand, as is the title page: 'Sinfonia / à 2 Violini / 2 Hautbois / 2 Corni / Viola / et / Basso / di Wolfgango / Mozart di Salisburgo / à la Haye 1766.' By the time this symphony and another by Leopold were presented to

Lambach Abbey – the parts are marked 'Dono Authoris 4ta Jan: 769' – Wolfgang, possibly with his father's assistance, had revised his own composition, mainly in the inner parts.

The Mozarts travelled homewards, breaking their journey in Paris and Versailles (from about 10 May to 9 July); during their stay, the family friend and writer Baron von Grimm included news of the visitors from Salzburg in one of his famous newsletters. Of Wolfgang he wrote:

> This marvellous child is now nine years old. He has hardly grown at all, but he has made prodigious progress in music ... [Now] he has composed symphonies for full orchestra, which have been performed and generally applauded here.[3]

Later, the young Mozarts played in Dijon, Lyons and in Switzerland, ending their tour at the Bavarian court in Munich. In many of these places Wolfgang's symphonies were performed.

On balance, Mozart's early symphonies are charming and, despite the occasional structural flaw, deftly fashioned. If Mozart's name were not attached to them, they would hardly be so frequently played and recorded today. When he returned to Salzburg, he seems to have received the occasional request for a symphony – not surprising at a court where Johann Michael Haydn was producing a constant stream of interesting and occasionally brilliant symphonic serenades, as well as actual symphonies.

On 11 September 1767, the Mozarts set out for what was to be their second trip to Vienna (they had been there in 1762 and had been received at the imperial court). During this visit, on 15 October, Archduchess Maria Josepha died of smallpox, which was raging in the city; a week later, in order to escape the epidemic, Leopold and his family fled to Olmütz. Even so, Wolfgang contracted the disease, as did Nannerl, but both recovered. During their long stay in Vienna, to which the Mozarts returned in January 1768, Wolfgang expected to produce a new opera, La finta semplice, which was however abandoned because of massive intrigues. While at Olmütz, he completed a serenely cheerful symphony in F (K.43) and, when he returned to Vienna, another, in D (K.51 [46a]) with trumpets and kettledrums, which he later used as the overture to the ill-fated La finta semplice (which Wolfgang brought back to Salzburg, where it was subsequently performed); when he revised the symphony as an overture, his changes included the omission of the minuet and trio and the reorchestration of the entire score.

Just before he left Vienna to return home to Salzburg, Wolfgang composed another D major Symphony (K.48), the autograph of which is dated 13 December 1768; this work was perhaps written for a private concert, about which nothing is known today. (Prince Galitzin was one of Mozart's patrons: as Russian Ambassador in Vienna, he kept an elegant palace and gave concerts to which members of the nobility were invited.)

Like Michael Haydn, Mozart composed large-scale orchestral serenades for various happy occasions in Salzburg – weddings, the end of the academic year at the university, the raising of a family to the nobility – all of which could call forth a bright, multi-movement serenade. Many such works had miniature concertos or concertante movements built into them – for trombone solo in one of Michael Haydn's, for trumpet in another by him, for wind band in Mozart's 'Posthorn' Serenade (K.320) and for solo violin in his 'Haffner' Serenade (K.250). After the event for which the serenade was written, composers would often turn these long works into shorter symphonies by removing some of the more boisterous solo movements and a minuet/trio. The first such serenade that Wolfgang wrote was in D (K.100 [62a]), performed some time during 1769. Its original nine movements were reduced to four to make a symphony. Although these compressed 'symphonic' versions are very effective as concert pieces, and were enjoyed as such in the eighteenth and nineteenth centuries, in the twentieth century it has been more usual for the long, 'serenade' versions to be performed. Recently, however, since the publication of the 'symphonic' versions in the *Neue Mozart-Ausgabe*, the shortened versions of several Serenades (K.85 [167a], 203 [189b], 204 [213a], 250 ['Haffner', K.248b] and 320 ['Posthorn']) are beginning to enter the symphonic repertoire again – and rightly so. In one case (K.250) Leopold Mozart added a kettledrum part for the revised version. Of these attractive serenade-symphonies, which are incidentally all in the bright, trumpet-related key of D, the 'Haffner' and 'Posthorn' symphonies are outstanding and we shall return to them in more detail.

*   *   *

Mozart went to Italy three times in the period 1769–73. For his first journey, which began on 13 December 1769, Leopold Mozart was not only granted leave-of-absence, but Archbishop Schrattenbach gave him 120 ducats (600 gulden). In a second document, dated 27 November 1769, Wolfgang was not only granted official permission to travel to Italy, but was also appointed to the unpaid but prestigious position of *Conzert-Meister*, with the promise that, when he returned from Italy, he would receive 'the remuneration due to that office.'[4] The main motivation for these three visits was, in each case, an opera commission from the Court Theatre in Milan, then under Austrian sovereignty (Archduke Ferdinand, one of Maria Theresa's many sons, brother of Emperor Joseph II and of Leopold, Grand Duke of Tuscany, was Governor and Captain-General of Lombardy). Apart from these operas, however, Wolfgang was called upon to give, or participate in, many orchestral concerts for which he urgently needed symphonies in the Italian style to open and close the long programmes which were fashionable at the time. It is thought that the Symphony in C (K.73 [75a]), of which the autograph is extant, was possibly composed between 1769 and 1772, in other words for one of the Italian journeys (scholars are still arguing the exact date). Other symphonies pose greater problems: K.97 (73m), very Italian in spirit and in D with trumpets and kettledrums, has no proper sources at all, while another D major work (K.84 [73q]) survives in a contemporary MS. copy (Gesellschaft der Musikfreunde, Vienna) bearing the contradictory inscription 'In Milano, il Carnovale 1770 / Overtura', followed by 'Del Sigre Cavaliere Wolfgango Amadeo Mozart a Bologna, nel mese di Luglio, 1770', which could mean that Mozart began the work in Milan and finished it in Bologna. It, too, is very Italian in spirit. The Symphony in G major (K.74) is on paper used by Mozart in Rome in April 1770;[5] it is one of those works where the first movement effortlessly merges into the second. When Wolfgang finally got round to composing the Overture to his new opera for Milan, *Mitridate, rè di Ponto*, he adopted the customary three-movement Italian *sinfonia* form, i.e. without minuet/trio. This was soon circulated as a concert symphony, and parts for trumpets and drums, missing in the opera sources, appear in a contemporary MS. at Donaueschingen.

On his return journey, with Leopold acting as mentor and agent, Wolfgang received a commission in Padua to compose Metastasio's *azione sacra* entitled *La Betulia liberata*, which he accordingly did in the summer of 1771. Those fortunate enough to have heard the performance of this extraordinary work at the Winter Festival in Salzburg in 1989 were astonished by its modernity and profundity. This music is in signal contrast to the prettily conventional Italianate symphonies which Wolfgang was then composing; and for the first time we are given an introduction to the stern, sometimes tortured world of the *Sturm und Drang* symphonies in the minor, composed principally by Joseph Haydn (now Kapellmeister to Prince Nicolaus I Esterházy), but also by his brother Michael in Salzburg: can it be a coincidence that in 1771 Michael wrote a darkly impassioned *Introduzione* to a drama called *Der büssende Sünder*, in which he included not two but four horns – an unusual feature also found in Mozart's Overture? The same ferocious repeated notes (quavers in Mozart, semiquavers in Haydn), the same relentlessly forward-moving music, inform both works to a degree of uncanny similarity. It was Wolfgang's first, and impressive, bid to achieve musical greatness.

The remaining symphonies composed, or probably composed, in Italy need not detain us except in a very general way. One, in C (K.96 [111b]) with trumpets and drums, existed in MS. in Germany (the sole source was destroyed in World War II), but may be an authentic work. The Overture to *Ascanio in Alba* (K.111), including trumpets and drums, was first performed in Milan on 17 October 1771 as part of the nuptial celebrations for Archduke Ferdinand and Princess Maria Ricciarda Beatrice of Modena. When he turned it into a concert symphony, Mozart replaced the original choral Finale with a new instrumental movement in 3/8 time (K.120 [111a]). Not long after the royal wedding celebrations, he had occasion to write the Symphony in F (K.112) for a private concert given in Milan by the keeper of the privy purse to Archduke Ferdinand: the autograph is dated 2 November 1771, and the work's layout shows it to be a real concert symphony, with the flanking movements and the andante marked with repeats (this practice was dispensed with in opera overtures, partly to save time). The series of Italian overtures that were turned into concert symphonies concludes with Mozart's third Milanese operatic commission, the grand and impressive *Lucio Silla* of 1772: its festive and somewhat cold three movements again contain parts in the flanking movements for trumpets and timpani. After its successful première on 26 December 1772, the work ran for twenty-six performances. Meanwhile a new Archbishop of Salzburg, Hieronymus, Count Colloredo, had been elected and was impatiently awaiting the kiss-of-the-hand which his *Conzert-Meister* was expected to give upon his return from his travels in Italy.

When the previous Archbishop, Siegmund von Schrattenbach, died in December 1771, the Mozarts lost a faithful and understanding prince, who had supported them and allowed them an extraordinary amount of freedom to travel. The way the new wind was blowing can be seen in the answer to Leopold Mozart's petition to the new Archbishop Colloredo for payment of some of his salary as Vice Kapellmeister (the confusion arose over the fact that when Leopold was away in Italy with Wolfgang, his own salary was withheld). The new Archbishop granted the payment, but added that his acquiescence was 'without precedent for the future, or for other court musicians absenting themselves.'[6] Life was not going to be as easy as it had been hitherto. Yet there was some good news, for Wolfgang would now receive a salary of 150 gulden p.a. as *Conzert-Meister*, a position which had previously carried no salary.[7]

In our discussion of these symphonies, we have included only those works for which there is ample evidence of authenticity. Even in the old Collected Edition published by Breitkopf & Härtel, there were some symphonies which scholars now believe were composed by Leopold. Although the *Neue Mozart-Ausgabe* includes without any apparent reservations a work like the Symphony in F (K.75), the only source for it was a set of parts in the archives of Breitkopf & Härtel, Leipzig, which are now lost; in fact, this particular work reveals many features which suggest that Leopold Mozart was its composer.

During the reign of Archbishop Schrattenbach, Wolfgang does not appear to have considered it necessary to supply the Salzburg court with many symphonies, and in the summer of 1771, when he was busy writing *La Betulia liberata*, he found time for only one, the symphony in G (K.110 [75b]). It is a merry little piece that reveals the influence of both Joseph and Michael Haydn, especially in the canonic minuet which is based on two symphonies in the same key, Joseph's no. 23 of 1764 and Michael's Overture to *Die Hochzeit auf der Alm* of 1768.

Between the second and third Italian journeys, however, Wolfgang's position underwent a significant change, for he would soon receive an official (if rather meagre) salary sanctioned by the new Archbishop. Wolfgang arrived back in Salzburg on 15 December 1771, and Schrattenbach died the day after. Two weeks after his return, Mozart had completed the first in a series of eight symphonies written before he left for Italy in October 1772 to compose *Lucio Silla*. Much of this sudden and quite unexpected burst of symphonic ardour was obviously designed to illustrate his powers to Archbishop Colloredo, who was appointed to the see in March. The works (with their respective dates from the autograph scores) are:

K.114 in A major, 30 December 1771

K.124 in G major, 21 February 1772

K.128 in C major, May 1772

K.129 in G major, May 1772

K.130 in F major, May 1772 (with the unusual scoring of flutes, two horns in C *alto*, two horns in F and strings)

K.132 in E flat, July 1772 (again with four horns, two in E flat *alto* – the only known instance of this pitch – and two in E flat *basso*, the normal pitch)

K.133 in D major, July 1772 (with trumpets)

K.134 in A major, August 1772 (with flutes and horns)

It was thus perhaps no coincidence that in August Wolfgang received notice of his official salary. However, it was obviously not just by the sheer weight of numbers that the musical and sensitive Colloredo was impressed; far more it is the quality of the material and the elegance and sophistication with which it is presented. Many of the new features appear in Haydn symphonies of the period, especially Joseph's: the experimentation with four horns (Symphonies 13, 31, 39 and – wildly out of place chronologically – 72), the sudden appearance of the flute in the slow movement of K.133 (nos. 24, 30, 41 – all predating these Mozart works), the quick-metred slow movements in triple time (3/8) in K.130 (nos. 38, 39 – both of the late 1760s).

Despite these influences, however, there is a very specially Mozartian quality about these works: as usual, Mozart has received the influence, assimilated it and turned it into his own special musical language. This is most clearly seen in the rightly celebrated Symphony in A major (K.114), which begins softly and with that peculiar delicacy which Mozart was soon to make his own. There is a wiry self-sufficiency in this music which bodes well for the future. Another work of the highest calibre is K.130 in F, with its bizarre Trio (modal harmonies and Haydnesquely high horn writing for Joseph Leutgeb, who would later move to Vienna and for whom Mozart wrote four magnificent horn concertos and a Quintet).

Some time after the performance of *Il sogno di Scipione*, a *serenata* composed for the installation of Archbishop Colloredo in May 1772, Mozart decided to turn its two-movement Overture into a symphony. In point of fact, the whole serenade had been composed for the previous Archbishop in 1771, and was brought out in 1772 when it was, perhaps, needed at very short notice. Some time between 1772 and 1774, Mozart composed a finale

(K.163), because originally the Overture had led into the opera after the slow movement; the resulting three-movement symphony (now K.141a) – which, confusingly, has another Köchel number, 161 – is one of Wolfgang's formal Italian *sinfonie*, coldly magnificent with trumpets and timpani and rather lacking in personality.

That last description is hardly appropriate for the next bout of symphonic activity – the orchestral music that Mozart wrote after his return from Italy in 1773. The works used to be bound in three volumes, as follows:

Vol. I:
Serenade in D (K.85 [167a]; probably August 1773)
March for the above Serenade (K.189 [167b])

Vol. II:
Concertone in C (K.190 [186e]; 31 May 1774)
Serenade in D (K.203 [189b]; probably August 1774)
Serenade in D (K.204 [213a]; 5 August 1775)
Serenade in D (K.250 [284b]; probably July 1776, 'Haffner')

The third volume, when sold at auction by Sotheby's in London in 1987, fetched the highest price ever for any collection of music: £2,935,000. A curious feature of this volume, which includes only symphonies, is that the dates have been tampered with, probably when Wolfgang had them sent to Vienna in the 1780s and wanted to palm them off there as 'modern' works. Most of the dates have been restored, though some questions still remain.

Vol. III: Symphonies
C major (K.162; 19 or 29 April 1773)
D major (K.181 [162b]; 19 May 1773)
B flat (K.182 [173da]; 3 October 1773)
G minor (K.183 [173dB]; 5 October 1773)
E flat (K.184 [161a]; 30 March 1773)
G major (K.199 [161b]; 10 or 16 April 1773)
C major (K.200 [189k]; 12 or 17 November 1774)
A major (K.201 [186a]; 6 April 1774)
D major (K.202 [186b]; 5 May 1774)

With this group of works, we arrive at a new level of inspiration. Mozart's technique has become flawless, and some of these works are great masterpieces. The first is the 'Haffner' Serenade – composed for a wedding in the

Haffner family, long standing friends of the Mozarts – which he shortened as a four-movement symphony, adding a kettledrum part. This Serenade is glorious *al fresco* music: of the slow movements, one has a meltingly beautiful violin solo (there are three movements with violin solo, all of them omitted in the symphony version), which is music for love under the starry Salzburg night; the slow introduction to the Finale is of moving dignity and depth; while the first movement has a majesty which turns surprisingly dark in the development section – here is the 'Great Precursor'. This, in my opinion, is Mozart's first truly great orchestral work.

Among the actual symphonies, and taking them in chronological order, the D major work K.181 (with trumpets) is a three-movement overture with no break between movements. There is a special D major brilliance in the first movement, which is in the best operatic *sinfonia* tradition – bracing chords, repeated semiquavers, dashing alternations of *piano* and *forte*; in short, all the tricks of the orchestral trade. All of which in no way prepares us for the Andantino grazioso, which starts out as if it were a typical 3/8 movement in the best serenade manner; but suddenly there is a swerve and the music becomes a miniature oboe concerto. The effect is magical, and we are in a spring night above the town of Salzburg, where the south wind softly moves the first leaves on the trees.

Another interconnected three-movement Symphony (also with trumpets) is in E flat (K.184=166a=161a), this time of sterner stuff than the charming D major K.181. In fact, it may have begun life (as indeed did K.181) as a real operatic overture for some serious drama. Not only does the first movement generate a real sense of passion, but the slow movement, in C minor, provides a sombre contrast. When Johann Böhm's theatrical troupe put on a play called *Lanassa* in the 1780s, Böhm used K.184 as the Overture, followed by much of the magnificent and stirring incidental music which Mozart wrote for *Thamos, König in Ägypten* (see the separate essay, pp. 38ff.).

The so-called 'little' G minor Symphony (K.183) has been much discussed. It forms part of the *Sturm und Drang* legacy of Austrian symphonists, foremost among them Haydn of the late 1760s and early 1770s with works (including symphonies, piano sonatas, string quartets and church music) in keys like F sharp minor, C minor, E minor, F minor and D minor. Not only Haydn but other Austrian composers, especially J.B. Vanhal and Carlos Ordoñez, between them developed a special 'passion' language –

melodies with wide leaps and syncopations, repeated quavers or semiqua-
vers, crashing chords, dramatic use of silence, and often four rather than the
usual two horns (Haydn, Vanhal, Ordoñez). The direct models for Mozart's
K.183 were Haydn's Symphony no 39 in G minor and a Vanhal Symphony
in the same key – both with four horns and the other characteristics of this
'Storm and Stress' school – which incidentally acquired its name from a
German play by Klinger of 1776, the Austrian music having preceded the
German literary movement by a decade. Although Mozart wrote only one
exercise in this manner in the mid-1770s, later, when he moved to Vienna,
he would return to it with a vengeance.[8]

The spirited Symphony in C major (K.200) was one for which Mozart
added a kettledrum part in autograph; it was sold at auction in 1929, but
contemporary copies have also been located in sources in Graz and Prague
(see the critical notes in the *Neue Mozart-Ausgabe*).[9] This has always been a
popular work, and it was one of the few early Mozart symphonies which
were available on records before World War II (Berlin College of
Instrumentalists, conducted by Fritz Stein, the man who found the 'Jena'
Symphony, then attributed to Beethoven). Two enchanting aspects are the
solo horn 'echoes' in the minuet and the trill-laden Finale.

Always the most popular and respected of this group of eight symphonies
has been the one in A major (K.210), for its grace, its craftsmanship and its
musical inspiration. The extraordinary beginning, with its strong rhythmic
sequence in the violins and the slow-moving minims with long legato slurs
in the lower strings, immediately reveals what an atypical work this is going
to be. An equally astounding moment comes towards the end of the stately,
very baroque, Andante, which sounds like a priests' procession: the music
stops, and the oboes and horns intone a fanfare; hitherto the strings have
been playing with mutes, which during the fanfare they lift off, entering
upon the fanfare's conclusion and repeating it as a stirring close. The Finale,
too, is a rushing but densely organized Allegro con spirito with high horn
fanfares towards the end which slice through the repeated semiquavers of
the strings: a daunting prospect for any but first-rate players.

In December 1774, Mozart went to Munich to supervise the production
of his new opera *La finta giardiniera* (K.196), which was first performed
there on 13 January 1775. Later, he took the two feathery movements of the
Overture and added a third to make a concert symphony; but the curious
thing is that this third movement (K.121 [207a]) is written on Italian paper

of a type used by Mozart in Milan principally between November 1772 and early 1773. Either he must have taken the paper with him to Salzburg, or the little movement was originally intended for another work.[10]

Similarly, Mozart created another three-movement symphony out of his new opera *Il rè pastore* (called 'serenata', K.208) by adding a finale to the original two movements which, according to the paper used,[11] was written in 1776 (K.102 [213c]). At any rate, Wolfgang took it with him on his trip to Germany and Paris two years later, performing it at the house of his friend and fellow composer, Christian Cannabich, in Mannheim on 13 February 1778. In this light-textured work (which includes trumpets) Mozart reverts to his previous Italian *sinfonia* language, but as always with Mozart the music displays great charm, especially in the Andantino slow movement, which in the opera was the music of the first aria (Aminta, the shepherd king); Mozart was able to do this by assigning much of the castrato soloist's vocal line to an oboe.

With this symphony-overture Mozart came to the end of his first Salzburg period. He was becoming increasingly frustrated and unhappy in this provincial town, and it was decided that he should seek his fame and fortune in Germany and Paris. Since Archbishop Colloredo would not grant Leopold Mozart leave for such an extended trip, and since it was rightly thought that Wolfgang was in many respects a naive and immature young man in need for a chaperone, they decided that his mother should accompany him. The trip was a financial failure and, as is well known, Mozart's mother died in Paris. Moreover, Wolfgang fell in love with a young singer, Aloysia Weber, in Mannheim, but by the time he caught up with her again in Munich, she spurned his attentions, leaving him broken-hearted. It is to the one symphony created during this unhappy trip that we must now turn our attention – the 'Paris' Symphony in D (K.297 [300a]).

Mozart composed this symphony for the Concert Spirituel in Paris, where it was first performed in public on the Feast of Corpus Christi, 18 June 1778: it had been given a trial run on the 12th at the house of Count Sickingen, Envoy of the Elector Palatine. Mozart wrote to his father on that day, saying that in the new work he had been careful not to neglect *le premier coup d'archet*, the grand orchestral opening for which the Parisian orchestras of the day were so famous. After the performance he wrote further that in the first movement there was a passage 'which I felt sure must please'. He continued:

The audience were quite carried away – and there was a tremendous burst of applause. But as I knew, when I wrote it, what effect it would surely produce, I had introduced the passage again at the close – when there were shouts of 'Da Capo'. The Andante also found favour, but particularly the last Allegro, because, having observed that all final as well as first Allegros begin here with all the instruments playing together and generally *unisono*, I began mine with two violins only, *piano* for the first eight bars – followed instantly by a *forte*; the audience, as I expected, said 'hush' at the soft beginning, and when they heard the *forte*, began at once to clap their hands. I was so happy that, as soon as the symphony was over, I went off to the Palais Royal, where I had a large ice, said the Rosary as I had vowed to do – and went home ...'[12]

Mozart's patron Le Gros (Joseph Legros), who was responsible for the Symphony being commisioned, disliked the original slow movement and requested another, which Wolfgang dutifully wrote. I consider the less familiar version (in 3/4 time rather than 6/8) to be the final one, for when Legros – to whom Mozart had ceded the rights – published the work with Sieber in 1789, he included not only the 3/4 movement but also extensive revisions in the other movements, among them different trumpet and drum parts, etc. – all patently Mozart's second thoughts. At the time, he wrote to his father:

> ... in order to satisfy him [Legros] (and, as he maintains, several others) I have composed another Andante. Each is good in its own way – for each has a different character. But the new one pleases me even more ... On August 15th, the Feast of the Assumption, my symphony is to be performed for the second time – with the new Andante ...'[13]

The Andante in 3/4 time has only recently been made available complete (the bassoon parts missing from all three movements in most known copies of the Sieber edition form an appendix to Zaslaw's book, pp. 564ff.)

Mozart carried a copy of the 'Paris' Symphony with him when he returned to Austria and there is evidence (see below) that he performed it on several occasions in Vienna and intended to revise it for Prague at the end of 1786. As a composition, K.297 is conventional but not without real flashes of genius; and unlike the other, later masterpieces, this work requires a great conductor to make the long stretches of D major orchestral writing come to life.

*   *   *

Mozart had been dismissed from the archiepiscopal service when he went on his long journey to Paris. Leopold managed to secure for his son the position of court organist following the death of Anton Cajetan Adlgasser (he had died in 1777, but the post was not immediately filled). Wolfgang arrived in Salzburg on 15 January 1779, and immediately submitted a petition to Archbishop Colloredo, begging submissively for the position; this was granted by a decree dated 17 January 1779, giving Mozart the annual salary of his predecessor, 450 gulden (much more than he had received as *Conzert-Meister*). Although Mozart detested Salzburg, he set to work on all sorts of tasks, using the large orchestra which consisted, in the years 1779 and 1780 when he remained in Salzburg, of twenty violins (they included a kettle-drummer and two trumpeters), two viola players, two cellists, four double-bass players, five oboists (doubling as flautists), three bassoon players and two horn players.

Mozart had returned from Paris a changed and saddened man. His style now became richer, more involved, more profound, with many dark sides to it. The key of C major, always associated with ceremonious music and settings of the Mass with trumpets and kettledrums in Austria, become especially ambivalent. In the C major church music of this amazingly productive final period in Salzburg, there are two large-scale Masses (including the celebrated 'Coronation' Mass, K.317) and two Vespers settings (see pp. 179f.). In all this music, we find not only a peculiarly heavy accent placed on brass instruments (the church music included three trombones which doubled the alto, tenor and bass voices in the choir), but Mozart began increasingly to cultivate a darker side to this music of Pomp and Circumstance. The same increase in variety and richness is also immediately noticeable in the three symphonies of this period and the 'Posthorn' Serenade. The first Symphony (K.318), dated 26 April 1779, is a powerful work in G with three interconnected movements, scored for four horns and two trumpets (in the original autograph, no timpani part is found). The trumpets were added to the autograph on separate sheets, and since they are on paper used mostly in Vienna in 1782 and 1783, it is presumed that the enlarged orchestration was created there.[14] The traditional kettledrum part (reproduced in small notes in the *Neue Mozart-Ausgabe*, derives from several early MS. copies, and it is likely that the work was first performed with an improvised drum part, as was often done in the eighteenth century. In view of the small scale of the work, many scholars have wondered if it was not intended as an operatic overture or the prologue to a spoken drama with incidental music; it is, however, a richly integrated and brilliantly orchestrated work with an exceptionally large wind band consisting of flutes, oboes, bassoons and four (rather than two) horns. Here, we find powerful Mannheim crescendos, as well as extraordinary shades of scoring, made possible by the large orchestration; towards the end of the Finale there is an explosion of sound when the bassoons, brass instruments and timpani (with a roll) – all marked *ff* – reach out to seize us in an unexpected switch into E minor (bar 259). This suddenly opens a vista into the kind of scoring that we find both in late Haydn symphonies and in early Beethoven.

The second Salzburg Symphony (K.319), in B flat and dated 9 July 1779, is quite another sort of work. It uses a delicate orchestration (oboes, bassoons and B-flat *alto* horns) and is in the long Austrian tradition of chamber symphonies, wherein there is a great deal of legato string playing which, in order even further to underline the unaggressive language, is set off by a principal theme with staccato quavers. There is no double bar in the first movement, and great is our surprise to find Mozart beginning a whole new section in the development based on the ancient Gregorian 'Credo' theme which, in the composer's most sinewy legato fashion, glides subtly from key to key with bewitching inner voices to accompany its beautiful metamorphosis. And the slow movement is all of the same general pattern – quiet, restrained, with a thoughtful juxtaposition of legato and staccato. The minuet and trio were added in Vienna on paper mostly used in the latter part of 1785, but sometimes found in scores of 1784.[15] In fact, the minuet has features very reminiscent of Joseph Haydn, a little like the minuet in his Symphony no. 43 ('Mercury'). The racy and racing Finale alternates triplets with series of dotted figures, and whole blocks of music where there are no triplets at all. This gives, in some curious way, a very light-hearted texture, so that this beautiful and sophisticated work is all of one piece: considering that the minuet was added some five years later, to have achieved this unity was no mean feat.

Artaria published K.319 in Vienna, together with K.385 ('Haffner') – part of an unrealized project whereby Mozart wanted to dedicate three symphonies to Prince von Fürstenberg. These two works were the only ones of Mozart's last nine symphonies – we exclude the symphonic version of the 'Posthorn' Serenade (K.320) from this list – to be published in his lifetime, a curious and not easily explicable phenomenon, when it is considered that

Artaria's edition was very widely circulated, also in England (where copies were imported by Longman & Broderip – one is in the Bayerische Staatsbibliothek in Munich) and Paris, as well as Germany.

The last of this great Salzburg trilogy – the grand C major Symphony (K.338) – is the most dramatic and symphonic of the group. Here it is time to speak of one of the most widespread of Mozartian 'fingerprints' (to borrow the term from the world of art and particularly the great American art-historian Bernard Berenson): the dotted rhythm ♩ ♪.♩♩ ♩ (or its equivalent in longer note-values ♩ ♩. ♪|♩ ♩).

In that E minor outburst, *ff*, noted in the last pages of K.318, it is characteristic that bar 259 is in this dotted rhythm, which pervades long sections of the opening movement in K.338. This is a marching rhythm which is every bit as all-embracing and pervasive as the march 'complex' frequently remarked upon in the music of Gustav Mahler. We find it in marked profusion in the opening movement of the 'Haffner' Symphony (K.385), in numerous piano concertos (the beginning of K.459, for example) and in all manner of other music, especially the operas (in *La clemenza di Tito* the Overture, final chorus etc.).

Another aspect of the hugely expansive opening of K.338 is the way in which, at the end of the exposition, the music begins to darken, as if black clouds were piling up in a brilliantly sunny sky – and what a touch are those 'toy' trumpets, underlining the final lead-back into the recapitulation! Note also that *opera buffa* – brought into the concert symphony by Haydn in the 1770s and 1780s – has now become a part of Mozart's questing spirit. The great slashing chords and dotted rhythm of the opening are suddenly echoed, softly by the strings and bassoons (those old comic figures) – it is reminiscent of a scene with Harlequin and Columbine in a tableau by Watteau. The slow movement is another study in delicacy: when sending a set of parts to Prince Fürstenberg's castle at Donaueschingen, Mozart changed his original marking 'Andante di molto' to 'Andante di molto più tosto Allegretto', and the additional instruction to all parts, *sotto voce*, indicates that the restrained, finely spun lines were to be played with the greatest delicacy. Between the first movement and this one, there was originally a marvellously symphonic minuet which Mozart seems to have torn out of the autograph: only a single page survives.[16]

The Finale, marked Allegro vivace, is again a kind of *perpetuum mobile* in 6/8 time and a virtuoso showpiece for any orchestra. It will be noted that the texture is like an insert into one of the great Salzburg serenades, with prominent parts for the two oboes. And this brings us to the last of the large-scale orchestral serenades of this period, that in D (K.320, 'Posthorn'), completed in 'Salisburgo li 3 d'Augusto 1779'. This – the most profound, the grandest and most symphonic of all Mozart's serenades – was composed for the end-of-term celebration at Salzburg University's Faculty of Philosophy. The work consists of nine movements (beginning and ending with a march), with two minuets/trios and an insert for wind band and strings with horns (Concertante and Rondeau), which Mozart later performed in Vienna as an entity in March 1783. When he came to compress the serenade into a symphony, he selected only the massive opening, with a slow introduction that is later introduced after the development without returning to the original time signature (the note-values are simply doubled, which means that there is a very precise mathematical relationship between the introduction and the Allegro con spirito). This is followed by an extremely sombre D minor Andantino and the original and brilliant Finale. Again, the tremendous energy of K.338 is to be found here, if anything with even greater nervous tension. The forward drive of this opening movement is something palpable: never have Mannheim crescendos sounded so electrifying, never has that famous dotted rhythm been used to such telling effect.

Mozart was ready for the capital city, Vienna, in more than one sense.

*   *   *

When he was summoned by Archbishop Colloredo in 1781 to proceed to Vienna from Munich, where he had just staged his new opera *Idomeneo*, Mozart had recently enjoyed a particularly happy period in the company of congenial colleagues. He felt insulted at having to occupy a place below the salt at the table used by the Archbishop's servants in the vast building of the Order of Teutonic Knights. Colloredo and his retinue were paying a state visit to the capital and his orchestra had accompanied him. Soon after his arrival there on 16 March, Mozart was caught up in a whirlwind of musical activity, playing at the house of the Russian Ambassador (Prince Galitzin) and then appearing for the first time in a large public concert, as part of the special event organized during Lent by the Society of Musicians (Tonkünstler-Societät). This famous organization, which boasted a volunteer orchestra of some 180 players, gave two more-or-less identical concerts at Christmas and another pair in Lent. With the Archbishop's grudging permission, Wolfgang gave his 'Paris' Symphony and played a piano concerto before an audience which included Emperor Joseph II. Mozart's Viennese career had begun, and with it his Salzburg career ended.

The history of the row between Archbishop Colloredo and Mozart is too well known to bear repetition here. In the end, the composer was booted out of the audience chamber by Count Arco, the Archbishop's chief steward (*Oberküchenmeister*). Mozart moved into the quarters of the Weber family (they had meanwhile moved to Vienna and Aloysia, his first love, had married the actor Joseph Lange), where he proceeded – much to Leopold Mozart's horror – to court and finally marry a younger daughter, Constanze. However, all that is peripheral to our symphonic history, which now moves forward to July 1782, when Leopold Mozart was commissioned to order a new symphony as part of the celebrations for the ennoblement of Sigmund Haffner. What Wolfgang actually wrote was another large-scale serenade, with an opening march and a second minuet (the latter is lost). On 7 August 1782, he sent it off with instructions as to how it should be performed ('The first Allegro must be played with great fire, the last – as fast as possible'). When Mozart needed the score for his concerts in the 1783 season, his father sent it to him in Vienna. On receiving it, he wrote, on 15 February 1783: 'My new Haffner symphony has positively amazed me, for I had forgotten every single note of it. It must surely produce a good effect.' The already good effect was further enhanced by the addition of two flutes and two clarinets in the first and last movements.

This was Mozart's farewell to the grand orchestral serenade in D major, a genre in which he had composed many excellent examples. Now, a change in Mozart's symphonic style is apparent: under the influence of music being played by Viennese orchestras (and not just works by Joseph Haydn) it has become tauter and less conventional. Haydn had meanwhile perfected a kind of monothematic way in which to treat broad-scale opening movements, and Mozart shows that he has once again assimilated to perfection a 'foreign' concept. This hugely symphonic first movement is largely based on the opening octave jump plus our old friend, the dotted figure. The second movement is still in the warm-hearted manner of the earlier Salzburg serenades, but there is one touchingly beautiful moment occurring after the first section (to be repeated). It is a wash of colour as Mozart provides a short but extremely poignant lead-back to the home key and the recapitulation. The remaining Minuet & Trio are concise, but again the Trio reveals that youthful and warm-hearted innocence which Wolfgang will soon hardly ever be able to recapture. And as for the Finale, to be played 'as fast as possible', it is a magnificent *tour de force*, featuring elements of *opera buffa* which alternate with vividly orchestrated *tutti* passages (note the dashing off-beat timpani rolls).

*   *   *

In 1783, Wolfgang took his new wife Constanze to Salzburg to meet his father and sister. At the end of this visit, Constanze sang the solo soprano part in the Mass in C minor (K.427 [417a]) at a performance in St Peter's Abbey on 26 October. After that, the couple left for Linz, where Wolfgang put on a hastily organized concert. He writes back to Salzburg, 'On Tuesday, November 4th, I am giving a concert in the theatre here and, as I have not a single symphony with me, I am writing a new one at break-neck speed …'. Between 30 October and 4 November, then, a space of five or six days for composing the new work, having parts copied, and rehearsing it, the 'Linz' Symphony (K.425) was born. It is in its composer's clear, radiant C major, solidly symphonic in the outer movements and with a tremendous innovation in the slow movement: here, for the first time in the history of the Viennese classical symphony, trumpets and kettledrums are retained in the slow movement. Their presence lends a solemnly ceremonious atmosphere to this majestic and often rather sombre Andante, which may have something of Haydn's slow movements in 6/8 time (like, for example, that for the 'Maria Theresa' Symphony, no. 48 of 1769). If Haydn's influence is also felt in the presence of a slow introduction, a very rare feature in Mozart's symphonic music, here again Mozart has taken the idea and turned it into his own. The last two movements return to the symphonic gaiety of the first, with the Finale providing a brilliant conclusion that differs in texture from the first movement only because it is in a quick metre (2/4) and therefore lighter. Throughout the development section, Mozart uses the theme in the new Viennese way, tossing it from instrument to instrument, which is both aurally pleasing and visually entertaining. In this dashing Finale there are also very serious moments, sometimes passages of considerable duration. This 'Linz' Symphony definitely represents a milestone in Mozart's symphonic career, the portal, as it were, to the last four works in the genre, where their composer elevates the whole form to a new level of inspiration and complexity.

*   *   *

During most of the nineteenth and twentieth centuries, the last three symphonies by Mozart were treated as an entity, the *non plus ultra* of his symphonic output; in recent years, however, scholars and indeed the general public have come to broaden that trilogy by including the 'Prague' Symphony in D (K.504), completed in Vienna on 6 December 1786. It may be that the work came into being through a very peculiar circumstance. Recently, Alan Tyson identified the paper used by Mozart for an autograph trumpet part to the 'Paris' Symphony (K.297). This paper was used by the composer largely in December 1786 and the trumpet part 'contains bizarre variants, suggesting either that it was written from memory or that Mozart undertook revisions to K.297.'[17] The Finale of K.504, which was written on paper of the type that Mozart used for Acts III and IV of *Le nozze di Figaro*, was presumably composed around the same time, i.e. in the first few months of 1786. Tyson therefore postulates that the Finale of K.504 was originally intended to replace the more conventional ending of K.297, composed in 1778, in a revised version. There also exist rejected sketches of a slow movement for K.504 (in the Mozarteum) and an 'Ultimo allegro per una sinfonia' (reproduced in Zaslaw, p. 418), which suggest that Mozart was very much preoccupied both with revising K.297 and then writing the rest of a new symphony in D major to go with his new Finale to K.297.

 The sketches for the first movement of the 'Prague' Symphony, like those for the string quartets dedicated to Haydn, show that not every kind of music came easily to Mozart's mercurial fingers. The towering intellectual structure of the first movement of K.504 has suggested to some critics that it might be considered the greatest symphonic opening movement of any in the Mozartian canon. The first surprising element is the opening itself, with its grand unison flourishes, for it is not until the second beat of bar 3 that we know whether the music is in D minor or D major (a similar ambiguity occurs at the outset of Haydn's Symphony no. 97, also with a remarkable slow introduction). And this ambiguity is played out on a mighty scale when, in bar 16 of this massive introduction consisting of 36 bars, the music shifts – using our omnipresent dotted 'fingerprint' – into D minor, where it

The Symphony in D (K.504): opening page of the autograph. This work forms part of the valuable collection of manuscript scores, formerly in the Preussische Staatsbibliothek, Berlin, which were transferred for safe-keeping during World War II to a monastery in Grüssau (then in Silesia) and subsequently disappeared; they are now in Poland, housed in the Biblioteka Jagiellońska, Kraków. Mozart's autograph, which was not available when the new critical edition of K.504 was prepared for the *NMA*, shows that, following his usual practice, the composer began by writing out the first violin and bass parts, that for flute I also being in the same ink; the remaining parts were added later in a paler ink, especially noticeable in the horns ('2 corni in [D]'), trumpets ('2 Clarini in D') and timpani ('tympani in D').
Reproduced by courtesy of the Uniwersytet Jagielloński, Kraków.

remains *until the end*. The following Allegro is one of Mozart's supreme contrapuntal gestures, worked out in staggering detail, and when it is not enmeshed in counterpoint other intellectual factors are present: there are two distinct second subjects, the first with a characteristic melody

which is then turned into the minor. When that happens, a variant of the theme is given to the bassoons as an accompaniment and, in order to bind the second of the two themes to the first, Mozart continues this bassoon accompaniment but assigns to it the actual beginning of the music it accompanies. It is no mean feat, and the point is to lead the listener through variety by retaining continuity – an old Mozartian principle. We might note the extraordinary turbulence and contrapuntal virtuosity of the development, wherein, characteristically, the music darkens and at the same time speeds up rhythmically: the semiquaver groups gradually take over. What follows is one of Mozart's supremely poignant lead-backs to the tonic and the recapitulation, as anguished and troubled – and beautiful – a sequence as one can find in the works of Gesualdo or other Mannerists.

The second movement continues this painfully intense chromaticism: in bar 3 the first violins move in such a pattern, and altogether the movement is remarkable for its veiled emotion and indeed ambiguous message. Who is to say if this music is happy or sad? And even to state the obvious – that it is both – does not entirely answer the questions that this quiet, troubled movement poses. Nor does the Finale, with its flamboyant unconventionality, solve the dilemma. (The fact that Mozart omits the customary minuet must have some significance, for this is the only work among his last six symphonies in which he does so.) Among the many novelties in this Presto, one notices the long wind-band solo at bars 31–46 and altogether the great freedom with which the wind instruments are treated – a clear reflection of the excellence of the Viennese *Harmonie* (wind band) established by Emperor Joseph II a few years before. In reality, this Symphony was not written for Prague but for Vienna; it acquired its nickname after Mozart visited the Bohemian capital early in 1787 and played it there. After the double bar, with its curiously unsettling timpani part, we arrive, via an increasingly complex instrumental palette, at one of the most startling passages in Mozart: a series of searing dissonances (bars 186ff.) which offer a syncopated top with a stable bottom and then, in the manner of double counterpoint, the same with top and bottom reversed. This pattern persists until bar 204. Little wonder, then, that many contemporary listeners considered Mozart's music to be verging on the lunatic fringe. The effect is very similar in spirit to the upward-moving dissonant progression in syncopations just before the coda of Beethoven's Overture *Leonore* no. 3.

The 'Prague' Symphony, together with Haydn's 'Paris' and 'Salomon' Symphonies, Mozart's final three and Beethoven's no. 1 (completed 1799?), belongs to the greatest symphonic legacy of the outgoing *settecento*.

*　　　　*　　　　*

Mozart's last three symphonies have become so celebrated and so surrounded with myth that it is very difficult to approach them with that objectivity which must be any critic's primary goal. The first myth is that they were composed in isolation, out of an overwhelming desire to crown the eighteenth century with three representative masterpieces, and that they were never performed in Mozart's lifetime. Otto Biba and, some years later, the present author have attempted to show that in 1788 Mozart put on a series of subscription concerts at the Casino in Vienna, at which these three works were first performed. And there is evidence that the revised version of K.550, with clarinets, was first performed at a concert given by the Tonkünstler-Societät in Vienna in April 1791. There is also a textual tradition of orchestral parts which derive, presumably, from these performances and not from the autograph manuscripts. Furthermore, Mozart must have taken these – his latest orchestral works – on tour in Germany in 1789 and 1790. Why would he have left them at home?[18] There can be little doubt that Mozart not only wrote, but subsequently revised these three works with very specific concert performances in mind.

The Symphony in E flat (K.543) of 1788 has an interesting scoring, including one flute, two clarinets, two bassoons, two horns, two trumpets and kettledrums, but without oboes. This was the same orchestration that the composer had used to such beautiful and original effect in the great E flat Piano Concerto (K.482), completed on 16 December 1785; and that brings us to the curiously autumnal sound of this E flat Symphony – which description is surely not seeking to inflict upon it any posthumous Romantic ideas, for this effect was quite simply a deliberate calculation on Mozart's part. The key of E flat is especially suited to wind instruments (this is for purely technical reasons which it is not necessary to relate in detail here) and has always occupied a very special position in the Viennese classical school – consider not only these works in Mozart's œuvre, but also the Serenade for wind band (K.375) or the big E flat concerted finales in his operas (for example, at the end of Act II in *Figaro*). And in Haydn we could mention two of the greatest London Symphonies, no. 99 (very autumnal, too) and the extraordinary no. 103 ('Drum Roll'), with possibly the most sinister opening in all eighteenth-century music. In Beethoven, one thinks of the 'Eroica' Symphony, as well as the 'Emperor' Concerto. There is something wistful and at the same time generous, like a bountiful harvest, in their use of E flat.

Mozart realized by this time that symphonies of this physical scale and spiritual magnitude needed to be more than four individual movements: the music must hang together, even if the desired result is achieved by means that reach only the listener's subconscious perception. German critics demonstrated long ago that there is a kind of *Ur-cantus firmus* that under-lines all four movements of the 'Jupiter' Symphony. And in the E flat work the long legato downward scales of the violins, which occur as soon as the opening *forte* of the massive slow introduction settles into *piano*, reappear in the ensuing Allegro, almost note-for-note. Notice, too, how the dotted chains in the introduction reappear in the Allegro, most spectacularly in the trumpets at the end of the first movement. The curiously unsettling timpani rhythm at the beginning may have Masonic overtones: we must remember that E flat is the principal key used in Masonic music in eighteenth-century Vienna and that it constitutes the golden thread in *Die Zauberflöte*.

The actual legato theme of the Allegro has also a spirituality and a haunt-ing quality which may derive from the fact that, like many of Mozart's (and *not* many of Haydn's) melodies, this one could be sung by a lyric soprano: hence the music's fragility mirrors human frailty: beauty, as Haydn noted in London a few years later, 'which will pass'.

Schubert remembered the explosive and profoundly upsetting character of those violent forages into the minor which occur in the slow movement of the E flat Symphony, a movement that in other respects is as inscrutably beautiful as the smile in Leonardo's *Mona Lisa*. These tremendous blocks of emotion occur in F minor (bars 30ff.) and, with ominous removal from the main key (A flat), in B minor (bars 96ff.). This kind of compositional proce-dure is, of course, exactly what will happen later in the second movement of Schubert's 'Unfinished' Symphony, where similar mountains of energy dis-place the quiet procesional music of the main theme.

In the Menuetto and Trio we find Mozart setting up a kind of Austrian *Ländler*: you can almost hear the county folk stamping their feet. But some of those feet are allied to the pretty feminine ankles for which Austrian women have always been famous – so that Mozart's accents are often deli-cate things (*mfp* is one – a sign never encountered in the whole of Haydn). In the Trio we have evidence of the profound influence which the clarinet-playing Stadler brothers had on Mozart's music. The first clarinet has the melody, framed with huge loving legato slurs, while clarinet II has the walk-ing, Alberti-bass accompaniment that is peculiarly suited to the instrument and which would soon become a standard device: here it is used almost for the first time in a symphony (though astute listeners could have been aware of this device in Mozart's concertos and operas, not to speak of the slightly later Clarinet Quintet of 1789).

The Finale is the most complicated and multi-structured of any thus far in Mozart's *œuvre*. It sounds at the beginning like Haydn, but its construction and continuation are profoundly Mozartian. It is predominantly monothematic – even little fragments derive from the opening material; and its tonal structure is dizzyingly original. As soon as the second section begins (both parts are to be repeated), we find ourselves in the extraordinary key of E major, and in the next few bars Mozart displays another technical device which he had learned from his friend, the horn-player Joseph Leutgeb, who was a specialist in producing so-called 'stopped' notes. This was done by inserting the right hand into the bell of the instrument, thus lowering the pitch by a half, a whole or even one-and-a-half notes. Here, in swift succession, we have six stopped notes in both horn parts. It is doubtful if any members of the usual orchestras of London, Rome or Paris could even *play* these notes on their horns – or indeed the clarinet parts (clarinet playing of this kind was largely confined to Vienna and Central Europe) – which also meant that circulation of this bold, innovative and profoundly personal work would be limited.

The Symphony in G minor (K.550) has always been regarded as one of Mozart's most personal revelations. It gave rise to a whole school of thought in the Romantic era. Nowadays, its violently neurotic and compulsive language is linked to a theory that Mozart was prey to bouts of depression of a nearly maniacal sort. There is, after all, a whole series of works, some of which easily approach, if they do not outdistance, this anguished music of K.550 – for example, the Piano Concertos in D minor (K.466) and C minor (K.491), the String Quartet in D minor (K.421), the String Quintet in G minor (K.516); the list could be easily continued. Neurotic though this great and seminal Symphony may be, it is none the less brilliantly organized and contains as rigorous and intellectual a self-discipline as any music of the period. There is not an ounce of musical fat on its lean structure.

Originally, Mozart intended to use four horns, as he had done in the 'Little' G minor Symphony (K.183) – two in G and two in B flat *alto*; but probably from motives of economy – the work was after all intended for performance at concerts which he himself was organizing, hence he would have to pay the members of the orchestra; and what would the two extra horn players do for the rest of the evening? – the scoring for the second pair was cancelled after only a few bars. The first version of K.550 is scored for one flute, pairs of oboes, bassoons and horns, together with the usual strings. Because of the nature of valveless horns, Mozart had to write for one horn in G and one in B flat. In nineteenth-century performances the wild slashes of colour – almost rude intrusions – of these horns into the polished superstructure of, say, the Finale, used to be toned down to the extent that they were almost inaudible. This attitude towards the eccentricities of Mozart's, and indeed Haydn's, scores was partly the result of a different concept of orchestral sound and partly an attempt to bring into line those aspects of eighteenth-century music which transgressed the typical 'Rococo' view of Haydn and Mozart as mild, pre-Beethovenian 'great precursors'. As part of this 'smoothing' process, dynamic marks and odd bits of orchestral colour were subdued or, as in the case of Haydn, removed entirely. Played as they are nowadays, especially on period instruments, these horn intrusions underline the intrinsic violence of the score. This is music stretched to breaking-point.

When Mozart came to revise the score, possibly for the aforementioned Tonkünstler-Societät concert in April 1791 in Vienna, he not only added clarinets, but rewrote the oboe parts.[19] Some prefer the leaner original version, some the more opulent revisions. There is one passage in the slow movement, repeated later, which contains music that is very difficult for the exposed woodwind instruments (bars 29–32 and 100–103). At some time and for some performance, probably in Germany where the woodwind players were not as adroit as those in Vienna, Mozart rewrote this passage, giving the difficult downward-moving music to the more agile strings and giving the woodwind section long-held notes.[20]

There is one passage in K.550 which might sum up the whole message of innovation, *Angst* and compositional self-discipline. This occurs immediately after the double bar in the Finale (Allegro assai), where Mozart peers ahead a century-and-a-half by flirting with the Grim Reaper: he introduced, obviously to illustrate the point of tonal (and personal?) disintegration, the twelve notes of the scale – a pre-Schönbergian nightmare, perhaps? The way in which they are set forth, with jumps, a whirling triplet gesture and accented crotchets, is profoundly upsetting, as is the message of the Symphony as a whole.

It was the great impresario Johann Peter Salomon who christened K.551, the last work of this final trilogy 'The Jupiter'. Salomon had come to Vienna in 1790 to engage, if possible, both Mozart and Haydn; in the event he persuaded Haydn to accompany him on his return journey to England, and it was agreed that Mozart should follow another year. It is fitting therefore to preserve the connection between the leading impresario of the day and music's greatest genius through the Symphony which many consider the greatest of the eighteenth century.

This work in C major is rooted in tradition – Mozart's music always is: the use of C major as the key of princes, archbishops, of coronations (*La clemenza di Tito* is in C) and *Applausus* cantatas (Haydn's *Applausus* Cantata of 1768), of solemn Masses for festive occasions. Trumpets and drums in this key have a rich and sonorous character, less brilliant than D and not so mellow as (say) B flat. Haydn had composed many a symphony in C major for festive occasions, and the very sound represented all those things to the audiences of the time. So although the fugal Finale is one of the great *tours de force* of its kind in the history of music, its arrival on the C major scene was not, perhaps, entirely unexpected. Members of the audience would have been immediately reminded of the Credo theme in the Sunday Mass, because the first four notes of the *cantus firmus* are literally 'Credo in unum Deum' – and that in itself is significant, since Mozart was much more deeply religious than secular twentieth-century critics give him credit for – but everyone would have thought also of the splendid fugues that were traditionally used for the close of the Gloria ('In gloria Dei patris, Amen'); of the close of the Credo ('Et vitam venturi saeculi, Amen' – another hint as to what motivated this incredible music, 'world without end' and 'life everlasting, resounding down the centuries'); and most of all, the end of the Ordinary, 'Dona nobis pacem', the desire for peace felt by every civilized human being, a peace which was under threat when Mozart wrote this Symphony in the midst of a cruel, unprofitable and inflation-making war between Austria and the Ottoman Empire. So perhaps the conclusion of the Mass, 'Ite Missa est', is also the unwritten but perhaps deeply considered conclusion to Mozart's symphonic life: the blessing that the priest confers on the faithful after Mass, and Mozart's blessing too, with the 'Jupiter' Symphony, on a deeply threatened and fragile world order.

Mozart's Masonic music: a survey

I N THE EIGHTEENTH CENTURY, MUCH OF WESTERN EUROPE WAS SWEPT by Freemasonry, that secret society which was and is dedicated to the higher things of life, to life's meaning and spiritual content. The origins of Freemasonry are largely lost in the grey mists of early European history and there is some debate among Masonic experts as to whether the words 'Free Masons' actually came from the guild of master masons – masons were one of the most important of the early guilds, responsible, as they were, for the construction of medieval cathedrals and other large, important buildings. In any case, it would seem that the rise of medieval crafts and guilds was responsible for the Masonic Society. The Austrian Lodges, which were formed in the eighteenth century, regarded the English Grand Lodge as their 'parent' or Mother Grand Lodge: that of England was inaugurated on the Feast of St John the Baptist, 1717, and it is for this reason that this section of Freemasons was and is still known as the St John's Lodges or, in German, *Johannislogen*.

An old 'Charge' delivered to initiates tells something of Masonic intent and explains the old description of the Order as an 'Ancient and Honourable Institution'.

> Ancient no doubt it is, as having subsisted from time immemorial; and honourable it must be acknowledged to be, as by a natural tendency it conduces to make those so who are obedient to its precepts ... To so high an eminence has its credit been advanced that in every age monarchs themselves have been promoters of the art, have not thought it derogatory from their dignity to exchange the sceptre for the trowel, have patronized our mysteries and joined in our assemblies.

The members are classified in three degrees: (1) Entered Apprentice, (2) Fellow Craft, (3) Master Mason. Mozart was an ardent Mason and soon became a Master. On 5 December 1784, Mozart was proposed for membership in the small Viennese Lodge 'Zur Wohlthätigkeit' ('Beneficence'), one of the eight *Johannislogen* then in existance in the capital. On 14 December 1784, Mozart was accepted as an Entered Apprentice. Ten days later he visited the most famous Austrian Lodge of all, 'Zur wahren Eintracht' ('True Concord'), of which the Grand Master was the famous humanitarian scientist Ignaz von Born. Interestingly enough, Mozart probably persuaded his friend Haydn to become a Mason, and plans were made for Haydn to be initiated in the more fashionable Lodge 'Zur wahren Eintracht' on 28 January 1785. Mozart was there to receive him, but the news of the intended initiation had reached Eszterháza Castle, where Haydn was Kapellmeister to Prince Esterházy, too late and the formal reception was therefore postponed. On 11 February, when Haydn was initiated, Mozart could not attend because he was engaged in conducting and playing the première of his D minor Piano Concerto (K.466) at the Mehlgrube in Vienna. The day afterwards, Mozart gave his famous quartet party during which Haydn went up to Mozart's father, Leopold, who was visiting his son at that time, and uttered those much-quoted words, 'I swear to you before God and as an honest man that your son is the greatest composer I know, either personally or by reputation ...'. At the end of March, Leopold Mozart also joined the Masons and was rapidly promoted to Master by special dispensation. To complete this distinguished group of eighteenth-century musical Masons, one should perhaps add that Ludwig van Beethoven also became a Freemason. (In fact, it is interesting to note that the United States Declaration of Independence is in many respects a Masonic document, drawn up, as it was, primarily by a group of distinguished American Masons.)

In the turmoil of the wars with France, the Austrians grew panicky about the activities of secret societies; in the middle 1790s Masonry was forbidden in Austria and remained so until the end of World War I. The hard world of Metternich's *Realpolitik* could tolerate no secret societies dedicated to the brotherhood of man and to the abolition of political borders.

Mozart has left us a considerable heritage of Masonic pieces, most of them intended for actual use in Viennese Lodges. It is often said that in Freemasonry Mozart found a substitute for the Catholic Church; significantly, he had no real opportunity to write church music in the Austrian capital (since he was not officially affiliated to any of the big Viennese churches), but did compose some of his most interesting music for the 'Great Architect' – as the Supreme Being is called in Masonic circles.

K.148 (125h) Lied 'O heiliges Band'

For tenor solo with piano accompaniment. D major. Text by Ludwig Friedrich Lenz. Although supposedly an early work, it is unlikely to have been composed before Mozart himself became a Freemason in 1784. The title on the autograph manuscript reads: 'Lobgesang – Feyerlich für die Johannis-Loge' ('Song of Praise – Solemnly for the St John Lodge'). 20 bars, *Generalbasslied*. This little song is in the form of a vocal part with figured bass; it would seem to have been intended for use at the opening of a Viennese Lodge.

TENOR

O heiliges Band	Oh, holy bond
der Freundschaft treuer Brüder,	of the friendship of true brothers,
dem höchsten Glück	like unto the highest happiness
und Edens Wonne gleich,	and bliss of Eden,
dem Glauben Freund,	friendly to belief,
doch nimmermehr zuwider	yet never opposed
der Welt, bekannt	to the world, known
und doch geheimnisreich,	and yet full of mystery,
ja, bekannt	yes, known
und doch geheimnisreich.	and yet full of mystery.

K.429 (468a) Cantata (fragment) 'Dir, Seele des Weltalls'

For 2 tenors and 1 bass, with 2 violins, 2 violas, bass, 1 flute, 2 oboes, 1 clarinet, 2 horns and figured bass (organ). Text by L. L. Haschka (1749–1827). (1785 Vienna?)

 1 Chorus 'Dir, Seele des Weltalls, o Sonne'. Allegro moderato, E flat, 4/4
 2 Tenor aria 'Dir danken wir die Freude'. Andante con moto, B flat, 3/4

CHORUS

Dir, Seele des Weltalls, o Sonne,	To thee, Soul of the universe,
sei heut'	oh sun, let this day
das erste der festlichen Lieder	the first of the festive canticles
geweiht!	be devoted!
O Mächtige, Mächtige ohne dich	Oh, mighty one, without thee
lebten wir nicht;	we could not live;

(*variously*)

von dir nur kommt	from thee alone come
Fruchtbarkeit, Wärme	fruitfulness, warmth
und Licht!	and light!
O Sonne, o Mächtige!	Oh, sun, almighty one,
O Seele des Weltalls!	soul of the universe!

(*variously*)

Dir, dir, dir, sei heut'	To thee, this day, let
das erste der festlichen Lieder	the first of our festive canticles be
geweiht!	devoted!
Dir, dir, sei's heut' geweiht!	To thee, this day, let it be devoted!
Von dir nur kommt	From thee alone come
Fruchtbarkeit, Wärme, Licht!	fruitfulness, warmth and light!
Dir, Seele des Weltalls, usw.	To thee, soul of the universe, etc.

ARIA (tenor)

Dir danken wir die Freude	We thank thee for the joy
daß wir im Frühlingskleide	that once more we see the earth
die Erde wieder seh'n,	in the mantle of spring,
daß laue Zephiretten	that gentle breezes
aus süssen Blumenketten	waft scent to us
uns Duft entgegen weh'n.	from sweet garlands of flowers.
Dir danken wir, usw.	We thank thee, etc.
Dir danken wir,	We thank thee
daß wir im Frühlingskleide	that we see the earth once more
die Erde wieder seh'n.	clad in the mantle of spring.
Dir danken wir,	We thank thee,
daß laue Zephiretten	that gentle breezes
uns Duft entgegen weh'n.	waft scent towards us.
Dir danken wir, dir,	Thee, we thank, thee,
daß alle Schätze spendet	that bountiful Nature bestows
und jeden Reiz verschwendet	all riches on us and upon us
die gütige Natur,	showers every charm,
daß jede Lust erwachet	that all pleasure wakes
und Alles hüpft und lachet	and all things skip and laugh
auf segenvoller Flur;	in blissful pastures;
daß alle Schätze spendet, usw.	that bountiful Nature bestows, etc.

It is not known for which Masonic Lodge or upon what occasion Mozart thought to perform this little cantata. Since the work is unfinished, we may assume that Mozart gave up the idea. A friend of the family, Abbé Stadler, was later able to fill in the missing parts rather easily – Mozart wrote almost the whole score but left out some of the inner parts – and it is in this form that the work is played today.

K.468 *Gesellenreise* (*The passage to becoming a Fellow Craft*)

For tenor with piano accompaniment, 'Die ihr einem neuen Grade'. Text by Franz Joseph Ratschky (1757–1810). Dated Vienna, 26 March 1785. B flat, Larghetto, barred C.

TENOR

Die ihr einem neuen Grade	You who now approach
der Erkenntnis nun euch naht,	a new degree of understanding,
wandert fest auf eurem Pfade,	go steadfastly on your way,
wißt, es ist der Weisheit Pfad.	know it is the path of wisdom.
Nur der unverdross'ne Mann	Only the man who perseveres
mag dem Quell des Lichts	may draw near the source
sich nah'n.	of light.

As we have noted above, Leopold Mozart visited his son in Vienna in 1785 and himself became a Mason; Leopold was promoted to the second degree (Fellow Craft = *Geselle*) on 16 April 1785 at the Lodge 'Zur Wohlthätigkeit' and for this occasion Wolfgang composed *Gesellenreise*.

K.471 *Die Maurerfreude* (*Masonic Joy*)

Cantata for tenor and men's chorus 'Sehen, wie dem starren Forscherauge'. Text by Franz Petran. Instrumental accompaniment: 2 violins, viola, bass, 2 oboes, 1 clarinet and 2 horns. Dated Vienna, 29 April 1785. Allegro, E flat, 4/4

TENOR

Sehen, wie dem starren	To see how Nature by degrees
Forscherauge die Natur	reveals her countenance
ihr Antlitz nach und nach enthüllt;	to the unblinking, searching eye,
wie sie ihm mit hoher Weisheit voll	how she fills the mind with high
den Sinn	wisdom

und voll das Herz mit Tugend
füllt —
das ist Maurer Augenweide,
wahre, heiße
Maurerfreude.
Das ist wahre, heiße Maurer-
freude.
Sehen, wie dem starren
Forscherauge, usw.
Sehen, wie sie ihm mit hoher
Weisheit, usw.
Das ist Maurer Augenweide,
usw.

and the heart with
virtue —
that is pleasing to the Masons' eye,
true and fervent joy to the
Masons.
This is true, warm Masonic
joy.
To see how Nature by degrees
reveals, etc.
To see how she fills the
mind, etc.
That is pleasing to the Masons' eye,
etc.

Sehen, wie die Weisheit und die
Tugend
an den Maurer, ihren Jünger, hold
sich wenden,
sprechen: Nimm, Geliebter,
diese Kron'
aus unsers ält'sten Sohns, aus
Josephs Händen.
Das ist das Jubelfest der
Maurer,
das, das der Triumph der Maurer.

To see how wisdom and
virtue
turn graciously to the Masons, their
disciples,
and say: Take this crown,
beloved,
from the hands of our eldest son,
from Joseph's hands—
that is the feast of rejoicing for the
Masons,
this the Masons' triumph.

Drum singet und jauchzet ihr
Brüder!
Laßt bis in die innersten
Hallen des Tempels den Jubel der
Lieder,
laßt bis an die Wolken ihn schallen,
laßt ihn schallen, laßt ihn schallen!
Singt, singt, singt!
Lorbeer hat Joseph der Weise
zusammengebunden,
mit Lorbeer die Schläfe dem
Weisen der Maurer umwunden.

Sing, therefore, and rejoice, you
brethren!
Let the song's jubilation penetrate
resounding to the innermost halls
of the temple,
let it ring out to the clouds,
let it ring, let it ring!
Sing, sing, sing!
Joseph the Wise has twined laurels
together,
bound the temple of the wise man
of the Masons with laurel.

CHORUS

Lorbeer hat Joseph, usw.	Joseph the Wise, etc.

This cantata was first performed on 24 April 1785 in honour of Ignaz von Born, Grand Master of the Lodge 'Zur wahren Eintracht', and was performed in the presence of Wolfgang's father Leopold by the Brothers of another Viennese Lodge, 'Zur gekrönten Hoffnung im Orient' (Crowned Hope in the Orient'). The tenor solo was sung by the famous Valentin Adamberger. The author of the text, Franz Petran, was a lay priest and the house poet of the Lodge 'Zur gekrönten Hoffnung'. The piece was repeated on 15 December 1785 at the Lodge 'Zur gekrönten Hoffnung' at a musical academy for the benefit of two basset-horn players, David and Springer. Mozart on this occasion also played a piano concerto and improvised a fantasy. In August 1791, *Die Maurerfreude* was played in honour of Mozart's final visit to the Prague Lodge 'Zur Wahrheit und Einigkeit' ('Truth and Unity'). It was one of Mozart's most popular Masonic pieces.

The Masonic world was a restricted one, and it is fascinating to follow the careers of individuals who are now mere footnotes in the library of music, such as David and Springer. Later we find Springer – together with another travelling basset-horn player, Dvorák – in London in the spring of 1791, where the two musicians played a concerto for two basset horns in the Haydn-Salomon Concerts.

K.477 (479a) *Maurerische Trauermusik (Masonic Funeral Music)*

For 2 violins, viola, bass, 2 oboes, 1 clarinet, 3 basset horns, double bassoon ('gran fagotto'), 2 French horns. Probably composed about 10 November 1785 in Vienna. Adagio, C minor, barred C

This, Mozart's greatest piece of Masonic music, was composed following the deaths[1] of two aristocratic Brothers: Georg August, Duke of Mecklenburg-Strelitz (died 6 November 1785) and Count Franz Esterházy (died 7 November 1785). The piece was first performed at a memorial meeting (Lodge of Sorrows) at the Lodge 'Zur gekrönten Hoffnung' on 17 November. At the last moment Mozart added parts for two more basset horns (making a total of three) for the travelling players David and Springer, and the double bassoon part for yet another itinerant performer. In this imposing and sombre piece, Mozart shows that he was, as indeed most great composers were, religious in a far deeper sense than merely observing the obvious convention of regular attendance at church services. In the middle section of the *Maurerische Trauermusik*, Mozart turns to the agelessly beautiful Gregorian Chant for Passion Week, 'Incipit lamentatio', the Lamentations of the Prophet Jeremiah. Eighteenth-century Catholic audiences would have recognized the allusion to this well-known *cantus firmus*[2] immediately; Joseph Haydn had used it in several works, among them the famous *Sinfonia Lamentatione* (no. 26 in D minor). Thus Mozart combines his conventional Christian belief with the religion of his heart to produce one of his most profound and moving works.

K.483

Lied with three-part chorus and organ for the opening of a Freemasons' Lodge: 'Zerfließet heut', geliebte Brüder'. Text by Augustin Veith, Edler von Schittlersberg (1751–1811). Probably composed in December 1785 in Vienna. Andante, B flat major, 4/4

TENOR

Zerfließet heut', geliebte Brüder,	Melt today, beloved brethren,
in Wonn' und Jubellieder,	in bliss and songs of rejoicing;
Josephs Wohltätigkeit	for us, in whose bosom
hat uns in deren Brust	burns a three-fold fire,
ein dreifach Feuer brennt,	Joseph's good will
hat unsre Hoffnung neu gekrönt.	has crowned our hope anew.

CHORUS

Vereineter Herzen und Zungen	With united hearts and tongues
sei Joseph dies Loblied gesungen,	let this song of praise be sung to Joseph,
dem Vater, der enger uns band.	to the father, who has bound us closer together.
Wohltun ist die Schönste der Pflichten;	To do good is the loveliest of ; duties
er sah sie uns feurig verrichten	he has seen us ardently perform it
und krönt uns mit liebvoller Hand.	and crowns us with a loving hand.

TENOR

Dank euch der Schar, die eh' uns wachte,	Thank the host, which has ever watched over us,

der Tugend Flamm' anfachte	fanned the flame of virtue
und uns zum Beispiel war,	and been an example to us,
aus deren jedem Tritt	from whose every step
auf ihrem Maurergang	on your Mason's path has sprung
ein Quell des Bruderwohls	a fount of brotherly
entsprang.	good.

CHORUS

Das innigste, tätigste Streben	The innermost, most active aspiration
zu ihnen empor sich zu heben,	to lift ourselves up to them
ist Allen der herrlichste Dank.	is the most glorious thanks for all.
Drum laßt uns, verdreifacht die Kräfte,	So let us now, our strength tripled,
beginnen die hohen Geschäfte	begin the noble tasks
und schweigen den frohen Gesang.	and hush our glad singing.

K.484

Lied with three-part chorus and organ for the closing of the Lodge: 'Ihr unsre neuen Leiter'. Text by Augustin Veith, Edler von Schittlersberg. Probably composed in December 1785 in Vienna. Andante, G major, 2/4

TENOR

Ihr, unsre neuen Leiter,	Oh, you, our new leaders,
nun danken wir auch eurer Treue;	we thank now your loyalty, too;
führt stets am Tugendpfad uns weiter,	you conduct us ever further along the path of virtue,
daß jeder sich der Kette freue,	so that every man rejoices in the chain
die ihn an bess're Menschen schließt	that binds him to better men
und ihm des Lebens Kelch versüßt.	and sweetens life's cup for him.

CHORUS

Beim heiligen Eide geloben auch wir,	By the sacred oath, we, too, vow
am großen Gebäude zu bauen wie ihr, usw.	to build the great mansion, like you, etc.

TENOR

Hebt auf der Wahrheit Schwingen	To the throne of wisdom on the
und höher zu der Weisheit Trone,	pinions of truth it raises us higher,
daß wir ihr Heiligtum erringen	so that we attain her holy shrine
und würdig werden ihrer Krone,	and become worthy of her crown,
wenn ihn wohltätig für den Neid	when beneficently through us you
Profaner selbst durch uns	even drive the malice of the
verscheut, den Neid Profaner selbst	profane away, drive away even the
verscheut	malice of the profane.

CHORUS

Beim heiligen Eide geloben auch	By the sacred oath we, too,
wir, usw.	vow, etc.

The text of K.483 was printed in Mozart's lifetime and the work was performed, together with K.484, at the Lodge 'Zur gekrönten Hoffnung' on 14 January 1786. (Two other such works, the texts of which were printed, were set to music by Mozart, but the music is now lost.) The text of K.483 contains references to the Emperor Joseph II's decree of December 1785 which required a major reorganization of the existing Viennese Lodges – Joseph considered that there were too many separate Lodges (and possibly that it would be easier to control the activities of the Freemasons if they were combined into a handful of larger Lodges).

K. 619 *Eine kleine deutsche Kantate* (*A Small German Cantata*)

For tenor and piano. 'Die ihr des unermesslichen Weltalls Schöpfer ehrt'. Text by Franz Heinrich Ziegenhagen (1753–1806). Composed in Vienna, July 1791.

1 Andante maestoso, C major, 4/4, leading to a recitative
2 Andante, C major, 3/4, 'Liebt mich in meinen Werken'
3 Allegro, C major, 4/4, 'Zerbrechet dieses Wahnes Bande!'
4 Andante, D major, 6/8, 'Wähnt nicht, daß wahres Unglück sei auf meiner Erde'
5 Andante a tempo, D minor, 4/4, 'Seid weise nur, seid kraftvoll und seid Brüder!'
6 Allegro, C major, 4/4, 'Dann ist's erreicht, des Lebens wahres Glück'

RECITATIVE

Die ihr des unermeßlichen	You who honour the Creator
Weltalls Schöpfer ehrt,	of the boundless universe,
Jehova nennt ihn, oder Gott,	whether you call him Jehovah,
nennt Fu ihn, oder Brama,	or God, or Fu, or Brahma,
hört, hört Worte aus der Posaune	hear, hear words from the
des Allherrschers!	trumpets of the Lord of All!
Laut tönt durch Erden, Monden,	Their everlasting sound loudly
Sonnen ihr ew'ger	rings through earths, moons and
Schall,	suns,
hört, Menschen, hört,	hear, you men,
Menschen, ihn auch ihr!	hear it, too!

ANDANTE

Liebt mich in meinen Werken!	Love me in my works!
Liebt Ordnung, Ebenmaß und	Love order, proportion and
Einklang!	harmony!
Liebt euch, liebt euch, euch selbst	Love, love yourselves
und eure Brüder!	and your brethren!
Liebt euch selbst und eure Brüder!	Love yourselves and your brethren!
Körperkraft und Schönheit sei	Bodily strength and beauty be
eure Zierd',	your ornament,
Verstandestelle euer Adel!	clear understanding your nobility!
Reicht euch der ew'gen	Extend the brotherly hand
Freundschaft Bruderhand,	of eternal friendship,
die nur ein Wahn, nie	which only a delusion,
Wahrheit,	never truth,
euch so lang entzog.	deprived you of so long.

ALLEGRO

Zerbrechet dieses Wahnes Bande!	Break the bonds of this delusion,
Zerreißet dieses Vorurteiles Schleier!	rend the veil of this prejudice,
Enthüllet euch vom Gewand,	put off the garment
das Menschheit in Sektirerei	that clothes mankind in
verkleidet!	sects!
In Kolter schmiedet um das Eisen,	Hammer the iron, which till now
das Menschen-, das Bruderblut	has spilt the blood of men, of
bisher vergoß!	brothers, into ploughshares!

Zerspringet Felsen
mit dem schwarzen Staube
der mordend Blei
ins Bruderherz oft schnellte!

With the black powder which
often fired the murderous lead
into the hearts of brothers,
blast rocks!

ANDANTE

Wähnt nicht, daß wahres
Unglück
sei auf meiner Erde!
Belehrung ist es nur, die wohl-
tut,
wenn sie euch zu bessern Taten
spornt,
die, Menschen, ihr in Unglück
wandelt,
wenn töricht blind ihr rückwärts
in den Stachel schlagt,
der vorwärts, vorwärts euch
antreiben sollte.

Do not believe that real
misfortune
exists upon my earth!
It is only instruction, which does
good,
if it spurs you on to better
deeds,
which should drive you
forwards
when you men who walk
in wretchedness,
strike backwards into the
thorns.

Seid weise nur, seid kraftvoll,
und seid Brüder!
Dann ruht auf euch
mein ganzes Wohlgefallen,
dann netzen Freundenzähren
nur die Wangen,
dann werden eure Klagen
Jubeltöne,
dann schaffet ihr zu Edens-
tälern Wüsten,
dann lachet alles euch
in der Natur.

Only be wise, be strong,
and be brothers!
Then will my entire favour
rest on you,
then only tears of joy
will wet your cheeks,
then your cries will be
cries of rejoicing,
then you will transform
deserts into valleys of Eden,
then everything in nature
will smile upon you.

Dann, dann, dann,
ALLEGRO
dann ist's erreicht,
dann ist's erreicht,
des Lebens wahres Glück!

Then, then, then,

then it will be attained,
life's true happiness
will be attained!

The autograph of this piece is now in Uppsala, Sweden, where it arrived through the agency of Frederik Samuel Silverstolpe, a member of the Swedish legation in Vienna at the end of the eighteenth century. Silverstolpe became a friend of Haydn's and often visited Mozart's widow Constanze, from whom he procured this interesting *Kleine deutsche Kantate*.

This Masonic piece – one of the few by Mozart that were not written specifically for an internal Lodge celebration – was commissioned by F.H. Ziegenhagen, a businessman who was a member of the Lodge in Regensburg.

K. 623 *Eine kleine Freymaurer-Kantate* (*A Small Masonic Cantata*)

For 2 tenors, bass, 2 violins, violas, bass, flute, 2 oboes, 2 horns. 'Laut verkünde unsre Freude'. Text probably by Karl Ludwig Gieseke (1761–1833). Dated Vienna, 15 November 1791.
1   *Coro*. Allegro, C major, 4/4, 'Laut verkünde unsre Freude'. Recitative
2   *Aria*. Andante, G major, barred C, 'Dieser Gottheit Allmacht ruhet'. Recitative
3   *Duetto*. Andante, F major, 3/8, 'Lange sollen diese Mauern'
4   *Coro*. Allegro, C major, 4/4, 'Laut verkünde unsre Freude'

CHORUS

Laut verkünde unsre Freude	Loudly proclaim our joy,
froher Instrumentenschall,	glad sound of instruments,
jedes Bruders Herz empfinde	let every brother's heart echo
dieser Mauern Widerhall.	the reverberation of these walls,

(*tenor enters*)

Denn wir weihen diese Stätte	for we consecrate this dwelling
durch die goldne	through the golden chains of
Bruderkette	brotherhood

(*bass enters*)

und den echten Herzverein	and the union of true hearts
heut' zu unserm Tempel ein.	to be our temple today!
Laut verkünde unsre Freude, usw.	Loudly proclaim our joy, etc.

RECITATIVE (*tenor*)

Zum ersten Male, edle Brüder,	For the first time, noble brethren,
schließt uns dieser neue Sitz	this new domicile of wisdom

der Weisheit und der Tugend ein.	and virtue encloses us.
Wir weihen diesen Ort	We consecrate this place
zum Heiligtum unserer Arbeit,	to be the sanctuary of our work,
die uns das große Geheimnis	which is to unravel the great
entziffern soll.	mystery for us.
Süß ist die Empfindung des	Sweet is the experience of the
Maurers	Mason
an so einem festlichen Tage,	on a festive day such as this,
der die Bruderkette neu und enger	which locks the chains of
schließt;	brotherhood fast afresh;
süß der Gedanke, daß nun die	sweet the thought that now
Menschheit	humanity
wieder einen Platz unter Menschen	has once more won a place among
gewann;	men;
süß die Erinnerung an die	sweet the remembrance of the
Stätte,	place,
wo jedes Bruderherz ihm,	where, for every brother's heart,
was er war,	what he was
und was er ist, und was er werden	and what he is and what he may
kann,	become,
so ganz bestimmt,	is defined exactly for him,
wo Beispiel ihn belehrt,	where example instructs him,
wo echte Bruderliebe seiner	where true brotherly love
pflegt	cherishes him,
und wo aller Tugenden heiligste,	and where, of all virtues the most
erste,	sacred, the first,
aller Tugenden Königin,	of all virtues queen,
Wohltätigkeit,	charity,
in stillem Glanze thront.	reigns in quiet radiance.

ARIA
(*tenor*)

Dieser Gottheit Allmacht	The omnipotence of this godhead
ruhet	rests
nicht auf Lärmen, Pracht und Saus,	not upon noise, display and
nein,	bluster,
im Stillen wiegt und spendet sie	in stillness and quiet it considers
der Menschheit Segen aus.	and confers grace upon mankind.

Stille Gottheit, deinem Bilde
huldigt ganz des Maurers
Brust,
denn du wärmst mit Sonnenmilde
stets sein Herz in süsser
Lust.
Dieser Gottheit Allmacht
ruhet, usw.

Silent Godhead, the Mason's
breast swears allegiance to thy
image,
for thou warmest his heart
ever in sweet delight with the sun's
gentle radiance.
The omnipotence of this godhead
rests, etc.

RECITATIVE
(*tenor*)
Wohlan, ihr Brüder, überlaßt
euch ganz
der Seligkeit eurer
Empfindungen,
da ihr nie, daß ihr Maurer seid,
vergeßt.

Come, brethren, give yourselves
up completely
to your consciousness of
happiness,
that you may never forget you are
Masons.

(*bass*)
Diese heut'ge Feier sei ein Denkmal
des wieder neu und fest
geschloßnen Bunds.

Let this feast today be a memorial
of the covenant renewed and
steadfast.

(*tenor*)
Verbannts sei auf immer
Neid, Habsucht und Verleumdung
aus unsrer Maurerbrust,

Let envy, avarice and calumny
be forever banished from our
Mason's breast,

(*bass, tenor*)
und Eintracht knüpfte fest das
teure Band,
das reine Bruderliebe
webte.

and may harmony knit fast the
precious bond
that pure brotherly love has
woven.

DUET
(*tenor and bass*)
Lange sollen diese Mauern
Zeuge unsrer Arbeit sein,
und damit sie ewig daure,
weiht sie heute Eintracht ein.

Long shall these walls
be witness to our work,
and, that it may endure forever,
concord consecrates them today.

Laßt uns teilen jede Bürde	Let us share every burden
mit der Liebe Vollgewicht,	with the full weight of love,
dann empfangen wir mit Würde	then we shall worthily receive here
hier aus Osten wahres Licht.	true light from the east.
Diesen Vorteil zu erlangen,	To attain this benefit
fanget froh die Arbeit an.	begin the work joyfully,
Und auch der schon	and he, too, who has begun
angefangen,	already,
fange heute wieder an.	let him begin afresh today.
Haben wir an diesem Orte	If we have completely attuned
unser Herz und unsre Worte,	our hearts and words
an die Tugend ganz gewöhnt,	to virtue in this place
o dann ist der Neid gestillt,	oh, then envy is silenced,
und der Wunsch so ganz	and the wish that crowns our
erfüllt,	hope
welcher unsre Hoffnung krönt.	completely fulfilled.

CHORUS
(*as previously*)

Laut verkünde unsre Freude,	Loudly proclaim our joy,
usw.	etc.

This Cantata is the last piece of any size that Mozart completed. Constanze reports that towards the middle of November 1791, Mozart's health improved sufficiently for him not only to compose this Cantata, but also to go to the Lodge 'Zur neugekrönten Hoffnung' ('Newly Crowned Hope') on 17 (not 18) November and conduct its first performance. Probably Mozart's friend Valentin Adamberger sang the beautiful tenor part on that occasion.

The work was a great success, but within three weeks the 'great white wings of death' had come to claim him. After Mozart's death, the Lodge issued the work for the benefit of Constanze and her children. Later, with a new text, it was sung at the Lodge in honour of the Emperor Franz II on 8 September 1792. Gieseke was a member of Mozart's Lodge and he is cited as providing a new text for the work in 1792. Previously it was thought that Emanuel Schikaneder (author of *Die Zauberflöte*) had written the original text, but that is now considered unlikely.

K.623 Anhang (appendix)

F major, 3/4; this chorus, which appears not in Mozart's original manuscript, but in the first edition put out by the Lodge 'Zur neugekrönten Hoffnung' early in 1792, is described there as 'for the closing of the Lodge'. It is not certain whether Mozart himself wrote this music, which may well have been performed at the Lodge meeting of 17 November 1791 (and which has now, rather incongruously, become the Austrian National Anthem), or whether it was the work of one of the other Viennese composers who were members of the Masonic community, such as Anton Wranitzky or Mozart's friends the clarinet and basset-horn players Anton and Johann Stadler. Shortly after, the hymn became known with the text 'Laßt uns mit geschlungnen Händen'. In any event, the assembled Masons will have symbolically closed their circle by linking hands as the hymn was sung.

CHORUS

Laßt uns mit geschlungnen Händen,	With clasped hands, brethren,
Brüder, diese Arbeit enden	let us end this work
unter frohem Jubelschall.	in sounds of glad rejoicing.
Es umschlinge diese Kette,	May this bond tightly embrace
so wie diese heil'ge Stätte,	the entire globe
auch den ganzen Erdenball.	as it does this holy place.
Tugend und die Menschheit ehren,	To honour virtue and mankind,
sich und andern Liebe	and teach ourselves and others
lehren,	love,
sei uns stets die erste Pflicht.	let our first duty ever be.
Dann strömt nicht allein in	Then not in the east alone will
Osten	light shine,
dann strömt nicht allein in Westen,	not in the west alone,
auch in Süd und Norden	but also in the south and in the
Licht.	north

MUSIC DOUBTFULLY OR WRONGLY ASSOCIATED WITH MASONRY

There are various moments in Masonic ritual when it is possible to perform either short or extended pieces of purely instrumental music, for example, when the Brothers enter the Lodge. The Lodges in Vienna with which

Mozart was associated often boasted 150 members in attendance, and on such occasions a piece like the glorious Adagio for two clarinets and three basset horns in B flat (K.411 [440a]), lasting some 6½ minutes could have been conveniently used (and even repeated, if necessary). The use of wind instruments in Masonic ceremonies was typical not only of Austrian Lodges but also of those in Paris.

The shorter Adagio (K.410), in canonic form for two basset horns and bassoon (lasting less than 2 minutes), has been stated to have been conceived for some Lodge purpose, now long forgotten. The autographs of both pieces have survived, that for the short work (K.410) being in Sweden, while K.411 forms part of the important Mozart collection in the Berlin State Library; both may be dated 1782–3, according to the research of Alan Tyson. If this dating is correct – and there is absolutely no evidence to contradict it – then K.410 and 411 will both have been written *before* Mozart became a Mason in 1784.

A similar situation obtains with regard to the sombre Adagio and Fugue in C minor for string orchestra (or string quintet), K.546, composed on 26 June 1788 in Vienna, and described in Mozart's thematic catalogue as 'a short Adagio, à 2 Violini, Viola e Basso, for a Fugue which I wrote some time ago for 2 pianos', referring to K.426. This Adagio is one of Mozart's most sinister opening movements, an act of defiance and despair, and was perhaps intended as the prelude to one of Gottfried van Swieten's concerts of 'old' music, of which Mozart became the director after the death of J. Starzer. The Fugue is a brilliant transcription of a piano piece, featuring dissonances that make the work sound a hundred years ahead of its time.

It has to be stressed, however, that there is no evidence whatever that this quite exceptional music, either in its original version for two pianos, composed before Mozart became a Mason, or in its later adaptation, ever had anything whatsoever to do with any Masonic Lodge in Vienna in Mozart's lifetime. Nowadays, everything of import in Mozart's music tends to be regarded as having been either written for or influenced by the Masons. This does a double disservice, both to Mozart's free-ranging genius and to the serious purpose of a Viennese Lodge in the 1780s.

Johann Michael Haydn, Mozart and the Duos (Duets) for Violin and Viola (K.423 and 424)

O N 14 August 1763, Johann Michael Haydn, Joseph's younger brother, was engaged as 'Hofmusicus und Concertmeister' at the Archiepiscopal Court in Salzburg. His salary was 25 florins per month, with the privilege of eating at the officers' table; this income in cash and kind compares favourably with Joseph's salary of 400 florins (Rhine value) when he was engaged as Vice Capellmeister to Prince Esterházy in May 1761.[1] Previously Michael had been engaged at Großwardein (Oradea Mare in present Romania) in the late 1750s, and, just before Christmas 1762, he had been in the Hungarian Coronation Town of Preßburg (Bratislava). Before his contractual engagement in Salzburg, he had directed a *Tafelmusique* there. In the Court Diary of Franz Anton Gilowsky von Urazowa, under the date 24 July 1763, we read:

> The high princely table [of the Archbishop] was today in the hall at Mirabell [Castle] on account of the rainy weather. 24 Ordinari [people who usually dined at the court table] and 8 guests and *Tafelmusique*, which today was set forth by a foreign composer from Vienna by the name of Michael Heidn.

A few years later, on 17 August 1768, Michael married the soprano Maria Magdalena Lipp, daughter of the cathedral organist, by which time he had naturally gravitated into the orbit of the Mozart family: Leopold had been engaged as Vice Capellmeister at Salzburg on 28 February 1763. Relations between the Mozarts and Michael Haydn seem to have been friendly if not intimate. Leopold Mozart would often discuss Haydn's music in letters to the family. While he concluded, after having listened to *Andromeda e Perseo*, that Michael 'has no genius for theatrical music' (letter to his daughter Nannerl, 13 March 1787),[2] he nonetheless had the highest praise for other works. One such was the incidental music to Voltaire's *Zaïre*, which

Leopold mentions in a letter dated 30 September 1777 to his son, who was then in Munich:

> *Mon trés cher Fils!* Today was a rehearsal in the theatre this morning. Haydn had to provide entr'acte music for *Zayre*. As early as nine o'clock one performer after another began to turn up; the rehearsal started after ten and they were not finished until about half past eleven. Of course Turkish music was included [this means the extra percussion, triangle, cymbals and bass drum, as in Joseph Haydn's 'Military' Symphony], also a march. Countess v[on] Schönborn also came to the rehearsal driven in a chaise by Count Czernin. The music is reported to suit the action very well and to be good. Although there was nothing but instrumental music, the court harpsichord had to be brought over and Haydn played on it. [We see from this description that, even in fully scored pieces such as this, a harpsichord *continuo* was still considered necessary.]

On 2 October, Leopold adds:

> … the play is to be repeated on Saturday … Haydn's entr'acte music was so good that the Archbishop did him the honour of saying at the table *that he never would have believed Haydn capable of writing such a thing, and that instead of beer* [usually served at table to court servants and composers] *he ought to have nothing but Burgundy.*

Leopold adds, appalled at the Archbishop's tactlessness – little did he know! – 'What kind of talk is that!' Finally Leopold had a chance to hear the new music and on 6 October reported:

> Haydn's entr'acte music is really beautiful. After the first act there was an Arioso with variations for violoncello, flutes, oboe and so forth; and then, preceding a variation *which was piano*, there was one with the Turkish music which was so sudden and unexpected that all the ladies were terrified and everyone laughed. Between the 4th and 5th acts there was a cantabile movement where the *cors anglais* always played in between. Then the Arioso was repeated which, together with the preceding sad scene with *Zayre* and the following act, moved us very much.

Three days later, Leopold concluded his description, 'I hear that for his beautiful music Haydn only received from the Archb[ishop] six Bavarian thalers. *Che generosità!*'

Later in the same year, on 1 November, Leopold writes to his son, then in Mannheim, about Michael Haydn's new *Missa S. Hieronymi*:[3]

> This very moment I've come from the Cathedral, where the Hautboy Mass by Haydn was given, he himself conducted … I found everything [i.e. also the Offertory and Epistle Sonata] exceptionally fine, because there were present 6 oboes, 3 double basses, 2 bassoons and the castrato [Francesco Ceccarelli], who has just been engaged for 6 months at 100 f. monthly … The whole affair lasted an hour and a quarter, and for me that was too short, for the work was really excellently written … The fugues, especially the *Et vitam* in the Credo and the *Dona nobis*, then the alleluja in the Offertory, were written in a masterly style, the themes themselves of course, and there were no exaggerated modulations or sudden excursions …

At the same time, Leopold scoffed at Michael's tendency to drink too much. In a letter to his wife and son in Mannheim, Leopold writes on 29 December 1777:[4]

> Who do you think has become organist at Holy Trinity? – H[err] Haydn! Everybody is laughing, that's a fine organist who after each Litany downs a quarter litre of wine …

Six months later, in a letter of 29 June 1778 to his wife and son in Paris, Leopold writes:[5]

> On Trinity Sunday I dined, as usual, in the Priests' House. In the afternoon, Haydn played the organ during the Litany and Te Deum Laudamus, at which the Archbishop was present, but so appallingly that we were all shocked and thought he would go the way of the late Adlgasser [who had had a stroke while playing the Litany on 21 December 1777 and died the day thereafter]. But is was only a small attack of *tipsiness*, the *head* could not coordinate with the *two hands*. I've not heard such a thing since the Adlgasser affair.

In a letter of 3 December 1777, Wolfgang had referred to Michael Haydn as follows: 'H[err] Kap[ellmeister] Schweizer is a good, decent, upright man – dry and smooth as our Haydn, only the language is more polished'.[6] And in a letter sent from Paris, dated 18 July 1778, he writes sarcastically that he had played a '*galanterie* sonata in the fashion of and with the fire, wit and precision of [Michael] Haydn …'.[7] Mozart and his father nevertheless had a profound respect for Michael Haydn, and Wolfgang requested works by Michael to play in the Sunday morning concerts organized by Baron Gottfried van Swieten at the National Library in Vienna. In a letter from Vienna dated 4 January 1783, Wolfgang asks his father to send him some symphonies (K.204, 201, 182, 183) and adds,

> Tell me, are there in Haydn's latest Masses or Vespers, or both, any fugues of importance? – I would be most grateful if you would little by little make up a score of both things for me … [8]

We also have the scores of Michael Haydn's *Offertorium pro Festo SS. Trinitatis* 'Tres Sunt' and other works such as the *Offertorium pro Dominica Adventus (quarta)* 'Ave maria' in Wolfgang's own autograph copies.

*   *   *

We now come to the extraordinary story of Michael Haydn's six Duos (Duets) for Violin and Viola and their completion by Mozart. To reconstruct their history we must move forward, to 1806, when Michael died in Salzburg. Two years later, there appeared a 'Biographische Skizze von Michael Haydn' issued anonymously 'for the benefit of his widow' (Salzburg, 'Gedruckt mit Zaunrith'schen Schriften, und im Verlage der Mayr'schen Buchhandlung'), but in fact written by two of Michael's pupils, Schinn and Otto. On pp. 38f. of this interesting little book, we read:

> Michael Haydn was ordered by high authority [i.e. Archbishop Colloredo] to compose duets for violin and viola. He could not, however, deliver them at the appointed time because he became seriously ill and the convalescence lasted longer than had been expected, rendering him incapable of doing any work at all; the great man was unable to find a *quid pro quo* [i.e. sending in an already existing piece rewritten for violin and viola, or something similar]. He was threatened with the cancellation of his salary on account of the delay, probably because his patron was too little informed about Haydn's circumstances, or had been deliberately misinformed. Mozart, who visited him daily, found out about this, sat down and wrote for his upset friend with such uninterrupted speed that in a few days the duets were finished and delivered [to the Archbishop] under Michael's name. In later years, we reminded ourselves with delight

of this wonderful example of brotherly love; our master kept the original manuscripts as a sacred relic, in honour of the memory of the immortal Mozart.

As it happens, we have corroborative evidence of this in the Mozart literature as well. Wolfgang and his new wife, Constanze, went to Salzburg to visit Leopold Mozart and Wolfgang's sister, Nannerl, in the summer of 1783. It was on that trip that Mozart composed the torso of the Mass in C minor (K.427) and performed it at St Peter's Church on 26 October, just before he left for Linz and Vienna. When he returned to the Austrian capital, he wrote to his father on 6 December: '… I would ask you please to send me as soon as possible my *Idomeneo* – the two violin duets and Seb[astian] Bach's fugues …'.[9] On Christmas Eve, he wrote again to remind his father 'to send me the two duets'.

It had been a mark of respect on Mozart's part to perform this act of kindness for his colleague at Salzburg. When Wolfgang left Salzburg to go to Linz, he took with him at least part of a Symphony in D by Michael Haydn (Perger 43, *c.* 1780–1) copied out in his own hand on paper that he used only in the latter part of 1783. It is now supposed that this may have been the work that Mozart performed in his famous academy concert in Linz under the auspices of Count Thun.[10] For years it was thought that Mozart's K.444 (425a; the 'Symphony no. 37'), which consists of a Michael Haydn Symphony in G (Perger 16, 2 May 1783), to which Mozart added a slow introduction (= K.444), was performed by Mozart in his Linz concert; but recently it has been demonstrated by Alan Tyson that

> Mozart's manuscript is written on a type of paper that he used only after his return from Salzburg via Linz to Vienna in 1783, and mainly in the months February–April 1784.[11]

Probably Mozart intended to use the new composite Symphony in G (K.444) in one of his academy concerts in Vienna.

It is also entirely possible that Mozart acted as a go-between in Artaria's publication, in January 1786, of three new symphonies by Michael Haydn (B flat, D minor, C major; Perger 18, 20, and 19, respectively, all composed in 1784) – the first publication of any Michael Haydn by Artaria,[12] who was already Mozart's principal publisher, *inter alia* of the Symphonies, K.319 and 385 (1785), Piano Concertos, K.414, 413, 415 (1785) and, of course, the Six Quartets dedicated to Haydn (also 1785).

Michael Haydn had apparently intended to compose a set of six violin duets for the Archbishop, for the Berlin State Library owns copies of four such works (in C, D, E, and F major); and when we examine these four, it is quite obvious that: (1) Mozart's two, in G and B flat (K.423 and 424), were carefully designed to make up the whole set by choosing two obvious keys not employed in the four already composed by Michael Haydn; (2) Mozart took great pains *to compose in Michael Haydn's style.* Archbishop Colloredo was a connoisseur, and although he had dismissed Mozart from his service, he was well acquainted with Wolfgang's music and continued to have it played at the Salzburg court. Michael Haydn's four duets close in two cases with a rondo; Mozart does the same in K.423 in G. But also the way the themes are organized, with their chirping grace notes and trills (opening movement of K.423), and their popular tunes (finale of K.423), successfully camouflaged the true identity of their author. The Archbishop never suspected that Mozart was behind two of the six works, indeed one must bear in mind that one of Mozart's specialities was being able to imitate other composers perfectly. On 7 February 1778, he wrote to his father: 'As you know, I can more or less adopt or imitate any sort and any style of composition'. What must be emphasized here, however, is that Mozart became interested, indeed involved, in these duets and ended up by writing two miniature masterpieces. The autographs, incidentally, have survived and are owned privately in Mannheim. The works were not published in Mozart's lifetime, and appeared only in 1793 (J. André, Offenbach).

K.423 in G

I. Allegro. II. Adagio. III. Rondeau: Allegro.

A densely packed movement in the usual sonata form, the development section contains passages in close imitation of, or in what used to be called in those days, 'the severe style'. Michael Haydn was regarded as a leading contrapuntist by his contemporaries, and the fugues of his masses were widely respected, also by Mozart (who copied some of them out for study purposes): Mozart was therefore careful to write the kind of contrapuntal development section that the Archbishop would recognize as 'authentic' Michael Haydn. We have noted above the clever way in which Mozart fashioned the theme to sound like genuine Michael Haydn.

The songful Adagio is in itself, by the very use of the slow tempo, another of Mozart's camouflaging tactics. Mozart usually writes andantes rather than adagios as slow movements, whereas in the real Michael Haydn duets, three of the slow movements are marked 'Adagio' and the fourth is an 'Adagietto'. This is a short movement (only forty-nine bars) but of a peculiar intensity, the viola part providing a smooth legato accompaniment in 'walking bass' patterns. Sometimes Michael Haydn and Mozart use the viola as a substitute bass instrument, and this is particularly evident in the *Rondeau*, with its long contrasting section in the minor. In case astute listeners wonder about the 'Mozartian' chromatic slither with which the repetition of the main theme is introduced after the minor section, this too is as characteristic for Michael Haydn as for Mozart; we find an extraordinary series of chromatic slitherings in the slow movement of Michael Haydn's Symphony no. 42 in D (earliest MS. source: dated copy in Lambach Abbey, Upper Austria, 1778).

K.424 in B flat

I. Adagio – Allegro. II. Andante cantabile. III. Thema con [6] Variazioni: Andante grazioso.

'Tritonus', the tritone (in this case B flat to E natural), used to be called 'diabolus in musica'. Mozart was not afraid of this 'devil in music' and, on the contrary, planned the main theme of his great E flat Quartet (K.428) – one of the six dedicated to Joseph Haydn – around a tritone. Now it happens that this very Quartet had been composed in June or July 1783 in Vienna, just before Mozart left for Salzburg. We can be reasonably confident in assuming that he took with him this marvellous new work, and played it to Michael Haydn.

The Adagio introduction, with its 'diabolus in musica', will strike the modern listener as being the most Mozartian moment of the two works: not the fact that he used a slow introduction, for that was one of Michael's specialities, but the intensity and emotional 'pace' slightly bursts the Michael Haydn mould which Mozart had carefully set himself. The opening theme of the following Allegro is also Mozartian in its great poise and in the seamless flow of the music; then, as if he suddenly realizes that things were getting out of hand, we are launched into a series of typical triplets: typical not only of Michael but also of Joseph. And here we must introduce yet another red herring into the history of these duets: for it is quite clear that Mozart also knew and had carefully studied Joseph Haydn's Six Duets for violin and viola (Hoboken VI:1–6) – they were called 'Sonatas' – which had started to circulate within Austria in the 1770s. Some of Joseph's learned developmental technique, the closely packed working with small motivic fragments, can be observed in the first movement of K.424, but the second subject, with its chain trills for the violin, ♪♪♪♪♪ is once again an example of studied and observed *Michael* Haydn. Here we have a fabulous example of Mozart, the greatest assimilator ever to put pen to paper: in K.424, especially, we encounter a miraculous fusion of Joseph Haydn, Michael Haydn and Mozart himself.

The longing aspirations of the *Andante cantabile*, with its rocking, *siciliano* rhythm in the viola, seem to be again close to the Mozartian spirit: the chromatic shifts, the depth and intensity of the music might, perhaps, have made the Archbishop wonder if Michael Haydn had not entered a new and particularly rich period. It would do less than justice to Michael's duets, however, if we would refrain from pointing out their own sterling qualities. Like Joseph's, Michael's Duets are called 'Sonatas', which meant that they were serious studies. This is perhaps the reason that there are no minuets at all, either in Michael's four, or in Mozart's two, though Michael does include, as a finale to his Duet in D, a 'Tempo di Menuetto'.

The Finale of K.424 is a theme and variations of the type which Joseph Haydn had brought to a rare perfection with his chamber music of the 1770s', the form was also used in these Duets. We notice, in these vivacious Mozart variations, the difficulty of the viola part, which requires a real virtuoso. The extreme chromaticism towards the end reminds one in a startling way of its composer, but the progress of this movement, with its humorous cast, is very like similar movements in the 'Salzburg' Haydn.

The Duets were surely labours of love in every sense of the word. They reveal another side to Mozart's mercurial personality, or rather two sides: his warm generosity towards a colleague and his ability to submerge his own style if he considered it necessary or interesting to do so. (The same applied, incidentally, to the introduction for the Michael Haydn Symphony in G, where Mozart steeps himself completely in a symphonic style which he himself had long outgrown: to see what is meant, it is only necessary to compare K.444, Mozart pretending to be Michael Haydn as a symphonist, and K.425, the Adagio introduction, Mozart being himself as symphonist. Both were composed within months of each other.)

The Piano Quartets in G minor (K.366) and E flat major (K.493)

MOZART WROTE ONLY TWO QUARTETS FOR PIANO AND STRINGS, both commissioned by his friend and publisher, Franz Anton Hoffmeister (himself a very successful composer of chamber music). Actually, Mozart had planned to write a set of three quartets for Hoffmeister to publish, but for several reasons the plan fell through. For one thing, the piano quartet was a type of chamber music almost unknown in Vienna in the middle of the 1780s. Piano quartets were written by a few composers like Johann Schobert, a German who lived and published in Paris and whose works were known to Mozart from the two trips he made to the City of Light. In Vienna, however, the piano trio was the successful and fashionable form.

Hoffmeister issued the G minor Quartet in December 1785 as part of a series of chamber music pieces by various composers. Sales of Mozart's contribution to the series were disappointing, and Hoffmeister lost money on his edition of the work. He nevertheless began engraving the second of the projected set of three, the quartet in E flat (K.493), but became discouraged after completing the violin part and decided to cut his losses; engraving a work as considerable as a quartet was an expensive process. According to Georg Nikolaus Nissen,[1] who married Mozart's widow and published a biography of Mozart in Leipzig in 1828, Hoffmeister 'made the master a present of the advance payment already given' and asked to be released from his contract with the composer.

Fortunately Mozart was able to persuade Artaria & Co., the publishers who had issued his six string quartets dedicated to Haydn in the autumn of 1785, to take over the project. Artaria engraved the remaining three parts of K.493 and issued the work in July 1787. Apparently sales were not such as to encourage Mozart to compose the projected third piano quartet: this he never did.

Piano Quartet in G minor (K.478)

The autograph manuscript of this work bears the date and signature in Mozart's hand, '*Quartetto di Wolfgango Amadeo Mozart mp. Vienna li 16 d'Ottobre 1785*'. This G minor Quartet was a fairly avant-garde composition for the Vienna of the period and moreover was so full of technical difficulties in the piano part that the work required not only expert execution but attentive listening for full appreciation. The following excerpt from a report contributed in 1788 by an anonymous Vienna correspondent to a Weimar fashion newspaper, the *Journal des Luxus und der Moden*, gives some idea of how the work had been received following its earlier publication by Hoffmeister:

> Mozart has now arrived in Vienna as Imperial Chapel Master [*sic*]. And now a few words about a bizarre phenomenon which he (or his celebrity) brought about. A little while ago there appeared a single Quadro (for piano, violin, viola and violoncello), each single part engraved separately, and which is very intricate, requiring the greatest precision in all four parts; but even in a very lucky performance, this 'musica di camera' can and should please only musical connoisseurs.
>
> The rumour was: Mozart has composed a new and very special Quadro, and this or that princess has it and plays it. The rumour spread quickly, excited general curiosity and was responsible for the witless idea of producing this original work in large, noisy concerts.
>
> Many another piece can sustain a mediocre performance; this product of Mozart's is, however, scarcely bearable if it is performed by mediocre, dilettante hands and sloppily presented. This is what happened countless times during the past winter ...
>
> What a difference, when this much discussed work of art was played in a quiet room by four skilled musicians who have studied it well, where the suspense of each and every note did not escape the attentive, listening ear, and which was played with the greatest precision in the presence of only two or three attentive persons. But then there would be no *éclat*, no brilliant and modish applause to be reaped, no conventional praise to be culled.

In Austrian music of the late 1760s and early 1770s, there had been a sudden upsurge of dramatic, angry music written in minor keys. Later this whole period was lumped together with a German literary movement named after a play of 1776, *Sturm und Drang* (literally, 'Storm and Stress'), by Friedrich Maximilian von Klinger. But the musical *Sturm und Drang* occurred ten years earlier than its literary counterpart and was led by Joseph Haydn, who furnished classic examples of minor-mode compositions in various forms – piano sonata, string quartet, church music and symphony. Mozart himself had heard some of these new works when on a trip to Vienna with his father in 1773 and had produced one such symphony himself, the so-called 'Little' G minor (K.183 [173dB]).

Now, more than a decade later, he returned to this violent language, which had made Haydn a *cause célèbre*, and created in the opening movement of the G minor Piano Quartet a work that not only shocks by its violent impact but reveals a whole new side to his mercurial temperament. Haydn eventually renounced *Storm and Stress* in his music; Mozart continued – sparingly – to return to it, and to the key of G minor, for some of his most personal statements. Two of the greatest of these are the first Piano Quartet and the String Quintet (K.516).

The mood of the G minor Quartet is angry, proud, defiant. The opening of the first movement is dominated by the motto-like phrase with which the work begins; it haunts the music as surely as any Beethovenian 'fate knocking on the door'. One notes how this motto figure colours the whole transition to the beautiful, nostalgic second subject in B flat, the relative major of G minor: a more perfect contrast to the doom-ridden force of the opening could hardly be imagined.

The development section soon returns to the motto theme, which bestrides the dramatic accents like a colossus. It is profoundly pessimistic music, and the dark hues are greatly increased by exploitation of the piano's bottom range (this can be heard clearly throughout the middle part of the development section). This is music that could no longer be played effectively on the light-voiced harpsichord, though publishers were always trying to satisfy the *ancien régime* when they put '*pour le clavecin ou piano-forte*' on title pages. The recapitulation is prepared for by a series of scales that grow closer to each other and suddenly begin to incorporate the motto figure with which, in its original shape, the recapitulation proper begins. The extended coda, with its brilliant passagework for the piano, is a stylistic device that figures in much of the music by Johann Michael Haydn. Here it is used in a dramatic, valedictory and fateful way that presages Beethoven in an astonishing glimpse into the future.

The rest of this extraordinary work is in studied contrast to the opening movement – perhaps the most daring movement in all of Mozart's chamber music. The Andante is in B flat, and in what is known as a 'quick metre' – in this case, three quavers to the bar. This is used, rather than 3/4 time, to keep the tempo more fluid and the music lighter. But although the theme, announced by the piano alone, is gentle and quiet, there soon develops a certain unrest in the series of quickening notes. The whole movement is characterized by that sense of fatality, or melancholy, that was to become more and more a part of Mozart's psychological make-up in the last six years of his life.

The second theme is in F major, and is constructed around a quiet pedal point, or held note, in the cello, answered by a questioning phrase of the piano (later turned the other way around). This answering with a question is a typically Mozartian tautology (the great pianist-composer Ferruccio Busoni once wrote, 'Together with the puzzle he gives you the solution', but it might with equal justification be said, 'Together with the solution he gives you the puzzle').

Unlike many of Mozart's later works in the minor key, this quartet gradually lightens as it progresses. After the stormy drama of the Allegro and the profound, quiet beauty of the Andante comes a rondo of almost unmitigated optimism. Some critics have thought to discover in the sophisticated humour of the theme, with its characteristic pauses, Haydn's influence; and possibly the whole turn toward optimism is a nod to the master of Eszterháza, who had recently created two minor-key symphonies (nos. 80 and 83) in which a similar progression may be traced. As in Haydn's two works, the finale of the quartet is in the tonic major.

In the first subsidiary of this rondo (the 'B' section, as it is called in the textbooks), we are in D major, with a theme that Mozart used again, note for note, as the basis of his famous and lovely Rondo in D for solo piano (K.485), composed in January 1786 for a lady of the Viennese aristocracy. The next subsidiary section is more surprising: it is in the unexpected key of E minor. This E minor interlude, with its rough entries, reminds us of the work's beginnings; but it is not intended to disturb the high spirits and rollicking good humour of the finale's basic mood. In the coda there is a startling and sudden modulation to E flat. In any such change of key, the composer must find a graceful way to get the music back to the home key, and this Mozart achieves here with wit and charm.

Piano Quartet in E flat major (K.493)

On 1 May 1786, Mozart's great opera *Le nozze di Figaro* was performed at the Burgtheater in Vienna. A month later, on 3 June, he finished the second of his Piano Quartets, a work in E flat whose quiet confidence seems to reflect the joy he must have felt after producing *Figaro*, a great breakthrough on the operatic front. E flat was the classic key for *cors de chasse*, the hunting horns that accompanied the eighteenth-century aristocracy on their prodigious slaughters of stags, hares, partridges, pheasants or wild boar. We seem to hear echoes of the hunting horns in the nearby Vienna Woods when, at the conclusion of the majestic pedal point with which the first subject begins, the music suddenly breaks into dotted fanfares – but the piano's continuation shows us that it is not a serious hunt.

Hermann Abert[2] and other notable Mozartian scholars have thought that the opening may have owed its existence to similar beginnings in the piano quartets of Johann Schobert. E flat, apart from being the key associated with hunting, always exerted a special fascination for composers, and Haydn, Mozart and Beethoven always relished the key's rich sonority, the beauty of wind instruments in that tonality, and a certain majestic optimism that E flat generates. We see many of these qualities in this post-*Figaro* quartet, which has always been a speciality of Mozart connoisseurs, although it fascinates the public perhaps marginally less than its great G minor sibling.

The second subject of the first movement steals in brightly but softly with a lovely imitation, the piano initiating and the violin echoing; in the continuation, a hint of melancholy seems to spread gently over the music, almost suggesting the later writing of Franz Schubert. There is a melodious third subject that features violin and piano in a way that suggests a passage from a violin sonata. The end of the exposition is marked by a magical return to the stuff of the opening theme, with its walking-bass pedal point in the piano's left hand. The development is dominated by the second theme, which is treated contrapuntally, in the old Haydnesque manner. The series of semiquavers in the piano's right hand generates a growing tension, which is broken off by a straight repetition of the second theme in varied instrumental guise.

The music, with steadily growing unrest, modulates in slow arches toward the recapitulation, which is introduced *forte* after the preceding long *piano* passage. As regards form, this is a brilliant stroke, a device that looks forward to Beethoven. Another Mozartian feature is the lead-back itself, the four bars preceding the actual reprise of the main theme that lead the music and the listener down a series of patterns into the recapitulation. The sense of expectation, and the release of the tension that has been generated, are finely achieved.

Hermann Abert has called the Larghetto in A flat major 'the crown of the work', a movement of 'indescribable inwardness of concept'. One thing that must strike the sensitive listener is the uncommon grasp of the new piano-quartet idiom that Mozart now displays in all its fresh glory – the interplay of the stringed instruments with, against, accompanying, taking over from, the piano. At the beginning of the second section (development), there is a curiously affecting *pianissimo* passage for the strings alone, it looks forward to German Romantic music, as do the waves of crescendos leading to *fortes*, dropping down and beginning again. Throughout this intimate movement, we are reminded that Mozart's own performance of the piano part must have irradiated this Larghetto; Haydn once said that Mozart's playing 'went to the heart' and this lambent music must have inspired a heartfelt performance. The coda quietly but inexorably grows out of the closing material and brings the movement to a hushed close.

For the concluding Allegretto, we again have a rondo – sunny, immaculately composed, with that same miraculous interplay between piano and strings that distinguished the previous Larghetto. The piano part is hardly less difficult than that of the earlier G minor work. Again, we sense the omnipresent humour typical of Haydn, not least in the flippant lead-back to the main theme, where a series of grace notes ends in echo effects separated by Haydnesque pauses. The second interlude of the rondo is in C minor and features a series of triplets in the piano's right hand. At this point the rondo verges on the sonata-rondo form because this *minore* section develops its material in a manner that is close to the typical exposition-development-recapitulation of the sonata form.

At the end of the movement there is a surprise, just as in the G minor work: here it is the flight into A flat major, after a *fermata* (pause) in the piano part. The surprise is compounded by the fact that the piano is silent, leaving the strings to present this unexpected key change. The E flat piano quartet is indeed, as Alfred Einstein says, 'a flawless masterpiece'.[3]

The Haydn brothers (Michael and Joseph) and Mozart's String Quintets

—————————— ❧ ——————————

T HE TYROLESE COMPOSER GIACOMO GOTIFREDO FERRARI (1759–1842), who met Haydn in London in 1792, related his personal experiences in his memoirs published in Italian in 1830.[1] A translated extract from *The Harmonicon*, also published in 1830, states that

> Prince Lobkowitz asked Haydn why he had not written an instrumental quintett; the answer was, that he had never dreamt of such a thing till he heard the celebrated quintetts of Mozart, and that he found them so sublime and perfect, that he could not presume to put himself in competition with such a composer …

Quintet in B flat (K.174)

I. Allegro moderato. II. Adagio. III. Menuetto ma Allegro (in some sources: Menuetto ma Allegretto) & Trio. IV. Allegro. [note: there is a considerable difference in tempi and order of movements between the old editions and those of the *Neue Mozart-Ausgabe* (*NMA*)]

On 13 March 1773, Mozart and his father returned to Salzburg from their third Italian trip. Wolfgang had produced a new opera, *Lucio Silla*, for La Scala in Milan; but the most interesting new works he wrote in Italy were a series of string quartets (K.155–60), showing the young composer's awakened interest in chamber music. When he arrived back in Salzburg, he was confronted with a new kind of chamber composition for strings: the string quintet. Now it is quite possible that Mozart heard an occasional performance of string quintets by Luigi Boccherini, who had composed twelve in 1771 and six in 1772; but his immediate confrontation with the *genre* was surely at Salzburg in March 1773, for just a few weeks before the Mozarts returned, Joseph Haydn's younger brother, Johann Michael, had composed his first String Quintet, a work in C major (completed on 17 February).

Michael Haydn had been in the service of the Archbishop of Salzburg since 1763, and was already very well known for his sacred as well as his secular compositions. Michael's new Quintet was scored for two violins, two violas and violoncello and was thus different than Boccherini's quintets, in which there were two cellos and only one viola.

Mozart admired Michael Haydn, as we know from extensive evidence, but at the same time Mozart would often use a work by a contemporary as a source of inspiration for work of the same kind and, if possible, seek to improve on the original. Mozart's first Quintet (K.174) is believed to have been composed in the late Spring of 1773. Some months later, Michael Haydn wrote his second Quintet, in G, completed on 1 December. This new work seems to have made an equally profound impression on the young Mozart, who immediately proceeded to rewrite his own work, providing it with a new Trio and recasting the Finale (though still using the thematic material of the original movement). He now re-dated the autograph as 'Quintetto del Sgr. Cavaliere Amadeo Wolfgango / Mozart. à Salisb: / nel Decembre / 1773'. (This autograph, part of a series of autograph scores by Haydn, Mozart, Beethoven and other composers removed from the former Prussian State Library in Berlin, was recovered in Poland in 1978.)

One of the novelties of Michael Haydn's Quintets in C and G was the way in which the scores were laid out, the first viola having a prominent part and one which often 'echoes' the melody or line of the first violin. Mozart immediately seized on this idea. (The result can be heard easily at the beginning of K.174, where the whole opening melody is first given to violin I, accompanied by violin II, viola II and cello, and afterwards with the melody transferred to viola I.) The style of this opening Allegro moderato is a curious mixture between that of the old Austrian cassatio-divertimento (as practised by Joseph Haydn in his earliest works) and the modern quartet: the older cassatio-divertimento tended to set up the violins and violas as 'choirs' and play one off against the other, whereas the newer quartet integrated the four instruments more closely. Mozart is clearly influenced, in this work, not only by Michael but also by Joseph: it is always said that Joseph Haydn never wrote any quintets, but in fact he wrote two (Hoboken II:2 and II:1, the second of which was discovered in Czechoslovakia by the present writer in 1959). It is not, however, on Joseph Haydn's quintets Mozart's attentive eye was fixed, but rather on the string quartets, which he was, precisely at the period under consideration, closely studying. Among Leopold Mozart's effects, which passed in part to the Church of the Holy Cross in Augsburg, were found manuscript parts of Haydn's Quartets, op. 17 (1771), edited and annotated in Wolfgang's handwriting. Thus, when towards the end of the exposition of K.174, the music breaks into triplets, itself a very Haydnesque procedure, we are only faintly surprised. Mozart also follows Joseph Haydn's sudden concentration on these seemingly insignificant triplets during the development section: here they dominate the proceedings for twenty-two bars, only giving way in the retransition to the recapitulation. However, the most dramatically Haydnesque feature is certainly the mysterious off-key unison passage and ensuing modulation, just *before* that triplet passage in the exposition. We seem to be in the middle of Haydn's Quartets, opp. 9 (1769?) or 17. This mysterious and portentous music (bars 54ff.) is repeated in the recapitulation's appropriate place.

The opening of the Adagio is magical: all the upper strings are muted and the cello part is marked 'sempre piano'. The first two bars are a kind of ethereal curtain-raiser, and at bar 3 we seem to be in some enchanted eighteenth-century garden – perhaps not an Italian garden, but surely a garden with Italian string players, conjuring up a sleepy Tuscan landscape bathed in moonlight. The succession of melodies is always Italianate and often like a quotation from an opera (particularly the extraordinary solo for violin II at bars 7ff.). The middle section suddenly abandons this Italian languor for a tense crescendo, but it was only the wisp of a south wind, and the moonlit landscape again returns to its initial peace. Without Wolfgang's earlier experience of three visits to the land 'wo die Zitronen blühen', this Adagio would have been unthinkable.

The sturdy Minuet has something very Haydnesque about it – both the Haydn brothers liked this kind of rustic dance with a strong forward momentum. The Trio, in its second, revised version, centres around an old Baroque effect, which we find even in Bach's Christmas Oratorio: the echo. In this case, the echo is marked *pp* and is managed as follows:

Statement			Echo		
		violin I			violin II
f	{	viola I		pp {	viola II
		violoncello			violoncello

It is a Baroque conceit, of course, but not without charm.

The Finale, in its revised version, is a much longer and more complicated movement than the original. Mozart was consciously seeking to solve one of the principal problems of sonata form that existed in those days: the weight was always at the top end, i.e. the first two movements (opening allegro, slow movement), and gradually became lighter as the work progressed. Joseph Haydn had long searched for a solution and the year before had returned to fully-fledged fugues in his serious and weighty op. 20 Quartets. In K.174 the contrapuntal weight allotted by Mozart to the development section, with its turbulent interplay within the various groups, using fragments of previous material, is his way of increasing the Finale's importance.

There is another explanation for Wolfgang's revision, and one perhaps more cogent than the arrival on the scene of Michael Haydn's second quintet (though we should not discount that either). Meanwhile, Mozart had paid a long visit to Vienna, where he had studied all the latest music circulating in the capital city, and especially Joseph Haydn's revolutionary *Sturm und Drang* symphonies and quartets. Wolfgang composed his 'Little' G minor Symphony (K.183) under the influence of these stormy new minor-key works by Haydn, and there seems little doubt that the symphonic cast of the Quintet's new Finale owes its origin not only to Michael Haydn but perhaps even more to the epochal works by Joseph Haydn and his school (J.B. Vanhal). The symphonic element, the working with motives, the increased use of contrapuntal forms, all seemed more important than the older cassatio-divertimento grace; and so it came about that, as an almost unique feature in Mozart's *œuvre* at this period, the Finale was almost more important than the preceding movements. As the great Mozartian writer Hermann Abert observed, the Quintet 'has shifted the whole intellectual [*geistigen*] centre from the first to the last movement'.[2]

The Late Quintets, K.515, K.516, K.516b, K.593 and K.614

Various theories have been put forward as to the origin of the late string quintets, the music of which can only be described as alarming in the extreme. In 1786, Luigi Boccherini became Court Composer to the new King of Prussia, Frederick William, who had succeeded to the throne upon the death of Frederick the Great. Like his predecessor, Frederick William was passionately fond of music and was, moreover, a fine cellist, and Haydn composed string quartets for this music-loving monarch. Alfred Einstein[3] considered that Mozart may have composed these quintets with the king in mind. I regard this as doubtful, in view of notice inserted (a) in the *Wiener Zeitung*, Vienna's leading newspaper, on 2, 5 and 9 April 1788, and (b) in the

Weimar *Journal des Luxus und der Moden* of June 1788:

Musical Notice

Three new Quintets for 2 Violins, 2 Violas, and Violoncello, which I offer on subscription, handsomely and correctly written. The price for subscribers is 4 ducats or 18 fl. [gulden] Viennese currency. – The subscription formulae are to be had daily of Herr *Puchberg* in the Sallinzish [firm of Michael Salliet] offices on the High Market, where the works will be available from 1 July. Foreign music-lovers are requested to frank their orders.

Vienna, 1 April 1788.　　　Kapellmeister Mozart.
　　　　　　　　　　　　　in actual service of His Majesty.

I believe that Mozart simply wrote this set of three works speculatively and intended to sell them to amateurs by subscription. The works in question are:

K.515, dated 'Vienna, 19 April 1787' in Mozart's own Thematic Catalogue of Works.

K.516, dated 'Vienna, 16 May 1787' in Mozart's Catalogue.

K.516b (406), Mozart's arrangement of the Wind Band Serenade, K.388 (384a), probably made in the Spring of 1787.

Mozart played them with his friends for a year and then decided to sell them in manuscript copies. He had done the same with three new piano concertos (K.413–415) in January 1783, but times had changed. In 1783, Mozart was still the darling of the Viennese public, and his concerts were supported by members of the nobility. By 1788, he was no longer in popular favour and was, moreover, heavily in debt to Michael Puchberg, owner of the prosperous textile firm of Salliet & Co. Puchberg was a brother Freemason and had lent Mozart considerable sums of money.

Nevertheless, the shock of being abandoned by the fickle Viennese public must have been considerable; and what a shame for Mozart to have to print the following admission in the *Wiener Zeitung* of 25 June 1788:

Musical Notice

Since the number of subscribers is still very small, I am forced to postpone issuing my 3 Quintets until 1 January 1789. The subscription formulae are still to be had, against payment of 4 ducats or 18 fl. Viennese currency, of Herr Puchberg in the Salietzish [*sic*] offices on the High Market.

Vienna, 23 June 1788.   Kapellmeister Mozart,
                             in actual service of His Majesty.

Quintet in C (K.515)

I. Allegro. II. Menuetto (Allegretto) & Trio. III. Andante. IV. Allegro. [This is the order of the first edition, published by Artaria, Vienna, in 1789; the order in the *Neue Mozart-Ausgabe*, E.F. Schmid, 1967, based on the autograph in the Library of Congress, Washington, D.C., is I-III-II-IV.]

Those who know the six Quartets which Mozart dedicated to Haydn will remember that one of the very greatest was in C major (K.465) and showed that Mozart was eminently able to make C major a key of yearning pathos. Here, in K.515, the brilliantly original opening theme uses an old device (the broken triad) in a new way. Tension is generated, and maintained, by the repeated quavers in the middle voices; while the broken triad in the cello is answered by the first violin in a phrase of peculiar poignancy. This formula is repeated three times before the theme comes to fruition. Hardly has Mozart completed the theme, however, than the music comes to a dead stop. After a bar of rest the whole process is repeated in C *minor* and the roles of first violin and cello are reversed: the poignancy of what was formerly the first violin's 'answer' becomes darkly ominous when brought down *three octaves* to the cello's lowest register. From C major we also move into darker harmonies: at the end of the C major statement, Mozart shifts to the dominant seventh by an inverted Neapolitan sixth (bar 43), and this slightly sinister Italian south wind is prolonged and extended a few bars later until, with a crescendo, the music explodes back into C major (bars 55–7). Of the second subject group, one's attention is especially drawn to the long pedal point on the dominant key, G major. The texture of this section (bars 131ff.) is complex in the extreme and as such mirrors the emotional complexity of the whole movement, the whole work and the whole cycle. The fragmented rhythmic figure in the first violin ♩♩♩♩ ♩ 𝄽 is the characteristic landmark of this part of the movement and with it Mozart closes the exposition. In the development, a dramatic confrontation is arranged between the second and first subjects, and one realizes that the second subject's principal motif has a strong relationship to the main theme of the Overture to *Le nozze di Figaro*.

This is made doubly clear when, in the development (bars 171–3), the cello actually duplicates the entire rhythmic structure of the Overture's main theme (already heard once in the exposition); and this segment then passes, in the Quintet, from cello to viola II, viola I, violin II and, finally, violin I. It is almost as if Mozart were symbolically reproducing the Opera's Revolutionary ambivalence: gay aristocratic nonchalance backed by unrest and an atmosphere of growing fury in the servants' quarters. 'Se vuol ballare, Signor Contino …'.

In Artaria's first edition, which appeared in 1789, the Minuet comes second. (Obviously, the fact that Artaria printed K.515 and 516, in 1789 and 1790 respectively, suggests that when the MS. subscription failed, Mozart sold the two original works to him. In fact, Artaria probably acquired the C minor Quintet (K.516b) as well, because the firm printed this arrangement, though it did not appear until the year after Mozart's death.) Among the Minuet's many striking innovations, one (which also appears in *Don Giovanni*) has a profound influence on Ludwig van Beethoven, a great connoisseur and admirer of Mozart's music: the use of a crescendo leading to *piano*. This is the principal dynamic innovation of this Minuet, and it would become a stylistic 'fingerprint' in Beethoven. It is a device never found in Haydn, incidentally. Not only does Mozart use it in the Minuet proper, but it also marks the beginning of the Trio as well. Mozart uses the device in a very characteristic way in both places. The first time the crescendo leads to *piano*, but the second time, immediately after it, the crescendo leads, as is normal, to a *forte*. If this use of a crescendo must be regarded as ambivalent in the extreme, the harmonic basis at the beginning of the Trio is equally ambivalent: we do not reach the tonic until bar 9, and then the G sharp in violins I and II continues the harmonic instability.

Einstein believed that the present slow movement was a second thought: the sketch in the Mozarteum in Salzburg for an Andante movement for a string quintet, in F major (K.515a/Anhang 87), was, he considered, Mozart's first idea which was discarded after only ten bars. In this extremely personal movement, we notice the great individuality of the viola I part; it does more than share the melodic richness with violin I, indeed it almost seems to be that instrument's *alter ego*. (This brings up the theory, documentation of which is provided below in connection with the D major Quintet [K.593], that these two principal parts, for violin I and viola I, were shared out between Mozart and Haydn. It would be the kind of musical tribute that

Mozart liked paying to his older friend. In any event, it is a civilized and highly intellectual conversation between two friends.)

The Finale is a tribute to Haydn's famous sonata-rondo form, which the older composer had demonstrated, not long before Mozart's composition of the Quintet, in several symphonies, e.g. the finales of Symphonies nos. 77 in B flat and 85 in B flat ('La Reine'), written in 1782 and 1785–6 respectively. Some of the force, wit and formal dash which characterize Haydn's racy finales are found in this interesting and unexpected conclusion to the quintet. Very Haydnesque, too, is the humorous stuttering of violin I, all by itself, as it leads into the second subject, and also the excursion into E flat preceding a return to G major and the rest of the second subject. When, instead of beginning a development section, the music suddenly returns, rondo-like, to a statement of the main theme (bars 212ff.), we realize for the first time that a sonata-rondo is in store for us. There follows, much later in the proceedings, a huge development section, on the most magnificent scale and with a contrapuntal admixture of various elements. This is altogether a bold, assertive and dramatic movement, as if Mozart had resolved firmly to conquer the troubles which were beginning to darken his whole life, and from which, eventually, he was to succumb financially, if never spiritually.

Quintet in G minor (K.516)

I. Allegro. II. Menuetto (Allegretto) & Trio. III. Adagio ma non troppo. IV. Adagio – Allegro.

This is the most famous of the Quintets. Its unusual key, its dramatic power, its combination of tragedy and tenderness, have assured it a special place in the chamber-music repertoire. This work and the the great G minor Symphony (K.550, completed on 25 July 1788), constitute the most personal music, perhaps, that Mozart ever wrote. By May 1787, when he composed the Quintet, it must have been obvious to Mozart that, at least as far as the Viennese were concerned, he had failed completely as a composer. The success of *Figaro* was not permanent (only in Prague), and he was beginning to sink into debt. The G minor Quintet is a mirror of Mozart's personal tragedy: music's greatest genius was misunderstood and spurned by the only segment of society on whom he could count for financial support. When he was engaged by Emperor Joseph II as 'court chamber composer', the salary, 800 gulden, was little more than a token amount, and in fact Joseph much preferred music by the likes of Sarti, Paisiello, Cimarosa and Gassmann.

Mozart was no stranger to minor keys, and there can be little doubt that many in the Viennese audiences were alarmed when presented with the Piano Concertos in D minor (K.466, completed on 10 February 1785) and C minor (K.491, completed on 24 March 1786); but these concertos are in the main public works of public drama, whereas the Quintet is a private work of private anguish. Nothing quite like it had ever been heard before: Haydn's great minor-key Quartets from op. 20 (1772) were also private works, but there the tragedy is more classic, more impersonal.

The nervous desperation of the first subject is underlined by its under-statement: it is all *piano* and without a real bass at all. The theme is first presented with violins I and II and viola; it is then repeated with violas I and II and cello. The beginning is so unconventional that one is hardly surprised to find the second subject, instead of being in the relative major (B flat), starting in the tonic minor and then shifting quietly to B flat. But within the second subject, we note the unusual melodic skip of a ninth: it is no heaven-storming protest such as would begin to come from Bonn in a few years, because the skip only lands in *mfp* – a muted protest, an act of desperation. The development darkens even further: the dissonances are a series of private agonies, and we find the second theme in E flat minor, with that rather ominous ninth leap ending in C flat: the leap seems to become the music's motto, there is no way to escape it. At the end of the recapitulation, there is a coda, in itself introduced by a *fermata*: there follow two further *fermate*, as if the mood of the music was one of utter resignation.

In the Minuet we notice the angry off-beat *forte* chords, like cries of protest, but the Trio reverts to a mood of hopeless resignation again, each part ending on a quiet pedal point, with the cello offering a quiet trill-like succession of quavers, the offering accepted by the violins.

The Adagio ma non troppo is couched in an extraordinary atmosphere, which is engendered by the use of mutes on all five instruments. It is possibly the most personal and intimate music Mozart ever wrote. Its quiet, manly beginning in very soft E flat is like a private hymn but its normal progress is later interrupted swiftly and dramatically by the second subject. It appears, like some dread omen, in B flat minor, and introduces itself with a *sforzato*, a biting accent; the inner parts beat quietly in semiquavers. This ominous shadow is further darkened by viola II's arrival, whispering blackly (its thrusting progress encouraged by *mfp* markings). By contrast, the end of the exposition is in B flat major, the long violin melody underlined by that Mozartian paradox of quietly restless syncopations. The closing cadence of this section drops the dynamic level to *pp* and is of particular beauty.

Joseph Haydn sometimes began his finales with a slow introduction, but the procedure is rare in Mozart. If he does so here, in K.516, it is because he needs a foil to separate the slow movement from the G major gaiety of the final Allegro, with which it would not, he must have considered, be proper to begin the final movement. This introductory Adagio is like an accompanied recitative in an opera, with the first violin acting as dramatic soprano. Though restless, this introduction is perfectly suited to prepare the way for the sunny conclusion, a G major rondo where Mozart's depression disappears as quickly as a single cloud in a summer's sky. Not everyone was prepared to accept this totally unexpected conclusion, which is entirely different than the grimly rough, ironical and dramatic Finale to the G minor Symphony (K.550).

Quintet in C minor (K.406 [516b])

Mozart's arrangement of the Serenade in C minor (K.388 [384a]) for wind band: I. Allegro. II. Andante. III. Menuetto in canone & Trio in canone al roverscio. IV. Allegro.

Recent scholarship has rendered the origin of the Serenade even more obscure than it was previously. There now seems to be no evidence to connect the work with the statement in Mozart's letter to his father dated 27 July 1782 that he had to compose a 'Nacht Musique' for wind band (he composed other pieces for wind band at this period, too). Not only have we no idea for whom and for which band it was composed, but the work itself is a total mystery. Why would anyone want a dark-hued, ominous wind-band piece in C minor? It is so startlingly different from the usual serenade, which was music made to entertain on a starry summer's night, that any speculation about its origin is quite useless. There we have it in all its dark majesty. There is a contemporary arrangement for other groups of instruments (with cors anglais instead of clarinets, in the Archives of the Gesellschaft der Musikfreunde, Vienna). But when all is said and done, our knowledge of the work's history is limited to the date on the autograph: 1782.

Wind-band serenades were, in the eighteenth century, among the most fragile of genres: when the occasion for which such a work was written was finished, its *raison d'être* ceased to exist. That is no doubt the reason why Mozart decided, quite against his usual practice, to reach back to an earlier work to make up the third quintet of the trio which he offered by subscription. There were certain technical aspects of the original Serenade that would not automatically fit the new layout for strings, and Mozart was constrained to write an entirely new autograph manuscript (British Library). However, a recently discovered letter written by Mozart helps us to establish the C minor Quintet's proximity to that in G minor. (The autograph of the Quintet in C minor contains no dating, but the watermarks strongly suggest this proximity to K.516 as well.) This letter – written to an unknown person – was sold at auction by J.A. Stargardt (sale of 13 May 1965). It reads:

> I ask your pardon that I was latterly bold enough to take away the Haydn Quartets [perhaps MS. copies of the new 'Prussian' Quartets, op. 50, which Artaria published in December 1787] – but I always think that, *clown* that I am, I am entitled to exceptions. – I would ask you kindly to lend me my 6 Quartets [probably the ones dedicated to Haydn, K.387 etc.] – the Quintet *ex* G minor and the new one *ex* C minor. – I will send back everything tomorrow with thanks. – Good night.

Notice that this letter refers to the G minor Quintet and then the 'new one' in C minor. This strongly suggests that the letter was written after 16 May 1787 (date of K.516), and probably towards the end of the year or even at the beginning of 1788, when the idea of issuing the three Quintets by subscription occurred to Mozart. Perhaps the letter was addressed to Michael Puchberg himself; he was a great musical amateur. In any event, its content suggests that the C minor Quintet postdates that in G minor.

Referring to the Serenade version, Donald Mitchell writes that it 'flourishes its singularity through its choice of key (C minor), its tempestuous, impassioned, gloomy mood, and above all, through the complexity of its thematic invention.'[4] The composer Dittersdorf once gently complained to Emperor Joseph II that Mozart displayed *too* many ideas. The bewildering profusion of intellectual force with which Mozart crowds the opening theme of the Quintet in C minor is typical: there are no fewer than five separate sections, all in marked dynamic and motivic contrast one with the other: the gruff, rhythmically tight opening motif (*forte*) is immediately contrasted by a sinuously *legato*, murmuring passage (*piano*) while it, again, leads to another violent contrast, with intricate syncopations. The fourth idea takes up the final 'tail piece' of the first subject and proceeds to develop it, quietly, ominously, fatefully. As a fifth section, we have a jutting series of quavers which pile up and tumble down the scale into yet another passage. And so the movement proceeds. In order to establish a fixed centre after the bewildering diversity of the opening subject, Mozart introduces a quiet, *legato* second subject (bars 42ff.): it was beautiful in the wind-band version, and miraculously lends itself elegantly to Mozart's string writing. The softly lapping accompaniments shift perfectly from blown pipe to stroked string. The development is of a violence unprecedented in Mozart: all the coiled tension of the opening theme explodes into contrapuntal action (notice the canonic extension of bar 4 of the opening subject, now tossed back and forth from violin I to cello, bars 115ff.). The retransition to the second subject in the recapitulation is positively sinister, with the octave jumps straddling the long viola notes like some grotesque Harlequin on stilts.

The Andante is in E flat and its lyrical beauty and fastidiously elegant line are gently ruffled by the series of *sf-p* dynamic marks with which Mozart provides the upper lines (later transferred to the violas in imitational fashion). Its warmth and mellow sound – so characteristic of Mozart when writing in E flat major – are tempered with a certain nostalgic loneliness which will become more and more an integral part of the mature Mozart's music, whether for chamber, opera house or concert room.

The severe canonic minuet and trio (the latter in an inverse canon) takes as its model the equally gaunt E minor Minuet 'in canone' of Haydn's Symphony no. 44 ('Mourning'), composed about a decade before the Serenade. If the opening movement of the present Quintet (Serenade) was a surprising way to begin a 'night music', what can the ladies with their coy fans have thought when hearing this harbinger of doom? And if their evening was disturbed by the contrapuntal severity of the music, it was upset still further by the violent *sf-p* markings which were inserted in the second section. The whole Trio is held to a *piano* level, but the chromatic tension is as surprising as any loud dynamic mark.

The Finale, says Einstein, 'anticipates the spirit of the C minor Concerto (K.491)'.[5] Like its great successor, it is in the form of a theme and variations. In the theme's second section, we observe a certain fragmentation which is to characterize this restless and forceful music. Variation One presents us with a mock Baroque march, with the bass hammering away in repeated galloping rhythms, while the upper lines have exaggerated flourishes and jagged staccato notes. Variation Two is a quiet and flowing series of triplets in violin I with a slow moving accompaniment in the bass, while Variation Three has a series of unsettling syncopations. Variation Four is the most violent of all, with sharp rhythms in the upper lines and terse quavers 'walking' in the bass. Mozart suddenly accelerates the music's tempo by introducing a series of rushing semiquavers in the cello. Variation Five is like a heavenly ray of sun, returning to the lyrical warmth of E flat as we know it from the slow movement. The music then shifts slowly to C minor and proceeds to a kind of development, becoming more and more restless and fragmented. The conclusion of this section, which slows down the pace by introducing long note values, is of the darkest hue, with nudging series of *mfp*, like the ruffling of the surface of a grey northern lake by a cold wind. Time seems to stand still; the music gets slower and slower. In a sudden mercurial shift, a trait for which Haydn was more famous than Mozart, the music springs into C major, and in a hard, triumphant mood the work sweeps to its conclusion. What a Serenade! But also what a Quintet, and how clever of Mozart to make this sophisticated adaptation for the delight of a new audience of connoisseurs!

Quintet in D (K.593)

I. Larghetto – Allegro – Larghetto – [Allegro]. II. Adagio. III. Menuetto (Allegretto) & Trio. IV. Allegro.

Mozart composed this uniquely great work in December 1790, probably for Johann Tost, formerly leader of the second violins in Haydn's orchestra who then married Prince Nikolaus Esterházy's housekeeper and inherited factories in southern Bohemia at Znaim (Znojmo). Haydn had composed quartets for him. That Haydn was now intimately involved with the first performance of this D major work is attested by their mutual friend, Abbé Maximilian Stadler, who related his personal recollections to Vincent and Mary Novello in 1829:[6]

> … Haydn and Mozart were like Brothers. Mozart delighted in Haydn's writing and owned repeatedly that he was much indebted to him in forming his style. Stadler said that on his first arrival at Vienna and becoming acquainted with Haydn's work, Mozart naturally changed his manner of composing.

... Mozart and Haydn frequently played together with Stadler in Mozart's Quintettos; particularly mentioned the 5th in D major, singing the Bass part [incipit of cello part, beginning of K.593], the one in C major and still more that in G minor ... .

... Quintets of Mozart – 1st Violin Schmidt, 2nd Stock, 1st Viola either Haydn or Mozart in turn, 2nd Viola Abbé Stadler – Bass he could not recollect ... [27 July] ... Schmidt, now dead, was one of Mozart's most faithful and intimate friends. He was an admirable performer on the violin and used frequently to play quintets through with Mozart and Haydn (as l'Abbé Stadler had already mentioned to me [this latter note concerned a visit to the Streichers, Beethoven's friends]).

Hans Keller writes:[7]

K.515 ..., K.516 ..., and K.593 ... are the greatest and most original string quintets in existence and the greatest and most original symphonic structures of Mozart, chamber-music or otherwise.

Only in recent years has K.593 come to be appreciated by a wider audience, and perhaps its beauties are more approachable to connoisseurs than to any listener untrained in the subtle formal and tonal techniques of which Mozart makes masterly use throughout this inspired and brilliantly original work. As if in tribute to a great Haydn connoisseur, Johann Tost, Mozart opens with a typically Haydnesque slow introduction. But he has other plans in store for this Larghetto, in that (like the famous Drum Roll Symphony by Haydn, which owes the device to K.593), the Larghetto returns after the Allegro section, just before the end of the movement, to be followed by a superbly rhetorical flourish: the announcement of the Allegro's main theme, which finishes the movement. The Larghetto is frail and has the proud melancholy of a setting autumnal sun: the upper strings' comment on the cello's thrusting figure grows quietly but steadily more melancholic. The main subject of the Allegro has a manly force that reminds us that Haydn was closely involved in these last two works' performances, and it is highly probable that he persuaded Tost to give the commission to Mozart; what more delicately flattering way to repay the compliment could there be than to write a Haydnesque main theme (even down to the cascading triplets that break into the abrupt series of *f-p* figures)? Of course, we must admire the clever way in which Mozart binds this Allegro section to the introductory material, and what better way to draw the eye's and ear's attention to their individuality than by repeating the dotted figure with which the Larghetto ended: this figure now enters immediately upon the heels of the first subject, and dominates the texture of the next thirty bars. But the very shape of the first subject is in fact a transformation of the violin's first entrance in the Larghetto, as Hans Keller has pointed out.

The development is the most massively symphonic of all in the works under consideration. The confrontation of the various sections previously presented is dramatic, swift and, as in all mature Mozart, of a conciseness which makes it difficult to assimilate everything the first time one hears it.

The marking Adagio is in itself a tribute to Haydn, whose adagios were famous, whereas Mozart usually, though by no means always, preferred the slightly quicker andante tempo. Although the opening is in serene G major, the texture and mood darken, and to our astonishment we find ourselves in D minor for the restless second subject, whose triplet accompaniments and nervous cello commentaries remind us of the mood of the G minor Quintet. The most incredible passage in any of the Quintets comes in the middle of the development section, where the central construction of the entire work – the use of descending thirds – reaches a violent pitch of intensity. Charles Rosen writes of it:[8]

> The climax is the sudden creation of a void: a cadence, built up powerfully and with the fierce energy that the culminated descent can arouse, is, in measure 52, *not* played – not only postponed but permanently withheld. Instead of the cadence, all motion ceases, and with a sudden *piano* only the soft throbbing of the two violas is left. As the other instruments enter with a new sequence that leads directly back to the main theme, we find four completely different kinds of rhythm superimposed in a contrapuntal texture at once complex and deeply touching.

The *pizzicato* cello here almost anticipates Bartók in its bizarre strength.

The Minuet, proceeding on the motif of the downward third, actually manages to introduce a strict canon on its theme in the second part. The Trio is yet another tribute to Haydn; it is so unlike Mozart that the tribute is doubly heartfelt.

Alas, someone tampered with the theme of the Finale, hence we almost never hear its original, chromatic slither but a Bowdlerized version, prettifying it. This tampered theme was added (by Tost, after Mozart's death?) to the actual autograph, and it was this version that was also taken over and used in the first edition published by Artaria & Co.

Some light is shed on this curious textual situation by a manuscript from the Pfannhauser Collection, discovered in 1985 and now in the Gesellschaft der Musikfreunde, Vienna. It is the cello part of a volume of quintets copied in the early nineteenth century (*c.* 1800–10?), if not partially earlier, by sundry Viennese copyists.[9]

Now in the Finale of K.593, the first passage in which the cello has the theme in unison with the other strings – bars 37/8 with upbeat – has been tampered with. The MS. shows an approximation of the revised Artaria version but with a dubious octave jump from A to G sharp:

The next unison passage, at bars 101/2 with upbeat, gives us the Artaria version also with corrections (i.e. there was another reading, but this has been erased). However, bars 209/10 with upbeat have the Artaria reading without corrections. At the end, the last two bars (278/9 with upbeat) have also been corrected into the Artaria reading.

In the absence of the upper parts, it is, of course, difficult to reconstruct what happened to the manuscript, but it would seem clear that the crucial passages have been altered, and probably the MS. originally had Mozart's chromatic reading.

It is a long, fast and intensely involved movement, distinguished by its contrapuntal complexity. Here we find a profound spiritual level matched by a technical brilliance which reveals itself constantly in new ways (the fugal entries at bars 132ff., starting at the bottom of the score and working their way up in off-beat patterns). The other startling technical innovation is the enormous length of the opening theme, which extends to no less than thirty-six bars. This fact in turn dictated the prodigious size of the movement as a whole.

Quintet in E flat (K.614)

I. Allegro di molto. II. Andante. III. Menuetto (Allegretto) & Trio. IV. Allegro.

'The Quintet in E flat (K.614) is a tribute to Haydn', observes Charles

Rosen;[10] concerning what was to prove the last piece of chamber music that Mozart wrote, he points out the similarity of the Finale to that of Haydn's Quartet, op. 64, no. 6, composed for Johann Tost. The entry for Mozart's Quintet in his own Catalogue is dated 'Vienna, 12 April 1791'. Several months earlier, Haydn had left for England and the two men were never to meet again; in December 1790 they had had a last meal together before Haydn's departure, and as they parted, Mozart suddenly looked at his older friend and said, 'We are probably saying our last adieu in this life'.

> Tears welled into the eyes of both men. Haydn was deeply moved, for he applied Mozart's words to himself, and the possibility never occurred to him that the thread of Mozart's life could be cut by the inexorable Parcae [Fates] the very next year.[11]

So this may be seen as Mozart's tribute to his best musical friend *in absentia*. Rosen continues:[12]

> The work which – in its outer movements – combines a detailed treatment in Haydn's fashion of the dynamic qualities of the tiniest motifs with a typically Mozartean sonorous and complex inner part-writing, makes a few musicians uncomfortable, perhaps because it lacks the expansive freedom of the other quintets, and seems to concentrate its richness … . It is only fitting, after all, that in his last chamber work, Mozart should once again appear to submit to Haydn's instruction. It was Haydn who created this chamber style, made it viable, and endowed it with the power to bear dramatic and expressive weight without flying apart. In the quintets Mozart expanded the range of form beyond Haydn's range, and attained a massiveness that Beethoven himself never surpassed. The fundamental and imaginative vision, of chamber music as dramatic action, however, was Haydn's; and his conception and his innovations were a living presence in every work of this kind Mozart wrote.

The 6/8 metre of the opening Allegro di molto is not a customary one for first movements, and Mozart may have borrowed the idea from Haydn's Symphony no. 67 in F. The quick, nervous language is typical of Haydn, too, as is the massive concentration of motivic relationships and expansions. The suave delicacy of the second subject is Mozartian, and the development might be said to be a synthesis of Haydn's intellectual concentration with Mozart's sense of drama and breadth.

The Andante is of that late-period simplicity in Mozart that astonishes in *Die Zauberflöte* and in passages from *La clemenza di Tito*: it is supreme art, touching, direct and of an autumnal beauty that reminds us that music's greatest and most perfect genius would die before the year was out: the chromatic passages that follow that deeply portentous pedal point on the cello, as soon as the theme has been stated and repeated, are like the fading light of a Watteau *fête*, bathed in a melancholy that Mozart even at his most Haydnesque cannot possibly escape.

The Minuet has some details of consummate subtlety: in the second part, we see how the main theme is suddenly turned round and used against itself, most clearly when the cello picks up the inverted version at bars 26ff. In the Trio, the waltz rhythm is established at the outset, but what impresses even more is the fact that almost the whole Trio has a bass of E flat, like a forgotten toy music box that keeps quietly repeating its tune.

In size, scope, and developmental process, the Finale, with its Haydnesque tune, completes this great and touching act of friendship, one that rounds out Mozart's personal tribute to the two Haydn brothers, Michael and Joseph.

Sacred vocal works: Oratorios and Latin church music

‍

I N RECENT YEARS SOME FUNDAMENTAL CHANGES CONCERNING THE authenticity and chronology of Mozart's church music, both great and small, have been suggested, partly as a result of the discovery of new sources, some of which will be unknown to many English-speaking readers.

As an appendix to this essay, an up-to-date comprehensive catalogue of the known vocal church music by Mozart, except for very small sketches and drafts, has been provided. This chronological catalogue is a necessity because some of the interesting pieces listed there – especially the collection of single movements and of late-period drafts – were in part published for the first time in the *NMA* (edited by Monika Holl) in 1990, e.g. the D minor Kyrie (K.90), the Hosanna in G (K.223), Kyrie in D (K.Anh.14), Kyrie in C (K.Anh.13), Gloria in C (K.Anh.20), as well as the impressive Kyrie fragment in C (K.Anh.18) and the smaller Kyrie fragment in D (K.Anh.19), both dating from *c.* 1772. These were, of course, not available for inclusion in the listing which appears in *The Mozart Compendium,* also published in 1990.

ORATORIOS

La Betulia liberata (K.118 [74c]), 1771

The first mention of this work is also the one that does much to clarify its origins. It occurs in a letter (written in Italian) from Leopold Mozart, dated Salzburg 19 July 1771, to Gian Luca, Count Pallavicini, in Bologna, in which he states: 'Meanwhile my son is in the process of composing an Oratorio by Metastasio for Padua, commissioned by Sgr. Don Giuseppe Ximenes de Principi d'Aragona, and I shall send this oratorio, when I pass through Verona, to Padua to be copied, and when returning from Milan [for the opera *Ascanio in Alba* (K.III), first performed there on 17 October 1771] we shall go to Padua to hear the rehearsal.'¹ From Luigi Ferdinando Tagliavini's foreword to *Betulia liberata* in the *NMA* (1960) we learn that Giuseppe Ximenes, Prince of Aragona, lived in Padua, put on 'academies' (i.e. concerts) and was an enthusiastic music-lover, being especially fond of oratorios and sacred cantatas of the old school, since, as he wrote to Padre Martini on 15 January 1781, apart from Hasse, most modern composers were not to his taste. (A cantata for which Giuseppe Ximenes wrote the words – *Il Delirio umano*, 1768 – is extant.)

However, something seems to have gone wrong with the whole project. Wolfgang did indeed finish the Oratorio, but it was not performed, and in its stead the same text was set by one Giuseppe Callegari: a libretto in the Biblioteca del Museo Civico, Padua, is entitled: 'Betulia liberata del Sig. Ab. Pietro Metastasio, posta in musica del Sig. Giuseppe Callegari, Padova, Stamperia del Seminario, 1771'.

Mozart, after he had settled in Vienna, gave concerts with the Tonkünstler-Societät (Society of Musicians, established to support former members' widows and orphans), and apparently intended to revive *Betulia*, for in a letter of 21 July 1784 to his sister² he asks his father to send him 'the old Oratorio *Betulia liberata*'. He adds, 'I have to write this oratorio for the society here – perhaps I could use here and there some of the pieces ...'. However, this project also seems to have fallen through (the details may be seen in the *NMA*, p. VII). In other words, this striking evidence of Mozart's early talent was to our knowledge never heard in his lifetime. Curiously, however, it was one of the works that Constanze Mozart sold to the King of Prussia³ on 4 March 1792, together with the Requiem.

Although *Betulia* is seldom heard even now, an excellent performance (conducted by Walter Hagen-Groll) was given in January 1988 during the *Mozartwoche*, staged in the Great Hall of Salzburg University. The work proved to be extraordinarily impressive, beginning with the passionate, *Sturm und Drang*-laden D minor Overture with four horns (two in D, two in F) and two trumpets but no timpani – in those days it was not customary to use kettledrums in Italian churches except in oratorios with warlike subjects, such as Vivaldi's *Judith*.⁴ The Overture consists of three parts with a middle Andante also in D minor, which leads to a final Presto with thematic reminiscences of the opening movement. It would make a very effective concert piece.

Another number which has always impressed commentators is No. 4, Chorus with Ozià, in C minor, an Adagio in cut time, with divided violas. The chorus has the same serious tone as parts of *Thamos* or *Die Zauberflöte*. The large-scale accompanied recitatives in *Betulia Liberata* have also been remarked upon: some sections could have been lifted from an *opera seria*.

Certainly the most surprising and inspiring pages are in the final Chorus No. 16, 'Lodi al gran Dio', which use the famous old psalm tone, *Tonus pellegrinus*, which was also employed to striking effect in Michael Haydn's Requiem for Archbishop Schrattenbach composed at the end of 1771, and which figures prominently in Mozart's own Requiem twenty years later during the Introit ('Te decet hymnus'). The whole music in *Betulia* also shifts from E minor at the chorus's beginning to D major at the work's end, evidence that even at this stage Mozart was concerned with large-scale tonal structures – in this case from D minor to D major, a pattern that would be repeated in *Don Giovanni* sixteen years later.

It is curious that this strangely prophetic music has never really enjoyed the success it so eminently merits.

Davidde penitente (K.469)

Since a large part of this work was taken from the Mass in C minor (K.427 [417a]), which Mozart was unwilling to discard after only one performance in provincial Salzburg on 26 October 1783, we shall mention here only the two beautiful arias which he composed especially for this revival in Vienna in March 1785. The first, for tenor solo, is 'A te, fra tanti affanni', which with its delicate scoring for flute, oboe, clarinet, bassoon and two horns in B flat *alto* is a typical example of Mozart's ambiguous musical language, mysteriously beautiful. The Andante beginning merges effortlessly into an Allegro, where the bravura seems as natural as the semiquavers that creep up on us as the tenor sings 'delle tempeste in sen'. The other Aria is for soprano I and is in C minor, 'Tra l'oscure ombre funeste': in it Mozart seems to be discovering the universe. Again, the music merges into an Allegro, this time in a radiant C major, the key of the Mass itself. There is magnificent woodwind writing (oboes, bassoons) in double thirds, to illustrate the phrase 'quella gioia, quella pace', which occurs twice. And we must draw attention to the spectactular cadenza that Mozart inserts into the end of the former 'Cum Sancto Spiritu' fugue (four full pages of score in the *NMA*, pp. 129–32).

It is worth recalling that it was Abbé Maximilian Stadler who, as a friend of the composer, imparted to Vincent and Mary Novello in 1829 some interesting and probably authentic information:

> ... on enquiring [of Stadler] on what occasion Mozart had put the 'Davidde Penitente' into its present form, he informed me that when Mozart came to Vienna he was applied to for some piece in the Oratorio style. As the time allowed was not sufficient to write an entirely new piece, he took the greater part of a Mass ... to which the poet Da Ponte adapted other words, and Mozart added the fine Terzetto in E minor [actually the cadenza described above] and the two new solos in order to complete the work required.[5]

And Monika Holl, the editor of the work in the *NMA* (1987), has found the records of the first performances by the Tonkünster-Societät in March 1785: the first, on 13 March, was attended by some 660 persons, whereas on the second occasion, only about 225 were present to hear Mozart's latest work – a sombre portent of what was soon to happen regularly in terms of the decline in interest on the part of the Viennese audiences.

MASSES, MASS FRAGMENTS AND MISCELLANEOUS SACRED MUSIC, INCLUDING LITANIES, VESPERS AND VESPER PSALMS

The greater part of Mozart's church music was bound up with his situation in Salzburg – first because his father was Vice-Capellmeister and Wolfgang could, as he said, 'write as much [church music] as I want to' (letter to Padre Martini, September 1776), and later in 1779 and 1780 because of his own new appointment as *Conzert-Meister* and court organist. In the latter capacity, Mozart's output of great church music during his last two years at Salzburg is remarkable: two Masses, including his most popular work in that form ('Coronation' Mass), three instrumental 'Epistle' Sonatas, including his grandest composition in this form (K.329), as well as two extraordinary Vespers settings, one of which is particularly well-loved (*Vesperae solennes de Confessore*, K.339).

Some of Mozart's church music was, of course, written away from Salzburg – the late Motet 'Ave, verum corpus' and the Requiem of 1791 are two obvious examples – and as it happens all the earliest specimens were composed 'abroad'. The earliest surviving example, a Kyrie in F for choir, strings and organ (K.33), was composed (finished) in Paris on 12 June 1766, while the next work listed in the Köchel Catalogue is an Offertory, 'Scande coeli limina' (K.34), composed, it would seem, for the Feast of St Benedict, celebrated at the Bavarian Abbey of Seeon.

We have no idea why Wolfgang started to write a Mass in Paris, since the Ordinary was not usually sung in churches there (rather the music performed consisted of motets, cantatas and organ works, some on a grand scale). The competent music is in the style of an Austrian Kyrie for a *missa brevis*, such as Wolfgang will have heard countless times in his infancy in Salzburg. All the fragmentary works have been edited for the *NMA*, such as those included in the volume 'Einzelsätze und Fragmente' ('Single Movements and Fragments'), edited by Monika Holl and published in 1990. Particularly in the case of this volume, it was possible to make definitive and in part revolutionary use of the research by Wolfgang Plath[6] into Leopold Mozart's handwriting in general and Wolfgang's as it changed in the 1770s. A summary of Plath's research may also be consulted in *The Mozart Compendium* (1990).[7] Added to this, Alan Tyson's studies on the papers used by Mozart and their watermarks were invaluable.[8]

Monika Holl notes that the Kyrie (K.33) is signed and dated by the composer at the top of page 1 'a paris 12 Juni di wolfgang Mozart 1766', and that pages 1–3 are in Leopold's hand, his father acting as scribe. Wolfgang also entered the names of the various parts ('viol 1 / viol 2 / viola / soprano', etc.), the tempo ('larghetto') and the dynamic marks in the violins (but not those in the viola part, which are by Leopold) as well as 'volti' at the bottom of the page. From about the second crotchet of bar 18, Wolfgang begins to write the MS. himself, continuing to the end. In other words, this is a composite autograph, or a kind of fair copy that was made from an earlier complete draft, afterwards perhaps discarded. This brief description will show how invaluable is Monika Holl's contribution to our knowledge of these little-known church pieces.

The most important commission for church music that young Wolfgang had received to date was in connection with the frustrating visit he made to Vienna in 1767 and 1768, in the course of which he expected to stage his new opera *La finta semplice*. The amazing attempts to sabotage that opera, which eventually resulted in its not being performed in Vienna at all, have been recounted elsewhere, not least in Leopold's letters sent from Vienna to Salzburg.[9] The failure of the opera was, however, in large measure gainsaid by the commission to compose a solemn Mass and the offertory (offertories?) for the newly constructed Waisenhauskirche, or Orphanage Church, in Vienna, the consecration of which took place on 7 December 1767, the Feast of the Immaculate Conception, in the presence of Empress Maria Theresa, Emperor Joseph II, the Archdukes Ferdinand and Maximilian, and the Archduchesses Elisabeth and Maria Amalia. Leopold Mozart, writing to Lorenz Hagenauer from Vienna on 12 November 1768,[10] says that 'Wolfgang composed for him [Pater Ignaz Parhamer, the Institute's Director] a *Solenne Mess, offertorium* and a trumpet concerto for a boy ...'. As to the identity of the Offertory, scholarly opinion is divided, but in the case of the Mass (K.139 [47a]) we are on firmer ground, aided by an invaluable MS. Catalogue of Mozart's works drawn up by his father, extracts from which are included here.[11]

Catalogue

of Everything which this 12-year-old Boy
has composed since his 7th Year, and which
can be examined in the originals

...

A short Stabat Mater for 4 voices without
instruments [lost]

...

A fugue – for 4 voices [lost? unidentified?]

A Veni Sancte Spiritus for 4 voices, 2 violins, 2
oboes, 2 horns, trumpets, timpani, viola e
Baßo, etc: [K.47]

...

And now the opera Buffa *La Finta Semplice*, which
consists of 558 pages in the original score.
Moreover, a large Mass with 4 vocal parts, 2
violins, 2 oboes, 2 violas, 4 trumpets
[clarini], timpani, etc: [K.139 (47a)]
[Nannerl Mozart later added the date '1768']

A smaller Mass for 4 voices, 2 violins, etc: [K.49 (47d)]
A large Offertorium for 4 voices, etc: 2 violins,

etc: trumpets [clarini], etc: [either lost or
possibly K.117 (66a)]

The Mass is easily identified because of the scoring for four trumpets, an
unusual number (it was, of course, the norm to have two). In the case of the
Offertory, 'Benedictus sit Deus' (K.117) is certainly a likely candidate, but
on the other hand it may be that the work in question is lost, as is the trumpet concerto 'for a boy' which was played on the same occasion. According
to Alan Tyson the paper used for the autograph of the Mass seems to have
been purchased by Mozart 'in Vienna in the course of the year 1768 ... We
need not be surprised that he preserved a sufficient quantity of it to enable
him to write out K.108 (74d), the *Regina Coeli* of 1771, on it ...'.[12]

The *Wienerisches Diarium*, Vienna's official newspaper, reported on 10
December 1768 that

> Wednesday the 7th Her Imperial Royal Majesty [Maria Theresa] conde-
> scended to visit the Orphanage on the Rennweg, there to participate in
> the inaugural festive consecration of and religious ceremony for the
> newly built church ... . The entire music performed by the Orphanage
> choir during the Ordinary of the Mass was especially composed for this
> celebration by the twelve-year-old Wolfgang Mozart, little son of Herr
> Leopold Mozart, Kapellmeister in the service of the Prince Archbishop of
> Salzburg. Known because of his special talents, [Wolfgang] himself per-
> formed this music to general applause and admiration; he conducted
> with the greatest precision and also the motets were of his composition.

With its rich orchestration (three trombones, two high trumpets and two
low trumpets) and its almost miraculous command of the musical language
required for such an event, this Mass must be reckoned as a real milestone in
the young Mozart's career.

The work is in a form known as the 'Cantata Mass', in which the first
three sections of the Ordinary (Kyrie, Gloria, Credo) were subdivided into
several parts – a procedure which we find in Haydn's *Missa Cellensis* of 1766
and in Mozart's own Mass in C minor (K.427 [417a]) of 1783.

The 'Cantata Mass' was something of a Viennese speciality and intended
for especially festive occasions, such as the consecration of a new church, the
celebration of the Feast of St Cecilia (22 November), or one of the great
Feast Days (Easter Sunday, for example). Mozart had models on which to
base his work – not only by Haydn but also by Antonio Caldara and Georg

Reutter Jr, whose Viennese 'Cantata Masses' could be studied in many church archives. The spirited and interesting fugues in Mozart's Orphanage Mass ('Cum Sancto Spiritu', 'Et vitam venturi') show that the young man's knowledge of counterpoint was already extraordinary.

It is difficult to imagine for which purposes Wolfgang wrote the other Offertory 'Veni Sancte Spiritus' (K.47), with its large orchestration, though if we take the newspaper's words 'and also the motets were of his composition' literally, it must mean that more than one 'motet' (or offertory) was included in the Orphanage Church service; in that case 'Veni Sancte Spiritus', may have been composed along with the Mass, despite the slightly different orchestration in the two Offertory candidates: K.117 (66a) has two flutes, two horns and two trumpets, and K.47 has two oboes, two horns and two trumpets, while the Mass, K.139 (47a), has two oboes, no horns and four trumpets. In those days, however, it was customary for trumpet players to be able to play the horn and for oboe players to double on flute (as they did in Haydn's orchestra in 1761).

*   *   *

There was always a certain dualistic streak in Austrian church music of the eighteenth century. While, on the one hand, there were grand Masses and smaller-scale pieces in C major with trumpets and kettledrums and operatic soprano solos, as well as flourishing instrumental interludes, on the other it seems to have occurred to all these composers – and to Haydn and Mozart as well – that there was another equally 'real' church music tradition. This was variously called the 'stilo antico' (antique style), or the 'contrapuntal' or 'Palestrina' style, and as it happens in this very year 1768, Joseph Haydn in Eisenstadt had begun (and possibly completed) an extraordinary work in this severe church music tradition, the *Missa* 'Sunt bona mixta malis' in D minor, the autograph of which was discovered in 1983 in the attic of a country house in Northern Ireland: it consists of the Kyrie and a large part of the Gloria and is scored for voices and *basso continuo*, and its style is at once learned and very austere. Naturally, this kind of exercise – a sort of purge – was not limited to D minor, but it is surprising that so many of Haydn's and Mozart's contrapuntal church music pieces are in that very key. In the case of Haydn, not only the rediscovered Mass, but also the equally startling Offertorium 'Non nobis, Domine', also for voices and *continuo* only, as well as the beautiful *Responsoria ad absolutionem* 'Libera me' and the second movement of the *Responsoria de Venerabili* (XXIIIc:4), are all available on record.[13] With Mozart there is, apart from the canonic Kyrie in G (K.89 [73k]), the D minor Kyrie (K.90), the latter very much in the same language as Haydn's Mass of 1768; both Mozart works are now dated Salzburg 1772(?) in *NMA*. But the summation of this 'Palestrina' style comes in the monumental Offertory 'Misericordias Domini' (K.222 [205a]) in D minor, which Mozart sent to Padre Martini in Bologna on 4 September 1776 with a letter in which he wrote:

> A few days before my departure [from Munich], H.H. the Elector wanted to hear some of my music in counterpoint: hence I was obliged to write this Motet in haste so as to have time to copy the score for His Highness, and to copy the parts for performance on the following Sunday as an offertory during the High Mass [*Sotto la Messa grande in tempo del Offertorio*]. Dearest and most esteemed F[ather] Maestro! You are most ardently requested to tell me frankly, without reserve, what you think of it. We live in this world to learn with untiring industry ...'.[14]

In fact, Padre Martini (with whom Mozart had studied briefly when visiting Bologna in 1770) was most impressed with the *Offertorium de tempore* and wrote that he found in it 'everything that modern music requires, good harmony, rich modulations, moderate movement in the violins, the modulations in the parts natural and well plotted ...'. As usual, the astute Padre Martini put his finger on the most interesting and unusual part of the work, the modulations, some of them startlingly unexpected even today.

In 1774, when Mozart was eighteen, he seems to have become aware that church music, in the Salzburg environment, had a dimension far above and beyond the normal kind of music that the archiepiscopal court expected from its exceptional young *Conzert-Meister*. The first of his new and popular settings is the *Missa brevis* in F (K.192 [186f]), completed on 24 June 1774. This so-called 'short mass' is scored in its original version for two violins and *basso continuo* (organ, cellos, double basses), with three trombones doubling the alto, tenor and bass parts of the choir. With this Mass, one notices that Mozart's writing for voices has become more fluent, and the use of counterpoint more flexible, subtle and personal. The Credo is based on a famous old Gregorian chant, which haunted Mozart all his life – even in purely instrumental music, e.g. the development of Symphony no. 33 in B flat

(K.319) and, most spectacularly, the Finale of the 'Jupiter' Symphony (K.551). Later, Mozart added two trumpets to the scoring of this Mass, and since it was no longer fashionable to use high clarino trumpets in F, he wrote for them in C. These interesting and by no means conventional trumpet parts were first printed in *NMA*, edited by (the late) Walter Senn in 1975.

For Mozart it was a period of prodigious output in composing church music. In 1775 and 1776 he wrote, apart from the Offertory 'Misericordias Domini' in Munich, the *Litaniae de venerabili altaris sacramento* (K.243), no less than *five* complete Masses – in an attempted chronological order, K.262 (246a), K.258, K.220 (196b – of which the exact position is unclear), K.259 and K.257. It was an astonishing feat, even for Mozart. In the letter to Padre Martini from which a passage is quoted above in connection with 'Misericordias Domini', there is another instructive passage:

> ... My father is maestro in the Metropolitan Church [= Cathedral], which gives me the opportunity to write for the church as much as I want to, and moreover since my father has been already *in the service of this court for 36 years, and knowing that this Archbishop can not and will not see people of advanced age,* he does not take it to heart but devotes himself to literature, already his favourite form of study. Our church music is considerably different from that in Italy, and is becoming more so, since a Mass with everything = the *Kyrie, Gloria, Credo,* the *Sonata all'Epistola, the offertory or motet,* Sanctus and Agnus Dei, even the most solemn [Mass], if we name the Mass, the principal part of the same is not to last longer than three-quarters of an hour, and so a special study is required for this kind of composition, especially however since a Mass is to have all the instruments – trombe di guerra [literally: war trumpets], timpani, etc.: ah! we are far away from our dearest Sgr. P: Maestro, how many things I would have to tell you! ...[15]

The title of the *Missa longa* (K.262 [246a]) is in Leopold Mozart's hand, next to the incipit on a composite title page for five C major Masses by his son – K.262 (246a), 257, 258, 259 – now in the Berlin State Library. It points out an obvious characteristic of this impressive work: it is one of the longest of these Masses and certainly does not conform to the description of the typical Mass favoured by Archbishop Colloredo, as outlined in Wolfgang's letter of 4 September 1776. Actually, there were always exceptions to the general 45-minute rule for such works, e.g. Michael Haydn's compositions.

One feature of the autograph is that there is no timpani part, especially curious in a C major Mass with horns and trumpets. Fortunately, the original performance material from Salzburg Cathedral, formerly in Leopold Mozart's library and now in the Chorherrenstift Heilig Kreuz (Holy Cross Abbey) in Augsburg, does include a timpani part in Mozart's own hand, but without the Credo. Walter Senn, who edited the volume of *NMA* in which the *Missa longa* appears, writes 'in this form' (i.e. without the Credo) the Mass was

> either intended for performance during a minor Church feast occurring on a weekday, for the liturgy of which a sung Credo was not used, or, because of the length of the movement – with its 406 bars it is the longest Credo Mozart ever wrote – it was not used and another one from a shorter Mass composition was used instead. In the kettledrum part, room for the Credo was left open – Mozart intended to write the part later.

The missing Credo part was discreetly added in *NMA* by Walter Senn in small print. (Previously, i.e. before *NMA*'s publication in 1975, this work was performed without kettledrums.)

In this work of exceptional scope, the fugues are outstanding: that for the 'Cum Sancto Spiritu' is a double fugue with the counter-subject sung to the word 'Amen', while the most extensive is the 'Et vitam' fugue at the end of the Credo, of scintillating brilliance. In the letter to Padre Martini quoted above, Mozart wrote that these Masses 'require a special study', and there is no doubt that the popular success of these church works of 1775 and 1776 was the result of the composer's deliberate calculations, for they became popular in a way that hardly any of Mozart's instrumental music could have been at the time. Mozart's symphonies, concertos and serenades of this period were written for a small circle at Salzburg – either for friends or patrons (such as the Haffner family), or for performance at the archiepiscopal court. In both cases, the audience was very limited. Not so in the case of the church music, however. In the huge cathedral, even in the long-naved Monastery Church of St Peter's, or in the Collegiate Church, hundreds of worshippers could and did hear Mozart's latest church music. Not only that, its fame soon spread all over *Land* Salzburg and Upper Austria – the territories surrounding the archiepiscopal see. Early MS. copies of these works are in Lambach Abbey, in Kremsmünster Abbey, in St Florian Abbey, in Schlierbach Abbey, in the parish church of Gmunden, in the former

Abbey Church of Mondsee and elsewhere in Upper Austria. Haydn's *Kapelle* at Eisenstadt (Prince Nicolaus Esterházy) owned MS. copies of the 'Credo' Mass, the 'Piccolomini' Mass and the 'Organ Solo' Mass, among many other church pieces by Mozart. Thus, many thousands of people near and even in Salzburg came to know Mozart first (and, in the cases of older people, only) through his church music. While such works as the violin concertos composed in the 1770s remained unprinted and to all intents unknown except to a fortunate few in Salzburg, Augsburg or Mannheim (where Mozart played them), the church music circulated widely in Austria and Germany. By 1800, works like the 'Credo' Mass were well known in Austria, while Mozart's secular compositions languished in obscurity. These Masses and other church pieces were circulated in MS. copies. The first person to undertake a certain amount of such distribution was Leopold Mozart, who seems to have sold the occasional MS. to Mondsee Abbey and elsewhere.

Although the works of 1776 achieved a real and lasting popularity in Catholic Austria and southern Germany, they remain still largely unknown in Britain and America. There are many and complex reasons for this, of which two may be singled out: (1) the prejudice, in the nineteenth century, against church works of the Austrian *settecento* in general, and (2) the fact that these works, designed for the Church, were never performed in Catholic churches in Britain and America, and certainly not with the full orchestra. This tradition is unknown in Anglo-Saxon countries. And thus it has come about that these works, of great importance in Mozart's *œuvre*, are known there only to Mozart experts and through a few recent recordings. It is to be hoped that all this music, now that it has been issued by *NMA* in scholarly texts, will become known to English-speaking audiences, both in church and in concert performances.

The *Missa brevis* in C (K.258) is very economically scored for trumpets, timpani and strings (apart from the usual four vocal parts and organ) and follows the Colloredo pattern of brevity. Similarly, the 'December Masses' of 1775 and 1776 also have no trombones in the orchestra, contrary to the usual Salzburg tradition. In Salzburg, K.257 is known as the 'Spaur-Messe', referring to the Salzburg Canon, Ignaz Joseph, Count Spaur, who was coadjutor of Brixen in South Tyrol (now part of Alto Adige in northern Italy). The autograph of the *Missa brevis* (K.258) is dated (in Leopold Mozart's hand) December 1775 and cannot therefore have been composed for the installation ceremonies in November 1776; it is now believed that K.257, the elaborate 'Credo' Mass, was written for Count Spaur, and not K.258 (see below). Perhaps, however, both were written for him, since he was a friend of the Mozart family.

The work's other title, 'Piccolomini' Mass, has an even more grotesque explanation. It was formerly thought that Piccolomini must refer to the great Italian family of that name, which furnished a pope (Pius II, 1458–64) and owned huge estates near Siena; nothing of the sort, however, for 'Piccolomini' is simply a Bowdlerization of the Italian *piccolo*, little – in other words referring to the fact that K.258 is a short mass.

It is not known exactly when Mozart composed the Mass in C (K.220 [196b]), known in Germany and Austria as the 'Spatzenmesse' (literally, 'Sparrows' Mass) because of the chirping violins in the Sanctus and at the end of the Benedictus. In some sources the work is entitled *Missa brevis*, in others simply *Missa* or *Missa solemnis*, probably because it is in the festive key of C and includes trumpets and kettledrums. The work appears to have been composed in 1775 or early 1776, and its outward structure conforms to the new rule established by Archbishop Colloredo.

In this sort of hybrid Mass, Mozart was brilliantly original. K.220 is, of course, a festive work, but even its brilliant manner allows sudden flashes of inspiration hinting at later Mozart: consider, at the end of the Gloria, the sudden entrance of the solo soprano with the words 'Quoniam tu solus sanctus' (originally sung by Maria Magdalena Lipp, Michael Haydn's wife, for whose extraordinary voice Mozart always reserved moments of touching gentleness and beauty – see p. 180); the rest of the phrase is taken over by the tenor, 'Tu solus Dominus, Tu solus Altissimus', and then both sing the words 'Jesu Christe' together. It is a magical moment and one that might have caused Colloredo to think that his young *Conzert-Meister* might possess God-given talents.

The *Missa brevis* in C (K.259) has the same economical scoring as K.258: trumpets, kettledrums, two violins, bass, organ and the four voices (soli and choir). This work is again in the 'Colloredo tradition', i.e. the short mass, and in order to distinguish it from its companions, most of which are in the standard church key of C major (standard for solemn masses, that is), K.259 is known as the 'Organ Solo' Mass. The solo in question occurs in the Benedictus and thus follows a tradition well known in Austria: Haydn's *Missa brevis S. Joannis de Deo*, composed about a year earlier, features a similar, though more elaborate, organ solo. The whole of Mozart's Mass is very Austrian, even to the delightful Agnus Dei, with its songful first violin (later vocal) part and its mischievous *pizzicato* bass part – as innocently Baroque and worldly as many an altar in southern Germany and Austria.

The name given to K.257, 'Credo' Mass, comes, as might be expected, from the Credo movement, which is united by having the word 'Credo' repeated at intervals throughout. This is an old Austrian tradition, going back to the great Baroque composer Joseph Johann Fux. It is likely that the special occasion for which this Mass was composed was the consecration of the Salzburg Canon, Ignaz Joseph, Count Spaur, as Bishop of Brixen on 17 November 1776. The solemn ceremony of installing a new bishop would account for the radical departure from the '*missa brevis*' tradition otherwise favoured by Archbishop Colloredo. Ignaz Joseph, Count Spaur, was the nephew of the previous Bishop of Brixen, Leopold Maria Joseph, Count Spaur (who held the see 1747–76). Leopold Mozart and Wolfgang were friends of the Canon and on 11 and 12 December 1771 the Court Protocol of Brixen records their arrival from Milan and Verona:

> Wed. the 11th Mass at 7 o'clock and the cure continued, at 6 o'clock confession. Can[on] Count Ignati made music with the 2 Mozard [*sic*] and had dinner with them. The 12th Xber [December] Thurs. the Mass at 7 o'clock and the cure continued, the Mozard lunched with the Can. Count Ignati and in the afternoon made music, they also dined with the Canon in the evening.[16]

It was, therefore, not only for a dignitary of the Church but also for a friend that the young Mozart composed the new Mass (K.257). In any event, it is one of the most endearing of the young Mozart's church pieces: full of life, energy and youthful spirits, combined with a certain innocent devotion which often characterizes works of the Austrian school of that period. At the same time, the orchestra, with its typically brass-heavy construction – three trombones and two trumpets against only two oboes and perhaps a bassoon or two doubling the *basso continuo* – is of a brilliance that is often symphonic in splendour.

The final Mass setting of this particular group, the *Missa* in B flat (K.275 [272b]), was composed at Salzburg some time in September 1777, and was probably first performed at Salzburg after Wolfgang and his mother had left for Paris (23 September). Authentic parts for the additional wind instruments (bassoons and three trombones) have survived. Being in the *missa brevis* tradition, the work has 'telescoped' texts in parts of the Credo (two different texts sung simultaneously, which was one of the bad traditions of the *missa brevis* form in Austria) and is scored for two violins and *basso continuo*. Apart from the Cathedral performance – parts in the archives have survived – there was another, at the Abbey Church of St Peter's in Salzburg on Sunday, 21 December 1777, at which the newly engaged castrato (soprano) Francesco Ceccarelli (1752–1814) 'sang incomparably', as Leopold Mozart wrote in a letter to his son and wife. This must mean the long and very beautiful soprano solo throughout the Benedictus (up to the repetition of the 'Osanna'), which requires not only a flexible voice but one capable of reproducing the *messa di voce* parts (bars 23–6 and 35–8), where 'benedictus' is sung on four long repeated B flats. This was another genuinely popular Mass: at the end the 'dona nobis pacem' marked Allegro is such a fetching melody that everyone will have gone home from church with it in mind (and heart). The soft ending is infinitely touching: *Ite missa est* indeed …

*   *   *

If we survey the substantial amount of 'smaller' church music of this period, we might single out three works of special interest and merit, one from the pre-Italian years, one written in Milan, and one composed just before Mozart and his mother left on their fateful journey to Paris in 1777.

The first is a grand Te Deum (K.141 [66b]) in C of 1769, the true magnificence of which was, astonishingly, only revealed when the volume of *NMA* which includes it was published in 1963, edited by Hellmut Federhofer. In that edition, it became clear for the first time that there was authentic performance material with MS. additions in Leopold Mozart's hand in the Salzburg Cathedral Archives: this included four trumpet parts – two for *clarini* (high trumpets), two for lower *trombe*. The other MS. sources, in so far as they had trumpets and timpani, had completely different parts. Since the timpani part was missing from the Salzburg Cathedral material, a new one, corresponding to the authentic four trumpet parts, was skilfully reconstructed by the editor.

An interesting fact was revealed by the German scholar W. Kurthen[17] in 1920, namely that Mozart's work is based, almost bar for bar, on a Te Deum by Johann Michael Haydn completed at Grosswardein (now Oradea Mare,

Romania) on 1 April 1760, which Michael must have brought to Salzburg when he arrived there in 1763 – a set of MS. parts is in the Archives of St Peter's Abbey, Salzburg – and which is chronologically perhaps the first instance, among many cited in these essays, when Mozart submitted gladly to instruction by his older colleague. In that famous letter to Padre Martini of 1776 already quoted above, Mozart writes respectfully of 'altri due bravissimi Contrapuntisti', referring to Michael Haydn and Anton Cajetan Adlgasser.[18] (The relationship between Michael Haydn and Mozart is discussed in two other essays in this volume: see pp. 129ff. and 143ff.) Alfred Einstein perceptively writes,[19]

> And yet this work is as Mozartean as the Violin Concerto [in D, K.218, supposedly based on a work by Boccherini], constructed with a sure hand, enchanting in its choral declamation, and possessed of a certain South-German rustic grandeur even in the concluding double fugue – a worthy conclusion to Mozart's activities as a church composer before setting off on the Italian journeys.

The second piece – today the most familiar single work among Mozart's smaller church music – is the Motet 'Exsultate, jubilate' (K.198 [74c]), composed in Milan in January 1773 for the famous Italian castrato Venanzio Rauzzini, who would later go to live in England (Haydn stayed with him in 1794 during his second visit to England and wrote a canon in honour of Rauzzini's dead dog, 'Turk was a faithful dog and not a man').[20] Rauzzini had sung the role of Cecilio in Mozart's *Lucio Silla* (Milan, 1772), and it was natural that this Motet in F major should be couched in the ripest operatic language of the period, with dazzling coloratura in the quick outer movements and a serene charm in the Andante movement 'Tu virginum corona' (it is not known who wrote the text). The concluding 'Alleluia' has become one of Mozart's best-known church pieces. The work was originally scored for oboes and horns, but when Mozart returned to Salzburg, he rescored it with flutes in place of oboes (a discovery made by Robert Münster too late for the revision to be included in the *NMA* text). It is thought that Mozart made this change as (relatively) late as 1779.

The third work, the Gradual 'Sancta Maria, mater Dei', was always regarded as something out of the ordinary. The autograph manuscript of this piece, written for performance on the Feast of the Blessed Virgin Mary (12 September) in 1777, is signed and dated 'Di Wolfgango Amadeo Mozart mpria Salisburgo li 9 di sept: 1777' (Berlin State Library). In August, Mozart had petitioned the Archbishop to grant him leave of absence, but Colloredo, furious at the whole family, dismissed both father and son from his service. Leopold prudently decided to remain in Salzburg and persuaded the Archbishop to continue to employ him as Vice Capellmeister, while the headstrong Wolfgang set out for Paris. Travel always entailed something of a risk in those days, and it was towards an uncertain future, professionally, that Wolfgang left Salzburg accompanied by his mother on 23 September, travelling in their own *chaise*.

The great French Mozart scholars T. de Wyzewa and G. de Saint-Foix have postulated that this simple, moving 'Sancta Maria' was Wolfgang's private votive offering to the Virgin Mary, seeking her protection on their long journey.[21] Certainly this work throws a powerful light on the whole question of Mozart's relationship to the Church. There can be no doubt that Wolfgang was a true son of the Catholic Faith – as evidence of which see also his comments made when composing the Mass in C minor (K.427) quoted below (p. 182). Perhaps this simple act of faith in 1777 moves us more than all the grand trumpets and drums of the Mass settings of this period: as such, it seems to stretch a hand forward to that other simple but monumental act of faith – the Motet 'Ave, verum corpus', composed at Baden in 1791 for the Feast of Corpus Christi.

In the event, Mozart's prayer to the Virgin went unheeded: while in Paris, he would witness the death of his mother and, having found no position suited to his talents, he had to return, empty-handed, to another post in Salzburg which Leopold managed to arrange for his wilful, difficult son of God-given talents.

*　　　*　　　*

On his return to Mannheim after Paris, in 1778, Mozart found that the electoral court had transferred to Munich, since the Elector Palatine Karl Theodor had meanwhile become Regent of Bavaria. It was probably for an intended performance in one of the court churches in Munich that Mozart began to write a magnificent Kyrie in E flat (K.322 [296a]), scored for oboes, bassoons, horns, and – what was rather rare for Mozart at that period – trumpets and drums in E flat; there were also two violas. This work remained fragmentary, but was expertly completed by the Abbé Maximilian

Stadler, whose involvement is apparent as early as bar 8. The extent of Stadler's participation was first registered by Wolfgang Plath of the *NMA*. As to the dating, Alan Tyson has established that the fourteen-stave paper used by Mozart was identical to that on which he wrote the great Double Concerto fragment for violin, piano and orchestra (K.Anh.56 [315f]); this projected concerto is mentioned by Wolfgang in a letter to his father dated Mannheim, 12 November 1778,[22] hence the Kyrie could have been composed either during his stay in Mannheim from 6 November to 9 December, or begun/continued in Munich in December 1778 or January 1779. I have added the Sanctus (K.Anh.12 [296a/296c]) because it is also in E flat and reveals striking thematic similarities with this Kyrie. This has been done despite the warning by Monika Holl, who edited the Sanctus for the *NMA* in 1990, that it 'can hardly be connected directly with the Kyrie' because the writing is patently later than that of the Kyrie – but certainly not that much later (she dates the Sanctus 1779–80). I presume that Mozart intended to continue the work in Salzburg and that the Sanctus sketch is part of the whole operation. If it was indeed first designed for Munich, those who know and love *Idomeneo* (see the separate essay, pp. 25ff.) will immediately recognize that the rich orchestral accompaniment of the Kyrie owes its inspiration to the Mannheim (subsequently Munich) Court Orchestra. There is a bold flexibility in the part writing and in the dynamic range, and also a real sense of commitment (clearly evident in the heavenly 'Christe eleison', first in the soprano solo, then choir, then contralto solo) – and in all this the music darkens in a most moving fashion: see especially bars 18ff.

Mozart's musical language was changing after his visit to Paris. It is infinitely darker-hued, even sombre at times, and there is a permanent sense of drama, even in non-dramatic works. When he arrived back at Salzburg, Wolfgang was indeed a very different man, and one senses the change in all his music, both sacred and secular, written in 1779 and 1780. His appointment as organist and *Conzert-Meister* in the service of Archbishop Colloredo would certainly account for Wolfgang's increased interest in composing church music.

During the two years that the composer remained in Salzburg, 1779 and 1780, he wrote a substantial quantity of church music, foremost among which are two Mass settings (the 'Coronation' Mass [K.317] of 1779 and the *Missa Solemnis* in C [K.337] of 1780) and two settings of the Vespers (the

Vesperae de Dominica [K.321] of 1779 and the *Vesperae solennes de Confessore* [K.339] of 1780). All four works established Mozart as a major composer of church music.

There is a curious parallel in the popularity of the two works within each *genre*: whereas the 'Coronation' Mass can lay claim to being the most popular piece of church music that Mozart ever composed (except for the Requiem, of course), the other C major Mass – despite its many subtleties and beauties – is scarcely known except to connoisseurs. The same difference obtains in the case of the two Vespers settings: the *Vesperae solennes de Confessore* has always been among the composer's best loved, and admired, pieces of church music, while the *Vesperae de Dominica* has remained under the shadow of its slightly later sister composition.

There are, in the Roman Catholic liturgy, two kinds of *Confessore* Vespers: the first is the *Vesperae de Confessore Pontifice* (Latin: *Confessor Pontifex*), and the second the *Vesperae de Confessore non Pontifice* (*Confessor non Pontifex*). The difference between the two is easily explained: the order of the psalms for the *Confessor non Pontifex* is the same in both first and second Vespers, i.e. Psalms 109, 110, 111, 112, 116. In the *Confessor Pontifex* that order is preserved for the first Vespers, while for the second Vespers Psalm 116 (*Laudate Dominum*) is dropped and Psalm 131 (*Memento Domine David*) is substituted for it. It is, then, the *Confessore non Pontifice* – to use the Italian term that Mozart might have employed – that the composer set.

The Mozart family thought highly of Wolfgang's Vespers settings. After their first performances in Salzburg Cathedral, Leopold Mozart had MS. copies made for the great Benedictine Monastery of Lambach in Upper Austria, which he entitled *Vesperae solennes de Dominica*, a (wrong) title that seems to have originated with the first performance material which is preserved in the Archives of Salzburg Cathedral. And Wolfgang, in a letter to his father from Vienna of 12 March 1783, asks him to send both works so that he can show them to Baron Gottfried van Swieten, at whose Sunday morning concerts, held in the Court Library on the Josephsplatz, Wolfgang and the local composer Joseph Starzer presided. (It was there that the music of J.S. Bach, Handel and other Baroque composers was assiduously cultivated, much to Mozart's delight and profit.)

It was the tradition in southern Germany, Austria and northern Italy to combine elements of the old 'Palestrina' style with the latest vocal fashion when composing Vespers. Thus the setting of Psalm 112 (*Laudate pueri*) was generally in the *stilo antico*, with fugues and other contrapuntal devices, and that is the case in both of Mozart's settings. In K.339 the music is in D minor for that movement, and here, as we have seen above, we are presented with sober music written in the *stilo antico* tradition. On the other hand, it was considered that the setting of Psalm 116 (*Laudate Dominum*) could be couched in modern, 'rococo' language – as is indeed the case in Mozart's famous music with the text of this psalm in the *Vesperae solennes de Confessore* of 1780.

There are several other general points which ought to be made in connection with these great Masses and Vespers. One is the kind of music that Mozart composes for his solo soprano. Now it happens that these parts were taken by Michael Haydn's wife, Maria Magdalena Lipp. Michael Haydn had been with the Salzburg Court since 1763 and he and Mozart were on the best of terms. It was for Maria Magdalena that Wolfgang composed music of ravishing beauty, of which the *Laudate Dominum* in K.339 is the most celebrated example – and rightly so – followed closely by the Agnus Dei of the 'Coronation' Mass which seems to presage Mozart's writing for the Countess in *Figaro*.

Another basic point is the special kind of orchestration generally used in church music: it was extraordinarily heavy and could employ two horns, two (sometimes four) trumpets and three trombones, giving even a key like C major a dark, brass-heavy majesty which is very distinctive and producing a sound quite different from that of Haydn's C major church music. This is also apparent in the most celebrated Mass of the period, the so-called 'Coronation' Mass (K.317).

It is thought that Mozart composed this work for performance on Easter Sunday, 1779. This setting, scored for performance by the big Salzburg orchestra, includes no fewer than seven brass instruments (three trombones, two horns and two trumpets), the combination of which lends to the music not only weight and splendour but a curiously brass-oriented orchestration which is strikingly original. It was previously thought that the name 'Coronation' had to do with the coronation of a miraculous Image of Our Lady which is kept in the pilgrimage church of Maria Plain near Salzburg. Some years ago, however, documentary evidence emerged which revealed that the name was first given to the Mass in 1791, when it was performed in Prague during the ceremonies associated with the coronation of Leopold II as King of Bohemia, on which occasion Mozart's last Italian opera, *La clemenza di Tito*, received its première. The 'Coronation' Mass is in the rather terse style which Archbishop Colloredo favoured, but into its structure Mozart has infused a brilliance and drama of unprecedented dimensions. In the Credo movement, one notices the dramatic way in which the words 'Et incarnatus est' are introduced, with the tempo sharply braking from fast to slow and the strings putting on their mutes. In the final fast section, 'Et resurrexit', when the movement seems to be finished, Mozart makes an unexpected gesture of almost operatic grandeur in which the music swerves into the subdominant (F major) to greet the words 'Et in Spiritum Sanctum Dominum et vivificantem'. The words that preceded this seemingly new branching-out are 'cujus regni non erit finis', and the whole opening of this new musical vista literally describes the concept of 'the reign that hath no end'.

One work that seems to have been slightly lost in all the complicated redatings and reassignments of the church music of the pre-1780 period is the delightful *Regina coeli* in C major (K.276 [321b]), recently assigned to 1779. This votive Antiphon for the Blessed Virgin Mary, which lasts less that seven minutes, has all the stylistic characteristics of a movement from one of the Vespers settings or the 'Coronation' Mass – a festive, sparkling Allegro with trumpets and drums which makes expert use of the solo voices contrasting with the choir and especially of the soprano solo part which, if it was not originally sung by Michael Haydn's wife, may have been first performed by the leading castrato Francesco Ceccarelli, whose fine singing in the *Missa brevis* (K.275 [272b]) was so much admired by Leopold Mozart (see above, p. 175).

One curious feature of the *Regina coeli* might be mentioned: at the words 'Ora pro nobis' Mozart introduces a seemingly flippant appoggiatura figure in the first violins (rather like the case of the Sanctus in the 'Spatzenmesse'). Since he does this twice, first at bars 68ff., then at 123ff., the effect cannot be missed: without wishing to appear frivolous, one could say that this effect is almost as if Wolfgang had deliberately sought to mock the words. Was he thinking of his earlier unfulfilled prayer to the Virgin, the *Sancta Maria* of 1777? It is a concept almost too appalling to contemplate, because there is, indeed, a real sense of commitment in all four of these more substantial works; this is at its most severe in the *Vesperae de Dominica* (K.321) and the *Missa Solemnis* (K.337). Listen to the stark power of the Benedictus in the latter, and at its most gripping in the 'Coronation' Mass and the *Vesperae solennes de Confessore*, the greatest of his works composed for performance in the austerely imposing Salzburg Cathedral. Here is clear proof of the power of young Wolfgang's musical language before he decamped to Vienna and immortality.

At the time of Mozart's marriage to Constanze Weber, in St Stephen's Cathedral, Vienna, on 4 August 1782, Wolfgang seems to have embarked on the composition of a large-scale votive Mass. In a letter to his father Leopold of 4 January 1783, i.e. some months after he had begun composing the Mass, he writes:

> Concerning the vow, it is quite true; – it did not flow from my pen without premeditation – I have really promised it in my innermost heart, and hope to be able to keep it. – My wife was not yet married when I made it – since I was firmly persuaded that I would marry her soon after her recovery, I could make the promise easily – the time and circumstances prevented our trip [to Salzburg, which actually did take place later that year], as you yourself know, – as witness, however, that I fully intend to keep my promise, there is the score of half a Mass, which is lying on my desk in the best of hopes.

In rather opaque terms, then, Mozart is suggesting that the new Mass (K.427 [417a]), in C minor and on a very large scale, was connected with some illness that Constanze had contracted. In the biography of Mozart by Constanze's second husband, Georg Nikolaus Nissen, which was compiled with her collaboration, it is stated that the work was composed to celebrate the safe delivery of their first child, Raimund Leopold, on 17 June 1783. Perhaps K.427 was also a celebration of their marriage, which had been contracted in the face of considerable opposition and difficulties.

The presence of two huge fugues in the new work – at the end of the Gloria and for the 'Osanna' in the Sanctus – reflects Mozart's involvement with the Sunday morning concerts which were given by Baron van Swieten, prefect of the National Library and head of the Government Education Department. There, Mozart and other musicians performed great contrapuntal music of the past, especially works by Bach and Handel, and where Mozart made arrangements of Bach's *Well-Tempered Clavier* for string orchestra; later he was to re-orchestrate several works by Handel in order to avoid having to use obsolete high trumpets and the organ *continuo*. Referring to his own Fantasia and Fugue in C (K.394) for piano, Mozart writes, in a letter dated 20 April 1782, to his sister Nannerl in Salzburg:

> ... this fugue came into the world really because of my dear Konstanze. – Baron van Suiten [*sic*], to whom I go every Sunday, gave me all the works of Handel and Sebastian Bach to take home (after I had played them to him). – When Konstanze heard the fugues, she quite fell in love with them ... – since she often heard me improvise [such fugues] ... she asked me if I had ever written any of them down. – And when I told her no – she scolded me thoroughly ... and she never stopped entreating me until I wrote down a fugue for her, and that is the work's origin ... .

Constanze was otherwise deeply involved with the new work in other ways. It was from the outset intended that she should sing the solo part for the first soprano (the work contains two soprano solo parts), the technical difficulty of which shows that she must have possessed a fine voice. In the noble and lofty Kyrie, which opens in C minor, the music modulates to E flat with Constanze's first great solo, to the words of 'Christe, eleison'; that music is known to us from a vocal exercise, or 'solfeggio', of which Mozart composed several for his 'dear wife' during the early years of their marriage (K.393, no. 2).

This extraordinary Mass in C minor, which was destined to remain unfinished, is like a compendium, as if its composer wished to display all the current modes of writing church music, from solemn fugues to arias reminiscent of Italian opera ('Et incarnatus est'), and including old-fashioned choruses like the Handelian 'Qui tollis' for double choir.

Mozart took the Mass with him to Salzburg, where he had it performed, using the whole court chapel orchestra and choir, in St Peter's Abbey on 26 October 1783, the day before he and Constanze left. On this historic occasion Constanze sang the first soprano part, and the actual music, of which the original parts have partly survived, consisted of the Kyrie, Gloria, Sanctus and Benedictus, transposed from C to B flat minor (was there perhaps a problem with the organ's tuning, or was the music too high for Constanze?). It was the tradition, at St Peter's, to omit the entire Credo on 26 October, the feast of St Amand, Bishop of Maastricht, the second patron saint of the Abbey – except when the feast fell on a Sunday, which as it happens was the case in 1783. We shall never know what music was performed for the Credo and the Agnus Dei, both of which might have been done in Gregorian chant. Mozart sketched out the opening Credo chorus and the elaborate 'Et incarnatus est'. Those pieces and the missing second choir of the Sanctus and Benedictus have been reconstructed by me (1955).

*   *   *

We now come to the extraordinary collection of fragments of church music of the late 1780s, up to and possibly even including 1791. These redatings were primarily the work of Alan Tyson (see above) and have been confirmed by Wolfgang Plath of the *NMA* and their editor for *NMA*, Monika Holl. We can only guess the reason why Mozart felt obliged to begin these half-a-dozen pieces, along with copies of sundry older works by composers long dead: they include the Kyrie in D (K.91 [186i]), the psalm *De profundis clamavi* (K.93 [Anh.A22]) and the psalm *Memento Domine David* (K.Anh.22 [93a, Anh.A23]), all by Georg Reutter Jr. In some of the original fragments, we seem to imagine something of the 'Ave, verum corpus' atmosphere, in other words a certain monumental folk-like simplicity combined with polyphonic artfulness: this might be the *raison d'être* for the Kyrie in G major (K.Anh.16 [196a]), as well as for the D major Kyrie (K.Anh.14 [422a]). However, some of the others are harder to explain: the language of the C major Kyrie (K.323 [Anh.15]) is very like one of the 1776 Salzburg Masses, and the Gloria in C (K.Anh.20 [323a]) likewise, though in the latter a certain artful simplicity is again present. The Kyrie in C (K.Anh.13 [258a]), with its chirping organ solo, might also be a Salzburg piece of 1776 or 1777.

It is a quite different story in the case of the stern D minor Kyrie (K.341 [368a]), whose monumental style and massive orchestration seem to pose insuperable problems of chronology (the autograph is lost). At first, this piece was assigned to the period of *Idomeneo* in Munich, i.e. between November 1780 and March 1781; this dating was based on the large size of the orchestra, with four horns and clarinets (the latter not part of the Salzburg orchestra). In 1988, I suggested that this Kyrie might have been the installation piece at St Stephen's Cathedral in Vienna, where Mozart successfully applied for the position of *Domkapellmeister* (Cathedral Chapel Master) in 1791. The *NMA* dates it 1787–91, but John Arthur, who will be a contributing editor to the new Köchel Catalogue, rejects this late dating 'on stylistic grounds'.[23]

Another interesting theory was advanced by Monika Holl in the foreword to the Kyrie in the *NMA*. She writes:

The text as it has come down to us gives rise to doubts whether in fact Mozart himself actually completed the work, or whether Maximilian Stadler or even Johann Anton André fleshed out the composition which might not have been fully completed ...

The particular points to which Monika Holl objects are the markings for *ff* in bars 102 and 114/5: certainly the *ff* in the bassoons, horns, trumpets and drums at bar 102 is odd (as is the trumpet writing in that bar). The autograph was once owned by André, who issued the first edition based upon it ('Nach dem hinterlassenem Original-Manuskripte'). He had purchased this Kyrie, along with many other MSS. among the deceased composer's personal effects, from Mozart's widow, Constanze.

In the absence of the original manuscript, these are points which no one is in a position to judge with authority, and in any case they do not materially contribute towards establishing the work's chronology; however, the positioning of the work in the Munich years is without any foundation, and, as far as the work's style is concerned, Mozart tried to keep to a certain old-fashioned tradition (just as he would do in the Requiem). In that sense, the Kyrie is timeless: it could date from 1781, or 1791. It does, however, provide a useful transition to Mozart's last work, the unfinished Requiem (discussed in a separate essay, pp. 191ff.).

The final remarks concerning the Kyrie (K.341) have to do with a now famous sketch that Wolfgang Plath identified in 1962[24] as belonging to Mozart's Requiem. The sketch begins with part of the Overture to *Die Zauberflöte* (the transcription of which can be seen in the *NMA* edition of that Opera), and three staves later there is a sketch for a D minor 'Amen' fugue which, Plath assumed, was Mozart's concept for the conclusion of the 'Lacrimosa' section. But why did not his pupil Süssmayr, who after all had access to Mozart's sketches,[25] use this magnificent fugue sketch in his completion of the Requiem? Plath has suggested that 'It is a tragic-comic concept, which is in all probability the case: Süssmayr in possession of Requiem sketches with which he could do nothing because he could neither recognize nor read them'.[26]

While this conclusion suggests that Süssmayr was in fact even more obtuse than was probably the case, there might be another solution to the identification of the 'Amen' sketch. There is no evidence to confirm that this sketch was actually intended for the Requiem. What if it were intended for the concluding 'Amen' fugue of the 'Dona nobis pacem' in the

Installation Mass in D minor for St Stephen's Cathedral, of which, if my theory be correct, the Kyrie (K.341) is the beginning? And if this was the real use for which this 'Amen' fugue was intended, that fact could have been known both to Constanze Mozart and to Süssmayr. If K.341 does date from 1791, then Mozart's sketch-leaf, which opens with part of the Overture to *Die Zauberflöte*, could easily have contained a sketch for another part of the Mass in D minor: this 'Amen' fugue could also have served as the end of the Gloria's 'Cum Sancto Spiritu'.

Reconstructions of this 'Amen' fugue as part of Mozart's Requiem can be easily seen and heard, *inter alia*, as follows:

1 Richard Maunder's, Oxford University Press, 1988, recorded for Decca (Oiseau Lyre) by Christopher Hogwood. See also Richard Maunder, *Mozart's Requiem: On Preparing a New Edition*, Oxford, 1988.
2 Robert Levin's, 1991, recorded by Helmuth Rilling (Hänsler Classic).
3 Duncan Druce's, Novello & Co., 1991, recorded by Roger Norrington (EMI Classics).

Before leaving the subject, there is one caveat to be entered against a whole-hearted adoption of this 'Amen' fugue as part of the K.341 circle. The main theme consists of the strict inversion of the opening of the Requiem's choral section (bass part). Having said that, it must also be pointed out that the subject (and indeed counter-subject) of the fugue are Baroque stereo-types or models. Still, in view of Mozart's concern for unity in the Requiem, this relationship between the 'Requiem aeternam' and the 'Amen' fugue is worthy of consideration. (The three 'realizations' of the fugue noted above differ one from another, but this is obviously not the place to comment on that aspect.)

Catalogue

ORATORIOS

K.118 (74c) *La Betulia liberata* (Pietro Metastasio). Commissioned at Padua in Mar. 1771 and completed in Salzburg, summer 1771, but apparently not performed.
3 S, A, T, B, choir SATB, 2 fl/ob, 2 bn, 4 hn, 2 tpt, str., continuo

K.469 *Davidde penitente* (text attr. to L. Da Ponte), first perf. Burgtheater (Tonkünstler-Societät), Vienna 13 and 15 Mar. 1785, music taken from the Mass in C minor K.427 (417a) except for 2 arias (nos. 6 and 8), dated 6 and 11 Mar. in *Verzeichnüß* and an additional 'Cadenza' at the end of the former 'Cum Sancto'.
2 S, T, choir SATB, 2 fl, 2 ob, cl, 2 bn, 2 hn, 3 tpt, 3 trbn, str, continuo

MASSES, MASS FRAGMENTS AND MISCELLANEOUS SACRED MUSIC INCLUDING LITANIES, VESPERS AND VESPER PSALMS

K.33 Kyrie in F, autograph dated Paris, 12 June 1766
Choir SATB, str, continuo

K.34 Offertory 'Scande coeli limina' 1766–7?
S, choir SATB, 1 tpt, timp, 2 vn, b, org. Composed for the Feast of St Benedict at Seeon Abbey, Bavaria

K.139 (47a) *Missa Solemnis* in C minor-major, Vienna, autumn 1768?
S, A, T, B, choir SATB, 2 ob, 4 tpt, 3 trbn, timp, str, org. Probably the work performed at the dedication of the Orphanage Church in Vienna on 7 Dec. 1768

K.117 (66a) Offertory 'Benedictus sit Deus', Vienna, autumn 1768?
S, choir SATB, 2 fl, 2 hn, 2 tpt, timp, str, org. Possibly the 'lost' *grand offertory* K.47b, performed at the Orphanage Church on 7 Dec. 1768

K.47 Offertory 'Veni Sancte Spiritus', Vienna, autumn 1768?
S, A, T, B, choir SATB, 2 ob, 2 hn, 2 tpt, timp, str, org
Possibly for the same event at the Orphanage Church on 7 Dec. 1768 (see K.139 above)

K.49 (47d) *Missa brevis* in G, Vienna, autumn 1768 (autograph)
S, A, T, B, choir SATB, [3 trbn], str, org. Draft for Gloria (S, choir SATB, b, org; 18 bars) and alternative version of Credo, bars 182–95 (K.Anh.20a [626b/25, 15 bars]) survive

K.65 (61a) *Missa brevis* in D minor, Salzburg, 14 Jan. 1769 (autograph)
S, A, T, B, choir SATB, str, org. Perf. at Collegiate Church, Salzburg, 5 Feb. 1769. Sketch for Kyrie (4 bars) and 3 rejected versions of Benedictus in autograph score (9 bars; 8 bars; 13 bars) survive

K.66 *Missa* in C ('Dominicus' Mass), Salzburg, Oct. 1769 (autograph), first perf. St Peter's Abbey Church, Salzburg, 15 Oct. 1769, later revived in Vienna at the Jesuit church (Kirche am Hof), autumn 1773, conducted by Leopold Mozart
Draft for Gloria, bars 310–43 (SATB; 34 bars), and beginning and end of rejected original version of Credo, bars 134ff. (8 bars; 6 bars), survive in autograph score

K.141 (66b) Te Deum in C, Salzburg, end of 1769
4 tpt, [timp], 2 vn, b, org

K.85 (73s) *Miserere* in A minor, Bologna, July–Aug. 1770
ATB, continuo

K.86 (73v) Antiphon 'Quaerite primum' in D minor, Bologna, 9 Oct. 1770
SATB – Exercise for the Accademia Filarmonica, Bologna

K.108 (74d) Votive Antiphon BVM 'Regina coeli' in C, Salzburg, May 1771 (autograph)
S, choir SATB, 2 fl/ob, 2 hn, 2 tpt, timp, str, org

K.109 (74e) *Litaniae Lauretanae* BVM in B flat, Salzburg, May 1771 (autograph)
S, A, T, B, choir SATB, [3 trbn], 2 vn, b, org

K.125 *Litaniae de venerabili altaris sacramento* in B flat, Salzburg, Mar. 1772 (autograph)
S, A, T, B, choir SATB, 2 fl/ob, 2 hn, 2 tpt, [3 trbn], str, org. Cancelled first version of Viaticum (9 bars) survives in autograph score; Pignus shortened for a later perf. (*NMA*)

K.127 Votive Antiphon BVM 'Regina coeli' in B flat, Salzburg, May 1772 (autograph)
S, choir SATB, 2 fl/ob, 2 hn, str, org

K.142 (Anh.C3.04) *Tantum ergo* in B flat, Salzburg, c. 1772?
S, SATB choir, 2 tpt, str, org

K.187 (Anh.C3.05) *Tantum ergo* in D, Salzburg, c. 1772?
Choir SATB, 2 tpt, timp, str, org. For renewed proof of both works' authenticity, see the recently discovered MS. material from Salzburg Cathedral and elsewhere listed in *NMA*

K.89 *Kyrie a cinque con diversi canoni*, G major, Salzburg, 1772?
5 S parts

K.90 Kyrie in D minor, Salzburg, 1772?
SATB, b, org (figures by Leopold Mozart)

K.223 (166e) Hosanna in G, Salzburg, 1772?
choir(?) SATB, str, org

K.Anh.18 (166f) Kyrie in C (fragment), 49 bars, Salzburg, 1772?
choir SATB, 2 ob, 2 hn, 2 tpt, timp, str (2 violas), org

K.Anh.19 (166g) Kyrie in D (fragment), 12 bars, Salzburg, 1772?
choir SATB, 2 ob, 2 hn, str, org

K.165 (158a) Motet 'Exsultate, jubilate', F major, Milan, Jan. 1773, first perf. by Venanzio Rauzzini, Church of the Theatines, Milan, 17 Jan. 1773 (Wolfgang's letter of 16 Jan.)
S, 2 ob, 2 hn, str, org (later rev. with 2 fl in Salzburg, 1779?)

K.143 (73a) Motet 'Ergo interest, an quis', G major, Milan 1770? (new dating from *NMA*) or 1773? Autograph is perhaps a fair copy made 1772–4.
S, str, org

K.167 *Missa in honorem Sanctissimae Trinitatis*, C major, Salzburg, June 1773 (autograph)
choir SATB, 2 ob, 4 tpt, [3 trbn], timp, 2 vn, b, org

K.140 (235d Anh.C.1.12) *Missa brevis* in G major, Salzburg, 1773? Authentic?
S, A, T, B, choir SATB, 2 vn, b, org

K.195 (186d) *Litaniae Lauretanae* BVM in D major, Salzburg, [May?] 1774
S, A, T, B, choir SATB, 2 ob, 2 hn, [3 trbn], str, org

K.192 (186f) *Missa brevis* in F major, Salzburg, 24 June 1774 (autograph)

S, A, T, B, choir SATB, 2 tpt (added later by Mozart), [3 trbn], 2 vn, b, org

K.193 (186g) Psalm 'Dixit Dominus' and Magnificat in C major, Salzburg, July 1774 (autograph)

S, A, T, B, choir SATB, 2 tpt, 2 trbn, timp, 2 vn, b, org

K.194 (186h) *Missa brevis* in D major, Salzburg, 8 Aug. 1774 (autograph)

S, A, T, B, choir SATB, [3 trbn], 2 vn, b, org

K.222 (205a) Offertory 'Misericordias Domini' in D minor, Munich, early 1775

choir SATB, 2 vn, [va], b, org

K.262 (246a) *Missa longa* in C major, Salzburg, June–July 1775 (Tyson, 1987)

S, A, T, B, choir SATB, 2 ob, 2 hn, 2 tpt, [3 trbn], timp, 2 vn, b, org. Timp part added by Mozart to a later (?) performance in autograph on separate sheets

K.258 *Missa brevis* in C major ('Spauer' or 'Piccolomini' Mass, Salzburg, Dec. 1775 (Leopold Mozart's date on autograph, later altered – see Tyson, 1987)

S, A, T, B, choir SATB, 2 ob, 2 tpt, timp, 2 vn, b, org

K.220 (196b) *Missa brevis* in C major ('Spatzenmesse', literally 'Sparrows' Mass), Salzburg, 1775-6?

S, A, T, B, choir SATB, 1 tpt, [3 trbn], timp, 2 vn, b, org

K.259 *Missa brevis* in C major ('Orgelsolomesse', 'Organ Solo' Mass), Salzburg, Dec. 1775 or 1776

S, A, T, B, choir SATB, 2 ob, 2 tpt,

timp, 2 vn, b, org. Cancelled fragment of Sanctus (21 bars) survives in autograph score

K.243 *Litaniae de venerabili altaris sacramento* in E flat, Salzburg, Mar. 1776 (autograph)

S, A, T, B, choir SATB, 2 fl/ob, 2 bn, 2 hn, 3 trbn, str, org. Kyrie begun end 1774/early 1775, rest a year later (Tyson, 1987)

K.260 (248a) *Offertorium de venerabili sacramento* 'Venite populi' in D major, Salzburg 1776

double choir SSAATTBB, 2 vn ad lib, b, org

K.257 Mass in C major ('Credo' Mass), Salzburg, Nov. 1776 (autograph)

S, A, T, B, choir SATB, 2 ob, 2 tpt, [3 trbn], timp, 2 vn, b, org. Sketch for a Gloria (20 bars, possibly for K.257?) and sundry sketches for Credo survive on a single autograph sketchleaf

K.277 (272a) Offertory 'Alma Dei creatoris' in F major, Salzburg 1777

S, A, T, choir SATB, 2 vn, b, org

K.273 Gradual 'Sancta Maria, Mater Dei' in F major, Salzburg, 9 Sep. 1777 (autograph), for Feast of BVM, 12 Sep.

choir SATB, str, org

K.275 (272b) *Missa brevis* in B flat, Salzburg, late 1777, first perf. St Peter's Abbey Church, Salzburg, 21 Dec. 1777

S, A, T, B, choir SATB, 2 vn, b, org

K.322 (296a, Anh. 12, 296b) Kyrie in E flat, 1778-9?

S, A, choir SATB, 2 ob, 2 bn, 2 hn, 2 tpt, timp, str. Completed by Maximilian Stadler. With this Kyrie may be perhaps grouped the E flat Sanctus, K.Anh. 12(296a)

K.317 *Missa* in C major ('Coronation' Mass), Salzburg, 23 Mar. 1779 (autograph)
S, A, T, B, choir SATB, 2 ob, 2 bn, 2 tpt, 3 trbn, timp, 2 vn, b, org

K.321 *Vesperae de Dominica* in C major, Salzburg, 1779
S, A, T, B, choir SATB, [bn] 2 tpt, [3trbn], timp, 2 vn, b, org. There is a fragmentary Magnificat in C (K.321a) in Mozart's autograph

K.276 (321b) Votive Antiphon BVM 'Regina coeli' in C major, Salzburg, 1779?
S, A, T, B, choir SATB, 2 ob, 2 tpt, timp, 2 vn, b, org

K.337 *Missa Solemnis* in C major, Salzburg, Mar. 1780 (autograph)
S, A, T, B, choir SATB, 2 ob, 2 bn, 2 tpt, 3 trbn, timp, 2 vn, b, org. A large earlier version of Credo (Tempo di Ciaconna, 136 bars) survives in autograph score

K.339 *Vesperae solennes de Confessore* in C major, Salzburg, 1780 (autograph)
S, A, T, B, choir SATB, [bn], 2 tpt, [3 trbn] timp, 2 vn, b, org

K.427 (417a) *Missa* in C minor, Vienna, *c.* end 1782–*c.* Oct. 1783, Salzburg
2 S, T, B, choir (maximum) SSAA TTBB, fl, 2 ob, 2 bn, 2 hn, 2 tpt, 3 trbn, timp, str, org. Several sketches and drafts exist in autograph. Only Kyrie, Gloria, Sanctus and Benedictus perf. at Salzburg, St Peter's Abbey Church, 26 Oct. 1783, with Constanze as soprano soloist

K.Anh.16 (196a) Kyrie in G, Vienna 1787-9? with attempts to continue work by Maximilian Stadler (unfinished or lost at end?)

choir SATB, str, org (other instr not indicated)

K.323 (Anh.15) Kyrie in C, Vienna 1787-9? Fragment (37 bars)
choir SATB, 2 ob, 2 bn, 2 tpt, timp, str, org. Completed by Maximilian Stadler

K.Anh.20 (323a) Gloria in C major, Vienna 1787-9? Fragment (26 bars)
choir SATB, str, org (other instr not indicated)

K.Anh.14 (422a) Kyrie in D major, Vienna, 1787-9? Fragment (11 bars)
choir SATB, 2 ob, bn, str, org (partly orchestrated by Abbé Maximilian Stadler)

K.Anh.13 (258a) Kyrie in C major, Vienna, 1787-91? Fragment (9 bars)
choir SATB, 2 tpt, timp, 2 vn, org solo, b

K.618 Motet 'Ave, verum corpus' in D major, Baden, 17 June 1791 (autograph)
choir SATB, str, org

K.341 (368a) Kyrie in D minor. Previously dated Munich, 1780–1, now (*NMA* dated Vienna, 1787–91) or (Landon, 1988) Vienna, 1791.
choir SATB, 2 fl, 2 ob, 2 cl, 2 bn, 4 hn, 2 tpt, timp, str

K.626 Requiem, Vienna, 1791 (unfinished) – see the separate essay, pp. 191ff.

In addition to these vocal works there is a series of instrumental Epistle Sonatas (list, see *Mozart Compendium*, pp. 319f.), some of which are positively glorious, such as K.329, a powerful symphonic miniature written for the 'Coronation' Mass in 1779.

The Requiem (K.626): its historical
and textual problems

———————— ❧ ————————

WHEN MOZART DIED ON 5 DECEMBER 1791, AT FIFTY-FIVE
minutes past midnight, his widow Constanze was left with a
number of significant debts. The mystery surrounding the large
sum of 1,435 florins 32 kreuzer which her husband had recently been ordered
by the court to repay to Prince Carl Lichnowsky is discussed in a separate
essay (see pp. 213ff.). It is curious to note that that debt did not figure in the
Suspense Order prepared after the composer's death,[1] and there must have
been other sums outstanding which did not feature in that document,
notably the money lent to Mozart at intervals (amounting to roughly 1,000
florins) by his benefactor and fellow Mason, the banker and merchant
Michael Puchberg.

The Suspense Order lists a small sum 'in cash ... 60 fl.', from which the
burial and other immediate costs had to be met.' The widow, with her two
young sons, therefore had urgent need of cash for day-to-day expenses. The
first potential source of income was the Requiem, which a mysterious
stranger had commissioned from the composer earlier that year. In 1798,
Franz Xaver Niemetschek published a biography of Mozart based largely on
information supplied by Constanze and other reliable sources.[2] In it he
records that:

> Shortly before the coronation of Emperor Leopold, even before Mozart
> had received the order to travel to Prague, an unknown messenger
> brought him a letter without signature, which with many flattering
> remarks contained an enquiry as to whether he would be willing to
> undertake to write a Requiem Mass. What would be the cost, and how
> long would it take to complete?
>
> Mozart, who never made the least move without his wife's knowledge,
> told her of this remarkable request, and at the same time expressed a wish
> to try his hand at this type of composition, the more so as the higher

forms of church music had always appealed to his genius. She advised him to accept the offer. He therefore replied to his anonymous patron that he would write a Requiem for a given sum; he could not state exactly how long it would take. He wished, however, to know where the work was to be delivered when ready. In a short while, the same messenger appeared again, bringing not only the sum stipulated but also the promise, as Mozart had asked so modest a price, that he would receive another payment on delivery of the composition. He should, moreover, write according to his own ideas and mood, but he should not trouble to find out who had given the commission, for it would assuredly be in vain.

In the meantime he received a very flattering and advantageous offer to compose the *opera seria* for the Coronation of Emperor Leopold in Prague. It was too much of a temptation for him to refuse to go to Prague to write for his beloved Bohemians.

In that same year (1798), Friedrich Rochlitz, who had met Constanze when she was travelling through Germany in 1796, published a series of Mozart anecdotes, based largely – though not exclusively – on information she had provided. Since some of Rochlitz's numbered anecdotes were adopted more or less verbatim in the Nissen biography of 1828, published in Leipzig, they can lay claim to the same authenticity as Niemetschek. In the matter of the Requiem, however, Rochlitz's version is longer and raises problems of chronology above and beyond the time sequence as clearly outlined in Niemetschek. Rochlitz records that

One day, when he was sitting there … a carriage drew up and a stranger had himself announced. He [Mozart] received him. A middle-aged, serious, impressive man, of a very earnest countenance, not known to him or his wife, entered.

The man began:

'I come to you as the messenger of a very distinguished gentleman.'

'From whom do you come?', asked Mozart.

'The gentleman does not wish to be known.'

'Very well – what does he wish of me?'

'Someone very near and dear to his person has died; he wishes to remember the day of her death, quietly, but in a worthy fashion, and asks you to compose a Requiem for this purpose.'

Mozart – in view of his state of mind at that time – was already much moved inwardly by this conversation; by the mystery in which the whole affair was shrouded; by the man's solemn tone. He [Mozart] promised to do so. The man continued:

'Proceed with all possible diligence: the gentleman is a connoisseur.'

'So much the better.'

'You will not be bound to any period of delivery.'

'Excellent.'

'How much time will you require approximately?'

'About four weeks.'

'Then I shall come again and collect the score. What fee do you require?'

Mozart answered recklessly – 'one hundred ducats.'

'Here they are,' said the man, who placed the roll of coins on the table and departed. Mozart once again sank into deep reverie, did not heed his wife's entreaties, and finally requested pen, ink and paper. He started at once to compose the commission. His interest in the affair grew with every bar; he wrote day and night. His body could not stand the strain: he fainted several times over the work. Every exhortation to moderation was in vain. Some days thereafter, his wife persuaded him to drive with her to the Prater. He always sat quietly, lost in his thoughts. Finally he no longer denied it – he felt certain that he was writing this piece for his own funeral. He could not be dissuaded from this idea; he worked, therefore, like Raphael on his 'Transfiguration', with the omnipresent feeling of his approaching death and delivered, like the latter, his own transfiguration. He even spoke of very strange thoughts in connection with the curious appearance of and commission from this unknown man. If one sought to persuade him otherwise, he was silent but unconvinced.

Meanwhile, the departure of Leopold to Prague for the coronation approached ...[3]

In this version, the commission occurs some time before Emperor Leopold leaves for Prague (perhaps July?), and Mozart embarks on the Requiem at once, working himself into a state of exhaustion. Notice, however, that Constanze is in the picture and that she takes her husband for a carriage ride. In 1791, Constanze was taking the waters in Baden throughout June and until the middle of July; *Die Zauberflöte* was completed, except for the Overture and the March of the Priests, by the middle of July, as the entry in Mozart's own thematic catalogue makes clear. *La clemenza di Tito* must have been commissioned by the middle of July, though as yet without precise knowledge of which singers would take the leading roles. There was therefore simply no time for Mozart to start the Requiem on a large scale, hence the chronology of Rochlitz's report must be wrong: several episodes concerning the Requiem seem to have been conflated. In the version which I chose as the primary source, it is clearly stated that the stranger acting as intermediary arrived 'shortly before the coronation'. The fact that the account in the Nissen biography is based on the Niemetschek version (1798) suggests that it is nearer to the truth (that is to say, as Constanze remembered the events).

We may disregard the thousands of pages published between 1792 and 1963 on the subject of the Requiem, for it was not until 1964 that Otto Erich Deutsch astonished the scholarly world by publishing in full a long manuscript report written by someone with first-hand knowledge of the origins of the Requiem. Finally, 172 years after the first printed notices about the work appeared in 1792, the truth came out. Here is the translated text of this precious document, preserved in the municipal archives of Wiener Neustadt, 48 km (30 miles) south of Vienna.

True and Detailed History of the 'Requiem' by W.A. Mozart. From its inception in the year 1791 to the present period of 1839. [By Anton Herzog, Director of the Information Centre, the Region, the Main School, and *Regens chori*]

Herr Franz, Count von Walsegg, owner of the estates Schottwien, Klam, Stuppach, Pottschach and Ziegersberg, in Austria below the [River] Enns … lived since his marriage to Anna, *née noble* von Flammberg, in his castle at Stuppach, as a tender husband and true father to his vassals. He was a passionate lover of music and the theatre; hence every week, on Tuesdays and Thursdays, each time fully three hours long, quartets were played, and on Sundays there was theatre, in which the Herr Count himself, and Madame Countess and her unmarried Madame Sister, took part, as did all the officials and the entire, numerous household, all of whom had to act roles, each according to his or her capabilities. To help with the quartet-playing, Herr Count engaged two excellent artists, Herr Johann Benaro as violinist and Herr Louis Prevost as violoncellist; Herr Count played the violoncello in string quartets, and in flute quartets he played the flute, and usually I played the second violin or the viola. In those days I was engaged as teacher in the Patronat-School of the Herr Count, at Klam.

So that we would not lack for new quartets, in view of such frequent performances of them, Herr Count not only procured all those publicly announced, but was in touch with many composers, yet without ever revealing his identity; and they delivered to him works of which he retained the sole ownership, and for which he paid well. To name one man, Herr [Franz Anton] Hoffmeister delivered many flute quartets, in which the flute part was quite easily negotiable, but the other three parts extremely difficult, which caused the players to work very hard; and that made the Herr Count laugh.

Since Herr Count never wanted to play from engraved parts, he had them beautifully copied out on ten-stave paper; but the author was never noted. He generally made copies of the secretly organized scores in his own hand, and presented them for the parts to be coped out. We never saw an original score. The quartets were then played, and we had to guess who the composer was. Usually we suggested that it was the Count him-self, because from time to time he did compose some small things; he smiled and was pleased that we (as he thought) had been mystified; but we were amused that he should take us for such simpletons.

We were all young, and thought this an innocent pleasure which we gave to our lord. And in such fashion the mystifications continued among us for some years.

I have thought it necessary to furnish these particulars so that the ori-gin of the *Requiem,* which has been described as mysterious, can be better judged.

On 14 February 1791, death snatched from Herr Count von Walsegg his beloved wife, in the flower of her life [she was not yet twenty-one]. He wanted to erect a double memorial to her, and he had an excellent idea. He arranged through his business representative, Herr Dr Johann Sortschan, Court and Judicial Lawyer, in Vienna, that one of the very best sculptors in Vienna [Johann Martin Fischer, 1740–1820] should model a memorial; and Mozart should compose a *Requiem,* of which he [the Count] as usual reserved to himself the sole right of ownership.

The first item, which cost over 3,000 gulden, was after a time erected in the valley with the spring near Stuppach Castle; and the remains of the lady were taken from the family vault in Schottwien and placed there.

But the *Requiem*, which was supposed to be played every year on the anniversary of Madame the Countess's death, took longer than expected; for death overtook Mozart in the midst of this worthy task. What to do now? Who was going to dare to imitate a Mozart? Yet the work had to be finished; for Mozart's widow, who (as was well known) was not in the best circumstances, was to have received one hundred ducats. Whether prepayments had been effected we did not know for certain, although there are reasons for thinking that they were ...

When all the individual parts were written out, preparations for performing the *Requiem* were at once set in motion. But because in the region of Stuppach not all the necessary musicians could be brought together, it was arranged that the first performance should take place in Wiener Neustadt. Among the musicians, the choice of the instrumental and vocal soloists was made from among the best [performers] available; and so it happened that the soprano part was sung by Ferenz [a choirboy?] from [Wiener] Neustadt, the contralto part by Kernbeiß from Schottwien, the tenor part by Klein of [Wiener] Neustadt, and the bass part by Thurner of Gloggnitz – these were the soloists. On 12 December 1793 the general rehearsal was held in the evening, in the choir-loft of the Cistercian Abbey and Parish Church of Neustadt; and in that same church, on 14 December at 10 o'clock in the morning, a requiem memorial service was held, during which this famous *Requiem* was given for the first time in the fashion for which it was intended.

Herr Count von Walsegg conducted the whole. Of all the musicians who participated in it, as far as I know, and at the moment of writing, none is still alive except for myself and Herr Anton Plaimschauer, who is at present *Thurnermeister* [the leader of the town band] here in Wiener-Neustadt.

On 14 February 1794, on the anniversary of Mad. the Countess's death, the *Requiem* was performed in the Patronat Church of Herr Count, at Maria-Schütz on Semmering; and from this time on Herr Count made no use of it, except that he arranged it as a quintet for strings, the score of which I kept for many years. [He relates that the full score – supposedly but, as we have seen, not in fact written in Süssmayr's hand – had never been seen by him or anyone else in the entourage, but] the score which the Herr Count gave me to use for rehearsing the singers was in his own hand, which I would have recognized at once.

That the Herr Count wanted to mystify with the Requiem, as he had done with the quartets, was well known to all of us; in our presence he always said it was his composition, but when he said that he smiled ...[4]

Meanwhile, a group of Mozart's friends in Vienna had decided to organize a memorial service for the late composer. This service, of which there was no known record before the discovery in December 1990 of a list of expenses relating to it, took place, only five days after Mozart's death, in the Parish Church (*Hofpfarrkirche*) of St Michael, having been arranged by Emanuel Schikaneder and his co-director of the Theater auf der Wieden, Joseph von Bauerfeld. The document itself, discovered in the archives of St Michael's Church by Walther Brauneis,[5] reads in translation as follows:

Day	Rubrica	Class	Fl.	Kr
	Translat. [brought forward]		113.	52
[December 1791] Memorial Services				
10 For the (hon.)	[Fl.]	[Kr.]		
Herr Wolfgangus				
Amedäus Mozart	14	20		
[this amount not included in the total below]				
	Fl.	X [Kr.]		
Ringing the bells	3.	36		
Requiem Service	6.	–		
Robes for the Requiem Service	1.	30		
Antependium [*Kreutztuch*]	–.	45		
For the 2 candle-bearers	–.	18		
			12.	9
	Summa		126.	1

Jos. Prisfüller [Griesfüller?]
Sacristan

There were several contemporary newspaper reports about this service. In the *Auszug aller europäischer Zeitungen* (Extracts from all European Newspapers) No. 283 of 13 December 1791, under 'Wiener Nachrichten' (News from Vienna), it is reported that the directors of the Wiedner Theater were responsible for the memorial service at St Michael's, while on 16 December *Der heimliche Botschafter* records the startling fact that during the service the Requiem, written during Mozart's last illness, was performed ('das Requiem welches er in seiner letzten Krankheit komponirt hatte, exequirt wurde'). Another report, dated 31 December and published in the German periodical *Das Berlinische Musikalische Wochenblatt,* states 'One of his last compositions is said to be a Requiem Mass, which was performed at his memorial service.' ('Eine seiner letzten Arbeiten soll eine Todtenmesse gewesen seyn, die man bei seiner Exequien aufgeführt hat.'). Yet another report appeared in the *Salzburger Intelligenzblatt* of 7 January 1792:

About Mozart – Some months before his death he received a letter without signature, asking him to compose a Requiem, and to ask whatever fee he wanted for it. Since this idea did not in the least appeal to him, he thought, I shall ask so much that the amateur [*Liebhaber*] will surely let me go. The next day a servant came to fetch the answer; Mozart wrote to the unknown man that he could not undertake to do the work for less than 60 ducats, and he could not start, moreover, for two or three months. The servant came again, brought 30 ducats instantly, saying that he would enquire again in three months, and that when the Mass was finished, he would bring the other half of the money. Now Mozart had to write, which he did, often with tears in his eyes, always saying 'I am writing a Requiem for myself'; he finished it a few days before his death. When his death became known, the servant came again and brought the remaining 30 ducats, asked for no Requiem, and since that time there was no further enquiry. It will actually be performed, when it is copied, in his memory at St Michael's Church.

Now the curious facts arising from this information are: that it seems certain that at least part of Mozart's Requiem was played in Vienna on 10 December 1791 in St Michael's Church; and that this performance took place in public, notwithstanding any arrangements agreed with Count Walsegg's representative. Note, however, that in the list of expenses for the service on 10 December there is no mention of musicians' fees. This absence may be explained, according to Walther Brauneis, by the constitution of the Barnabite College of St Michael: the church was the seat of the former Congregation of St Cecilia, formed in 1725, made up of members of the Court Orchestra and Choir, who regularly celebrated the name-day (22 November) of their patron saint each year by performing a solemn Mass in St Stephen's Cathedral, and now, on 10 December 1791, would have offered their services *gratis* in memory of the *Kammermusikus* (chamber musician) officially engaged in 1787 and since 1790 listed on the pay-rolls as *Hofkompositor* (Court composer) – Wolfgang Amadeus Mozart.

Now let us consider the situation of the actual music of the Requiem in December 1791. Constanze, a trained musician, would, on examining the unfinished manuscript, have seen that her late husband had left the work was in the following state:

Introitus
'Requiem aeternam': completely orchestrated by Mozart.
Kyrie: only the vocal parts and *basso continuo* fully written out.

Sequence
'Die irae' – 'Confutatis': only vocal parts and *basso continuo* fully written out: rest occasionally notated.
'Lacrimosa': only the first eight bars present for vocal parts and *basso continuo*, with the first two bars for violins and viola notated.

Offertorium
Domine, Hostias: only the vocal parts and *basso continuo* fully written out: remainder occasionally notated.

Sanctus, Benedictus, Agnus Dei & Communio
Sketches (no longer extant): probably for vocal parts and *basso continuo*.

Obviously, within a period of only five days, the only movement that could be copied out in full was the beginning, the 'Requiem aeternam'. On the other hand, that section ended on the dominant and could not be performed satisfactorily as an entity. The Kyrie fugue existed in its essential parts, however, and all that was needed here was for a pupil to write in the doubling parts: in the structure of the fugue, the violins and basset horns doubled the soprano and alto, the bassoons the bass, the viola the alto part, etc. Only the trumpets and timpani needed to be newly composed. These tasks were entrusted to two of Mozart's pupils: Franz Jakob Freystädtler, from Salzburg, who was a friend of the family, copied the doubling parts (though with some mistakes in transposition for the basset horns),[6] while the trumpet and kettledrum parts were added by Franz Xaver Süssmayr, whose role in the completion of the Requiem will be discussed below.

In practical terms, these are the only two sections which could have been performed at the memorial service on 10 December 1791, although nothing of this performance material is known to exist, unless we consider a curious manuscript found among the effects of Süssmayr acquired after his death by Prince Nicolaus II Esterházy (now in the Országos Szechényi Könyvtár, Budapest): this is a copy, in Süssmayr's hand, of the 'realized' organ part of a section of the Introitus, from bar 21 ('Te decet hymnus') to the end of the Kyrie fugue, very hastily written out and accompanied by remarks intended for a copyist, for example 'put this in the G clef' ('–NB setz' es in V[iolin]S[c]hl[üssel]'). This otherwise slightly incomprehensible procedure, does, however, make sense in the context of the memorial service now known to have taken place on 10 December.[7]

Despite this evidence, Constanze herself related that it was not to Süssmayr that she gave the Requiem to be completed after this extract had been performed, but to another pupil, Joseph Eybler. Many years later, in a letter dated Salzburg, 31 May 1827, addressed to Abbé Maximilian Stadler, a friend of the family, she states her wish

> ... to relate to you and all Mozart's friends the history of the Requiem, which consists of this: that Mozart ˙never thought of beginning a Requiem [at any other time], and often said to me that he undertook this work (i.e., the one commissioned by Anonymous) with the greatest pleasure, since that was his favourite genre [i.e., church music] and he was going to do it and compose it with such fervour that his friends and enemies would study it after his death; 'if I can only stay alive that long; for this must be my masterpiece and my swansong.' And he did compose it with great fervour; when he felt weak, however, Süssmayr often had to sing, with me and him [Mozart], what he had written, and thus Süssmayr received a real lesson from Mozart. And I can hear Mozart, when he often said to Süssmayr: 'Ey – there you stand like a duck in a thunderstorm; you won't understand that for a long time,' took the quill and wrote down principal parts which, I suppose, were too much for Süssmayr. – What Mozart can be blamed for is that he wasn't very orderly with his papers and sometimes mislaid what he'd started to compose; and so as

not to search for it endlessly he simply wrote it again; that is how it could happen that some things turned up twice, but the second [version] was no different from the first; for once he had made up his mind from the mass of thoughts, that idea was as solid as a rock, and was never changed; that is something you can see in his scores, too, so beautiful, so efficient, so cleanly written, and certainly not a note altered. – Let us assume the case that Süssmayr finds something left by Mozart (for the Sanctus, etc.), that would mean the Requiem is after all Mozart's work. – My proposal that Eybler should finish it occurred because I was then (I don't remember why) annoyed at Süssmayr, and Mozart himself had thought highly of Eybler. I thought myself that anyone can do it, since all the principal sections are written out. And so I had Eybler sent to me and told of my wish; since he at once turned me down with beautiful excuses, he wasn't given it ...[8]

In fact, however, Constanze did entrust the score to Eybler. On 21 December 1791, he received the score of the Requiem from her and signed a receipt which seems to have been written by Sophie Haibel (Constanze's younger sister), who had been present when the composer died. This receipt,[9] now in the archives of Wiener Neustadt, reads as follows:

The undersigned hereby acknowledges that the widow Frau Konztanzia Mozart has consigned to him the Requiem begun by her late husband, with a view to completing it; that I propose to complete it by the end of this coming Lent, and at the same time I promise that I will not allow either it to be copied or to pass to any hands other than those of the Frau Widow. Vienna, 21 December 1791. [Signed] Joseph Eybler mpria.

The extraordinary thing about Eybler's additions is that they were made directly on Mozart's unfinished autograph. Eybler began his work with the 'Dies irae', which of course confirms the theory that the Kyrie fugue, immediately preceding it in the autograph manuscript, must have been already completed by Freystädtler and Süssmayr before 21 December 1791: otherwise Eybler would have been obliged to start with the Kyrie and not with the 'Dies irae'. The fact that Eybler's corrections were entered directly on Mozart's manuscript does, however, raise an interesting possibility: could Eybler have made these corrections before Mozart died and thus under the composer's direct supervision? This rather bold hypothesis might be confirmed by the following authentic statement. In an autobiographical note written for the *Allgemeine Musikalische Zeitung,* Eybler stated: 'I had the good fortune to retain his [Mozart's] friendship undamaged up to his death, so that I could help him during his painful last illness, lifting him, laying him down and waiting on him …'[10] It is entirely possible that Eybler actually filled in those parts from the 'Dies irae' to the 'Hostias' (which Mozart had only written in *particella*) under Mozart's direct supervision: not only are they entered on Mozart's manuscript, but they are incomparably better than Süssmayr's additions, particularly the trumpet and kettledrum parts of the 'Dies irae'.

Eybler's additions, then, comprise the music from the 'Dies irae' to the 'Lacrimosa', and while this additional orchestration is not entirely complete, it is sufficiently far advanced to permit it, with very small additions, to be issued in practical form, which was the method I adopted for the new edition published by Breitkopf & Härtel in 1993.

After Eybler declined Constanze's proposal 'with beautiful excuses', she gave it to Süssmayr, who not only completed the sections from the 'Lacrimosa' to the end of the Offertorium, but also the Sanctus, Benedictus, Agnus Dei and Communio. He also completely recomposed the parts that Eybler had only partially completed – probably a rival pupil's pride prevented him from using much of Eybler's additions.

The completed score now had to be presented to Walsegg's emissary. In order to avoid giving the impression of several handwritings being present, Süssmayr used – of the Mozart autograph – only the 'Requiem aeternam' and the Kyrie fugue. He then recopied all the rest of the Mozart fragment and to this second manuscript he added his own orchestration. Since Süssmayr's handwriting was very similar to that of his former master, it would have been relatively easy to pass off the whole thing as Mozart's autograph, especially since even the paper used was rather similar in most of the MS. and, in the case of the final 'Dona eis' fugue (was this, then, the first operation in the Süssmayr reconstruction?), identical to the second part of the Mozart original. Süssmayr then forged Mozart's signature on the title page and, inexplicably, added the date '1792'. Given that it was general knowledge that Mozart had died in December 1791, what could he hope to accomplish with this extraordinary misdating? The only tentative explanation that I can offer is that Süssmayr, who might have considered the whole affair slightly sinister, wanted to leave a small indication that all was not right with the final score.

And when was Süssmayr's completion ready for delivery to Walsegg's famous grey-clad emissary? On 4 March 1792, Baron Jacobi, Freiherr von Klöst, the Prussian Emissary to the Court of Vienna and a member of Mozart's Freemasons' Lodge 'Zur neugekrönten Hoffnung', bought a collection of music by Mozart from the composer's widow. Mozart had been admired by King Frederick William II of Prussia, who now generously assisted the widow by purchasing *La Betulia liberata* (K.118 [74c]), an oratorio (probably *Davidde penitente* [K.469]) and two Litanies: Jacobi borrowed the original scores and had them copied. On the reverse side of the sheet is the note: 'N.B. copying charges for the four pieces 40 florins and for the Requiem 450 florins or 100 ducats, [total] 490 fl.' ('NB Copiatur deren 4 Stücke 40 flt / für daß Requiem 450 fl. / 490 fl.'). The cost of copying – 450 florins – is a significant amount, and it is highly unlikely that Constanze would have sold Mozart's *incomplete* Requiem to the Prussian Court for 100 ducats, hence it must be presumed that by 4 March 1792 Süssmayr had completed all the missing parts and movements and had delivered them to Count Walsegg.

*   *   *

There exist, then, two manuscripts of the Requiem. The first is the fragment, starting with the 'Dies irae', of which Eybler orchestrated the 'Dies irae', 'Tuba mirum', 'Rex tremendae', 'Recordare' and 'Confutatis'; there then follows Mozart's incomplete 'Lacrimosa', breaking off at bar 9 (the soprano part of bars 9 and 10 added by Eybler), and afterwards his *particella* sketch of the 'Domine' and 'Hostias'. The second manuscript consists of Mozart's completed movement, 'Requiem aeternam', with the false signature, the Kyrie fugue (by Mozart, Freystädtler and Süssmayr) and the rest of the work completed and copied by Süssmayr. A complete facsimile of both manuscripts,[11] accompanied by a detailed introduction, is now easily available to students.

The purpose of the new edition which I prepared was to combine the work of the three pupils who had been involved in completing Mozart's commission – Süssmayr, Eybler and Freystädtler. The mistakes that Süssmayr made – parallel fifths and octaves, etc. – are well known, and it was not considered necessary to correct them for the new edition, but those who are interested may consult other modern editions. To reiterate, my new edition was based on the extant autograph material as follows:

Introitus and Kyrie
Mozart's completed autograph of the 'Requiem aeternam'. Kyrie fugue by Mozart (vocal parts and *basso continuo*), completed by Süssmayr (trumpets and timpani) and Freystädtler (basset horns, bassoons, violins I and II, viola, all doubling the vocal parts).

Sequence
'Dies irae': (1) Mozart's *particella* sketch, instrumentation by Eybler with small additions by the editor. (2) Süssmayr's autograph including his own additions.
'Tuba mirum': as above.
'Rex tremendae': as above.
'Confutatis': as above.
'Lacrimosa': (1) Mozart's sketch, bars 1–8 with an unused addition of two bars by Eybler. (2) Süssmayr's autograph with his additions.

Offertorium
'Domine': (1) Mozart's *particella* sketch. (2) Süssmayr's autograph with his additions.
'Hostias': as above.
Sanctus, Benedictus, Agnus Dei and Communio: Süssmayr's autograph. The only known authentic source for the theme of the Benedictus is found in Barbara Ployer's sketchbook.[12]

A sketch which has been identified as the fugal completion of the 'Lacrimosa' is published in the *NMA* edition of the Requiem. This sketch was not used by Süssmayr, but I have put forward the suggestion that it may have been for the unfinished Mass in D minor, of which the Kyrie (K.341 [368a]) has now been redated from Munich *c.* 1780–1 to the last period of Mozart's life.[13] The sketch is on a sheet containing *inter alia* a section from the Overture to *Die Zauberflöte*, a piano piece,[14] a sketch to the Amen fugue of a choral work in D minor and a draft of part of the 'Rex tremendae' in the Requiem. The sketch, if it were intended for a Mass, might have been used either for the end of the Mass ('Dona nobis pacem. Amen') or for the end of the Gloria, with the words 'Cum Sancto Spiritu in gloria Dei Patris. Amen'. The sheet in question is among the Mozartiana in the Preussische Staatsbibliothek, Berlin.

The Offertorium and the Role of Abbé Maximilian Stadler

Those familiar with the family correspondence in the *Mozart Briefe* will know that Abbé Stadler (1748–1833) was a remarkable musician and composer, and a friend of the Mozart family. As a confidant of Constanze, he undertook to complete many of the fragments which her late husband had left in an unfinished state. That he was involved with the Requiem is well known, though a less familiar aspect is his involvement at a textual level.

Stadler made two copies of Mozart's manuscript, one of which is in the Stadt- und Universitätsbibliothek in Frankfurt-am-Main (Mus.Hs.211). This consists of the 'Dies irae' in score (22 sheets), which Stadler gave to J.A. André in Vienna on 21 August 1828, together with the 'Lacrimosa', which also includes the 'Domine' and 'Hostias' (8 sheets). There is the following note by J.A. André: 'The present copy of the appropriate part of Mozart's Requiem is, note for note and sheet for sheet, exactly after Mozart's manuscript and was prepared for me by my esteemed friend Herr Abbé Stadler'.[15] The second copy is in the Music Division of the Österreichische Nationalbibliothek (Cod. 19.057), and that library also owns an even more interesting Stadler copy – that of the Offertorium (S.m. 4375) – which he sent to André, and from whose heirs it was purchased in 1931. The astonishing thing about this MS. is the fact that it is a copy not of the Mozart *particella*, but of the instrumented completion by Süssmayr, where however the faulty Süssmayr text of bar 4 has been improved: this improved version is the one which has also come down to us in the first edition published by Breitkopf & Härtel in 1800.[16]

The question now arises: was Stadler perhaps responsible for the orchestration of the Offertorium which has hitherto been ascribed to Süssmayr? Constanze relates clearly that, in addition to Eybler and Süssmayr, she also approached other composers to undertake the completion of the Requiem. Given that Stadler was her confidant, would it not have been logical for her to approach him? If Stadler was in fact responsible for the additions of the Offertorium, we should have to revise our general view of Süssmayr's participation in the completed Requiem score. Even if it could be proved that the watermarks of these MSS. are indeed of the period 1828 and do not date from as early as 1791/2, one must add a cautionary word that perhaps there once existed a Stadler version of 1791/2 which has since disappeared. In any event, on the available evidence the Offertorium text as it appears in the Süssmayr autograph of 1792 holds chronological primacy.

A Document detailing Mozart's income
and expenses (1786 or 1787?)

────────── ～❧～ ──────────

O
N 31 JANUARY 1993, DR ULRICH DRÜNER, A GERMAN ANTIQUARIAN
bookseller in Stuttgart, wrote to me saying that he had recently
purchased, at a sale in Basle on 19 September 1992, a Mozart document which had never been properly reproduced – there are only extracts in
Mozart *Briefe*[1] – and which was last heard of when sold at auction in 1929 by
D. Salomon (sale catalogue, lot no. 54, item 9978). Dr Drüner kindly sent
me a photograph of the first page of the document and asked for my opinion
of its contents and interest. Having transcribed the document, I felt that it
seemed to represent a very interesting statement regarding Mozart's finances
in the mid-1780s, but having suggested this to Dr Drüner, I did not attempt
to analyze the document further, since I was involved with other urgent pro-
jects at the time.

Meanwhile, Volkmar Braunbehrens and Ulrich Drüner have prepared a
long article for inclusion in the *Mozart-Jahrbuch 1993* (forthcoming).
However, an English translation entitled 'A newly discovered Piece of Paper
in Mozart's Handwriting' by Bruce Cooper Clarke was published in extracts
in the *Prince Lichnowsky Newsletter* (Issue No. 6, 28 February 1994), but
complete some months earlier (November 1993), and this, in the absence of
the *Jahrbuch* article, has been of great value. The second page of the document was also published in this *Newsletter*. By combining the photograph of
page 1 – see the reproduction opposite – and the information taken from the
Prince Lichnowsky Newsletter, we may reproduce the content of the two
pages as follows, also incorporating in the process the corrections suggested
by Ulrich Konrad, whose contribution to the document's value will be discussed below.

As a reminder of the currency in use in Vienna, the terms florin (fl.) and
gulden are synonymous, and the abbreviations 'x.', 'xr.' or 'kr.' all signify
kreuzer (60 kreuzer = 1 florin/gulden). The ducat was equivalent to 4½

florins/gulden. A *Banco Zettel* was a bank cheque and was used instead of cash, i.e. at no discount (for details see note 3, below).

[Page 1:]

line

1 Meine Cassa bestund verflossenes Jahr aus

kayserlich und Cremnizer   Salzburger

2 295 Duckaten zu 4 fl: 30 x. – aus 119 Ducaten zu 4 fl: 20 x. holländer aus 88 ducaten zu 4 fl: 18 x.

3 aus 101 Souvrain zu 13 fl. 20 x: – aus 250 Thaler zu 2 fl. 30 x: aus 25 banco zettel zu 50 fl.

4 aus 18 banco zettel zu 25 fl. – aus 50 banco zettel zu 10 fl. und aus 90 banco zettel zu 5 fl: –

5 – Dieses Jahr durch habe ausgegeben wie folgt. –

6 99 kayserliche Ducaten. – 5 Salzburger. – 33 holländer. – 66 Souvrains. – 88 thaler

7 zu 2 fl: 30. – und überdies noch 539 fl: 56 x:. – Den Rest dann habe in 5 theile getheilt.

8 Nun ist die frage wie viel Jeder bekommen hat? –

9   W. A. Mozart's Handschrift
                                                              André

[Page 2:]

10 Originalpartituren   3777
11 was Artaria herausgege[ben]

12 Leon // Die Ged[i]chte Freimaurers[chen]

13 kiere til [?] Silv[er]stolpe
14 Ja eller Nei

15 Musenalmanach Mozarts Musik

16 Vorstehende Zeilen sind v. Nissens
17 Handschrift A./.

[written upside down in Carl Mozart's hand:]
18 Von Carl Mozart zum Andenken
19 Mayland am 1. Oktober 1818

In translating the sections of page 1 which do not deal purely with figures, we have in Mozart's hand:
line 1 – my cash during the past year consisted of
line 5 – during this year I had expenditures as follows
line 7 – … in addition 539 fl: 56 x:. – I have divided the rest into 5 parts.
line 8 – Now the question is, how much did each one get?

Page 2, being interrupted by the fact that the sheet was cut in two – see below – presents more difficult problems:
line 10 – Original scores   3777 [catalogue number?]
line 11 – which were published by Artaria
line 12 – Leon // The poems of Masonic content
line 13 – Dear Mr Silv[er]stolpe
line 14 – Yes or no
line 15 – Musenalmanach Mozart's Music
line 16 – Above lines are in v. Nissen's
line 17 – handwriting A[ndré]
line 18 – From Carl Mozart to an unknown recipient as a remembrance
line 19 – Milan, 1 October 1818

The Mozart document is written in a rather pale crimson ink on thick paper measuring 229 mm x 84 to 91 mm (9 in. x 3½ in. max.); the watermarks show chain lines about 24 to 25 mm (1 in.) apart. Johann Anton André's note regarding the paper's authenticity is in a dark ink. Mozart used reddish ink of one kind or another for *inter alia* the Canon (K.507 [1786?; British Library]), K.537a (Anh.57, sketch to a piano concerto, 1786?; Mozarteum, Salzburg), Horn Concerto in E flat (K.495 [26 June 1786; private possession]), Piano Trio in G (K.496 [8 July 1786 private possession, Paris]). The autograph of K.507 is attached to that of K.508 (another canon) and a sketch to the Piano Quartet in E flat (K.493), also in red ink.[2] In other words, it seems that Mozart's use of this red ink was confined to the year 1786. The descriptions of the various ducats – Imperial and Cremnitz, Salzburg and Dutch – were insertions between lines 1 and 2. And this leads us to the conversion rates noted by Mozart.

The exchange rates for these ducats and the double souverains d'or (golden double sovereign) were fixed by imperial decree. On 1 September 1783 they were fixed as of 15 September as follows:

Kremnitz ducats	4 fl. 22 kr.
Salzburg ducats	4 fl. 20 kr.
Dutch ('Holländer')	4 fl. 18 kr.
Double souverains d'or	12 fl. 51 kr.

Another decree of 12 January 1786 changed some (not all) of these rates, effective 1 February 1786:

Kremnitz ducats	4 fl. 30 kr.(+ 8 kr.)
Salzburg ducats	4 fl. 20 kr.
Dutch ('Holländer')	4 fl. 18 kr.
Double souverains d'or	13 fl. 20 kr. (+ 29 kr.)

On 9 February 1788 the value of the Dutch ducat was officially increased to 4 fl. 26 kr. (+ 8 kr.).[3]

Using these tables, it is apparent that Mozart's exchange rates were calculated at the rate effective from 1 February 1786, until 9 February 1788. It is also evident that Mozart was speaking of one year, despite the curious terminology ('verflossenes Jahr', 'dieses Jahr'). If 1786 is meant, Mozart's income would have included the fees for both K.486, *Der Schauspieldirektor* (50 ducats or 225 florins) and K.492, *Le nozze di Figaro* (100 ducats or 450 florins). How much Mozart earned from his benefit concert at the Burgtheater on 7 April 1786 is not known. If 1787 is meant, income would have been from the journey to Prague and the benefit concert there on 19 January ('Prague' Symphony, etc.), as well as a possible benefit evening of *Figaro*. The second trip to Prague included the income from *Don Giovanni* (probably 100 ducats or 450 florins),[4] first performed there on 29 October 1787 and probably a substantial amount arising from a benefit performance on 3 November. This was also the year in which Mozart received 1,000 florins from his late father's estate.[5] Naturally, there are large gaps in our reconstruction of Mozart's income both for 1786 and 1787, but the amounts given in his summary are as follows:

Cash balance		4,193 fl. 14 kr.
Banco Zettel	2,650 fl.	
	———	
Total		6,843 fl. 14 kr.

The expenses 'this year' amounted to 2,465 fl. 40 kr., which if subtracted from the assets leave 4,377 fl. 68 kr. Divided, as far as possible, into five equal shares, we arrive at 875 fl. 30 kr. with 4 kreuzer left over. In other words, the division is a theoretical one, because the smallest coin in use in Mozart's time was the ¼-kreuzer piece (equal to 1 denar).

Braunbehrens and Drüner now pose the question: what does the content of this sheet actually signify? They offer three possible solutions:

1 It represents a problem in arithmetic using invented numbers. In this version, 'the entire matter is to be seen as an exercise in mathematics prepared for the fun of it'. One aspect of the document might lead to this supposition: the sequence of numbers under the expenditures – 99, 55, 33, 66, 88. They note that 'one could well imagine some symbolic numerical cipher (stretching even into Freemasonry) buried behind such a series. On the other hand, such a striking row of numbers is limited to line 6, while all the other number series exhibit nothing out of the ordinary.'

2 It represents a problem in arithmetic using real numbers. 'In this interpretation', write the authors, 'the paper [uses] numbers drawn from Mozart's daily life. One is perhaps surprised at the magnitude of the amounts, but recent research has suggested that Mozart earned quite substantial sums of money at this period, and it will be remembered that Leopold Mozart wrote to his daughter on 19 March 1785 that Mozart, if he had no debts, could deposit 2,000 florins in the bank "today"'. The authors point out that it would be curious for Mozart to lay bare his own financial

circumstances if there were no need to do so (supposing that the details set down were the basis of a puzzle for society games). 'If the purpose was a problem ... using actual numbers ... then some more discreet formulation, such as "The cash situation of a merchant" (or something similar) would seem more likely than the frankly revelatory "*My* cash ..."'.

3 A document reflecting some actual financial business.

This is the interpretation which the authors favour. They suggest that the cutting of the paper in two 'can also be interpreted as resulting from a deliberate intent to conceal something. In this case, the slip of paper can be read as the record of the outcome of a meeting of creditors at which Mozart was obliged to swear an insolvent debtor's oath.' The authors are not, however, inclined to believe in the insolvency theory, given the lack, at present, of 'further circumstantial evidence'.

The second side of the sheet contains several items. The first is Nissen's comments. He was engaged in preparing his large biography of Mozart, with Constanze's assistance, and these notes were *aides-mémoires* along those lines: (1) Which scores by Mozart were authentic, i.e. original, among those published by Artaria? (2) Gottfried Leon (1757–1830), superintendent of the Vienna Court Library, was a Mason, his *Gedichte* (Vienna, 1788) included two poems which Mozart may have set to music, 'Des Todes Werk' and 'Vollbracht ist die Arbeit der Meister' (both lost, Köchel *desunt*).[6] (3) There was, indeed, some Mozart published for the first time in the *Wiener Musenalmanach für 1786*, edited by J. F. Ratschky and A. Blumauer, Vienna, printed by Georg Philipp Wucherer: *Lied der Freiheit* (K.506, text by Blumauer). The first eight lines (10–17) are crossed out with two parallel strokes of the pen. The entry about Silverstolpe is also part of Nissen's attempt to collect musical and biographical material: Frederik Samuel Silverstolpe (1769–1851), who was one of Nissen's friends, was a member of the Swedish Legation in Vienna from 1796 to 1803. As an admirer of Mozart, he collected relics from Constanze, including the autograph of the Cantata, K.619. The remarks in lines 13 and 14 are in Danish and Swedish.

Here, one would have thought, the matter might have rested, but the forthcoming *Mozart-Jahrbuch 1993* is to include another article which is at present only available in the pre-translation (November 1993) by Bruce Cooper Clarke as part of the *Prince Lichnowsky Newsletter* series: Ulrich Konrad's 'And just what is "Interpretative Violence"? – Comments on interpreting the rediscovered piece of paper in Mozart's handwriting'.

In brief, the proposition here put forward may be summed up in the author's own words at the end of the article:

The piece of paper described here is concerned with the first document written in Mozart's hand that contains sums in the form of a mathematical problem. With reasonable confidence, the document can be dated to the years 1786 and 1787. The document does not allow us to draw any conclusions, direct or indirect, regarding Mozart's financial circumstances in this period. The text has the appearance of a serious exercise; it is characterized by an inner logic and, so far as the currencies named are concerned, conforms with the circumstances of Mozart's life. It is only the solution to the problem posed that is unrealistic. This last fact could suggest Mozart had written down a text that was meant perhaps as a joke (devised by himself? found elsewhere?) in connection with some occasion (*Fasching*? [i.e. 'Carnival']) not otherwise known to us. To magnify the text into more than a mathematical problem, possibly with a highly speculative basis for the numbers used, would mean doing interpretative violence to the words he wrote.

In other words, the document is not a serious evaluation of Mozart's income, but may actually represent a problem taken 'from a contemporary arithmetic book or from some course of instruction for business people'. At one point the author makes the following suggestion:

To judge from the writing, it could be the text of some homework which Mozart had to solve in connection with his hitherto unknown application for the position of practice teacher at the school in Himmelpfortgrund; his solution may have been written on the part of the paper which has been cut off.

No doubt this rather heavy-handed humour was intended to discomfit Volkmar Braunbehrens and Ulrich Drüner, but it is difficult to see precisely why Ulrich Konrad should be so thoroughly annoyed at the modest and sensible results of the Braunbehrens-Drüner investigations. It is true that Mozart was an inveterate prankster, but one fails to see why the composer should have set up such an elaborate series of figures in line 6 if the whole exercise were only a party game. It seems clear that although the last words on the subject of this mysterious document have yet to be spoken, we would do well not to hold it in scholarly disdain.

Some recently discovered documents concerning Mozart's last year

T HE OCCASIONAL DISCOVERY OF CONTEMPORARY DOCUMENTARY evidence relating to the events of 1791 and their significance for our understanding of Mozart's mixed fortunes in the months preceding his death proves that there are still unexpected aspects – notably the lawsuit brought by Prince Carl von Lichnowsky discussed below – which call for detailed examination and analysis. Since scholarly interpretation of new evidence tends to be restricted to specialist journals or to be published in German, I have brought together a number of items of interest which help to throw new light on Mozart's standing in Viennese society and on the attitude of others towards him, especially the new Emperor Leopold II (who succeeded his brother Joseph II in 1790) and his consort, the Empress Maria Luisa. It has always to be remembered that, with the decline in Mozart's public following in the late 1780s, patronage was a key feature in his ability to survive financially and to avoid further indebtedness to his friends and Masonic brothers.

The Lichnowsky Lawsuit of November 1791

In the summer of 1991, Walther Brauneis published a summary court record (recently discovered in the Hofkammer Archives in Vienna),[1] relating to a previously unknown lawsuit between Prince Carl von Lichnowsky (1756–1814) and Mozart. The composer was ordered by the Lower Austrian Court to pay the Prince 1,435 gulden 32 kreuzer, together with court costs of 24 gulden; the record of the lawsuit was registered in the Hofkammer Archiv on 12 November, and the relevant entry (reproduced here in pl. 9) reads as follows:

> 4384. N: Ö: Landrecht erinnert unterm [fol. 1587r] 9ten et prs: [=praesentatum] 12 = 9mb: 791: Daß Karl / Fürst v: Lichnowskj Ca dem K: K:

Hof = Kappelmeister [*sic*] Wolfgang Amadé / Mozart wegen schuldig-
ungen 1435 f / 32 Xr samt 24 f Gerichts Kosten / sowohl die Pfändung, als
auch die / Erfolglassung dessen Besoldungs / Hälfte bewürkt habe.

Translation: '[No.] 4384. The Lower Austrian Court advises under
date 9th and recorded on 12th Nov. 1791 that Prince Karl Lichnowskj
contra K: K: Hof Kappelmeister Wolfgang Amadé Mozart, for indebtedness of 1,435 florins 32 kreuzer together with court costs of 24 florins, has
shown cause for both attachment [of property] and withholding of half
his salary.'

(Hofkammerarchiv Vienna Camerale Protokoll 1791, fol. 1586v–1587r;
facsimile by courtesy of Hofrat Dr Gottfried Mraz).

The reasons why this record lay undiscovered for nearly two hundred
years are in any case twofold. First, it is only a digest of the original transcript of the hearing, which was stored in the Justice Building (housing the
relevant documents of the Lower Austrian Court) until it was burned down
in 1927; in the absence of that transcript one can only surmise that the sum
of money mentioned could represent unpaid debts plus compound interest
(1,435 f 32 xr would otherwise be a slightly odd figure as the basis of a claim
for judgment in favour of the Prince). The second reason is altogether more
mysterious: the lawsuit and its ramifications have never been mentioned
elsewhere in connection either with Lichnowsky or with Mozart, nor was
this episode ever discussed by Constanze Mozart after she became a widow.
It does not even figure in the Suspense Order drawn up after Mozart's death
on 5 December, less than a month after the court's decision.

Before proceeding further, let us hark back to 1789, when the composer
embarked on a journey to Prussia, via Prague and Dresden, in the company
of the Prince, who invited Mozart to travel in the same coach. As to how the
Lichnowsky family came to know Mozart, we may simply cite later documents in which it is stated that both Prince Carl and his younger brother,
Count Moritz, considered themselves pupils of Mozart (for one such document, see p. 217).

At the beginning of April 1789, Mozart and Prince Lichnowsky set off
from Vienna, travelling first to Budwitz in Bohemia. While away on this
journey, Mozart sent whole series of letters to his wife Constanze, who
remained in Vienna. Thanks to the survival of much of the family correspondence, we know that Lichnowsky's name figures casually in many of the
earlier letters – for our present purposes it is hardly worth quoting extracts.

Once Mozart had reached Berlin, he wrote to Constanze on 23 May with something of interest about the Prince:

> My dear little wife, you will have to content yourself with looking forward to seeing *me*, more than seeing any *money*. – 100 Friedrichs' D'or are not, however, 900 fl. but 700 fl. [probably an advance honorarium for six string quartets intended for Frederick William II of Prussia and for six piano sonatas for the king's daughter, Princess Friederike], at least that is what they told me. –2ndly, Lichnowsky had to leave me because he was obliged to hasten away in the morning and hence I was forced to look after myself (in that expensive place Potsdam). –3rdly, I had to lend him 100 fl., because his purse was emptying; I could hardly avoid doing so, you know why [the Prince was a fellow Mason]. –4thly, the academy concert in Leipzig, just as I predicted, was a failure, so I had to backtrack 32 miles almost for nothing; Lichnowsky is entirely to blame for it, because he would not leave me in peace unless I returned to Leipzig. – Still – more about this when I see you. – There is, firstly not much to be made from an academy concert and 2ndly – the king does not look upon it with favour. – You must be satisfied with me and with this, that I am fortunate enough to be in the king's good graces; what I've written to you must remain between us …'[2]

Although the language is very guarded, a hint of a certain lack of understanding might be construed. Could this have been the occasion – sometime during this trip – when Mozart had reason to borrow money from the Prince? It has been cautiously suggested that Mozart's need might have been settling a gambling debt, but there is no evidence for that or indeed that Mozart gambled in any serious fashion.

It was not unheard of for a Prince of the Holy Roman Empire of German Nations to sue a commoner, but for Lichnowsky to sue Mozart in the circumstances does seem extremely odd. Even odder is the fact that the debt was patently 'hushed up' immediately after Mozart's death. Is there any clue to all this in the characters of the Prince or his wife Christiane, *née* Countess Thun? She was one of the famous 'Three Graces', daughters of the liberal, free-thinking Maria Wilhelmine, *née* Countess Ulfeld (1747–1800) and her eccentric husband, Franz Joseph, Count Thun-Hohenstein (1734–1800), a member of Haydn's Masonic Lodge 'Zur wahren Eintracht'. The 'Three Graces' were Elisabeth, married in 1788 to Andreas, Count Razumovsky,

Beethoven's quartet patron and later Russian Ambassador in Vienna; Christiane (born 1765), married in 1788 to Lichnowsky; and Maria Carolina, married in 1793 to Richard Meade, Earl of Clanwilliam, the British Attaché in Vienna.

Most of the documentation concerning Prince Carl and his wife dates, it is true, from some years later, when the young Beethoven was befriended by the Lichnowsky family: the Princess was regarded as a substitute mother for the hot-headed young composer. Some documents dating from the post-Mozartian period will, perhaps, help shed some light on the characters of the princely couple.

Frau von Bernhard came to Vienna when still a girl in order to complete her training as a pianist. While there she moved in the Lichnowsky circle, which also included Ludwig van Beethoven, and later recorded her impressions of her youthful experience:

> When he [Beethoven] came to us, he used to stick his head in the door and make sure that there was no one there whom he disliked. He was small and plain-looking with an ugly red, pock-marked face. His hair was quite dark and hung almost shaggily around his face. His clothes were very commonplace, not differing greatly from the fashion of those days, particularly in our circles. Moreover, he spoke in a strong dialect and in a rather common manner. In general his whole being did not give the impression of any particular cultivation; in fact, he was unmannerly in both gesture and demeanour. He was very haughty; I myself have seen the mother of Princess Lichnowsky, Countess Thun, going down on her knees to him as he lolled on the sofa, and begging him to play something. But Beethoven did not. Countess Thun was, however, a very eccentric woman.
>
> I was frequently invited to the Lichnowskys, in order to play there. He was a friendly and distinguished gentleman and she a very beautiful woman. Yet they did not seem happy together; she always had such a melancholy expression on her face, and I heard that he spent a great deal of money, far beyond his means. Her sister [Elisabeth, married to Count Razumovsky], who was even more beautiful, had a husband who was a patron of Beethoven. She was almost always present when music was performed. I still remember clearly both Haydn and Salieri sitting on a sofa on one side of the small music-room, both carefully dressed in the old-fashioned way with perruque, shoes and silk hose, whereas even here

Beethoven would come dressed in the informal fashion of the other side of the Rhine, almost ill-dressed.[3]

Carl Czerny, a pianist, composer and colleague of Beethoven's, wrote about the Prince as follows:

In 1804 I was presented by [Wenzel] Krumpholz to Prince Lichnowsky, Beethoven's friend and most active supporter. The Prince, as well as his brother, Count Moritz, had previously both been pupils of Mozart and later of Beethoven; they were great connoisseurs of the arts as well as the most amiable and humane of men. It was Prince Lichnowsky who had brought the young Beethoven to Vienna and enabled him to study with Haydn, Salieri and Albrechtsberger. He treated him like a friend and brother and persuaded the whole of the high nobility to support him.'[4]

Ferdinand Ries, Beethoven's pupil, left a valuable testament as to the conduct of Beethoven as well as that of Lichnowsky at the time when the composer was living as a guest of the Prince:

Beethoven, who had been brought up under straitened circumstances and at the same time under guardianship, though merely that of his friends, had no idea about the value of money and was anything but economical. To give an example: dinner-time at Prince Carl Lichnowsky's was set for four o'clock. 'Now I'm supposed to be home every day at half-past three,' said Beethoven, 'shave, change into something better, etc. I could never endure that.' So it happened that he often went to inns, where he came off badly, as in all matters of economy, since he did not, as stated above, have any understanding of the value of things or of money. The Prince, who had a very loud metallic voice, once gave an order to his valet, in the event that he and Beethoven rang at the same time, to attend the latter first. Beethoven overheard this and on the same day engaged a servant of his own. In the same way, the Prince made available to him a mount from his well-filled stable. Beethoven thereupon procured a horse of his own when he was taken with the notion, but soon abandoned the idea of learning to ride ... This Andante of the Waldstein Sonata has left me with a sad memory. When Beethoven played it to Krumpholz (whose death in 1817 upset Beethoven greatly) and myself for the first time, it gave us the utmost pleasure and we tormented him unceasingly until he repeated it. On my way home, passing by the house of Prince

Lichnowsky, I went in to tell him about Beethoven's wonderful new composition and was obliged to play him the piece as well as I could remember it. As I remembered more and more of it, the Prince requested me to repeat it once more. So it came about that even the Prince learned a part of it. In order to surprise Beethoven, the Prince went to him the next day and told him that he, too, had composed something which was not at all bad. Beethoven's firm declaration that he did not wish to hear it went unheeded; the Prince sat down and played, to Beethoven's astonishment, a good part of the Andante.

Beethoven was very annoyed about this, and it was because of that occasion that I never heard Beethoven play again. For he would never again play in my presence and several times insisted that I should leave the room when he played. One day, when a small party, which included both Beethoven and myself, breakfasted with the Prince after the concert in the Augarten (at eight o'clock in the morning), it was suggested that we should go to Beethoven's house in order to hear his as yet unfinished opera *Leonore*. When we arrived there, Beethoven requested, even this time, that I should go away. Since the insistent requests of all those present were fruitless, I left with tears in my eyes. The whole company noticed it. Prince Lichnowsky, coming after me, asked that I be allowed to wait in the anteroom; since he had been to blame for the whole occasion he now wished it to be settled. My offended sense of honour would not allow it. I heard afterwards that Lichnowsky was very violent with Beethoven on account of his behaviour, for it was only his love of Beethoven's works which had occasioned the whole affair as well as Beethoven's resulting anger. But the only outcome of these remonstrances was that henceforth he never again played at private parties.[5]

To conclude this series of documents concerning relations between Beethoven and Lichnowsky, I have chosen two complementary descriptions of the famous altercation between the two men which took place in the Prince's castle at Grätz. The first is by the physician Max Ring (1817–1901), who visited Grätz and recorded the recollections of the old castellan, while the second is from the personal physician to Prince Lichnowsky, Dr Anton Weiser.[6] Dr Ring wrote:

The old castellan, to whom we had a recommendation from a high official, told us about a number of the famous composer's characteristics. He was firmly convinced that Herr van Beethoven was not quite right in his mind; he would often run, bareheaded, without a hat, around in the great park of the castle hours on end, even if it were raining with lightning and thunder. On other occasions he would sit for whole days shut up in his room without seeing anybody and not speaking a word.

But the most insane behaviour of Herr van Beethoven occurred when the French occupied Grätz after the battle of Austerlitz [1805]. The Prince had aroused the hopes of the French General, a very fine gentleman and a great music-lover, of meeting the celebrated composer and hearing him play on the pianoforte. To this end, a great musical soirée was arranged at the castle and the composer was to play his latest compositions. Beethoven, however, refused although the Prince repeatedly and earnestly requested him to do so. Nevertheless, the Prince still hoped to persuade the obstinate musician, and invited the French General and other distinguished guests to the intended soirée. On the appointed evening the company was assembled, eagerly awaiting the promised treat, but Beethoven was nowhere to be seen. The Prince sent one attendant after the other, but the musician would not come. Finally the major-domo who had also been sent to Beethoven, brought the news that the artist had left the castle secretly and only a letter to the Prince had been found in his room. In it he explained that he could not play to the enemies of his country. In order to avoid any further pleas or solicitations, Beethoven had fled on foot to the town of Grätz in the cold winter night. This, the old castellan added, was a clear indication of his madness.

According to Dr Weiser's version,

In order to humour them [the French officers], it was promised that after dinner they would have the pleasure of hearing the famous Beethoven, who was then a guest at the castle, play. 'They went to table; one of the French staff officers unhappily asked Beethoven if he also played the violin.' Weiser, who was also at table, 'saw at once how this outraged the artist ... Beethoven did not deign to answer his interlocutor.' Weiser could not attend the rest of the dinner since, as Director of the Troppau Hospital, he had to make a professional call there. He heard the rest of the story from Beethoven himself. When the time came for Beethoven to play, he was nowhere to be found. He was looked for. The Prince wanted to persuade him – to cajole him – into playing. No use. An unpleasant, even vulgar, scene took place. Beethoven immediately had his things packed, and hastened, despite the pouring rain, on foot to Troppau, where he spent the night at Weiser's. It was because of the rain that the Sonata in F minor op. 57, the *Appassionata*, which Beethoven was carrying with him was damaged by water ... Weiser tells further that the next day it was difficult, without the Prince, to get a passport to return to Vienna. Finally it was procured. Before he left, Beethoven wrote a very self-willed letter to Lichnowsky which is supposed to have read as follows: 'Prince! What you are, you are by circumstance and by birth. What I am, I am through myself. Of princes there have been and will be thousands. Of Beethovens there is only one ...'. Unfortunately, it seems that the march from Grätz to Troppau induced a considerable worsening of Beethoven's deafness. An exaggerated tradition even tells us that Beethoven's deafness was the result of the chill.

The last and most curious document is from the Memoirs of Lulu von Thürheim, whose sister was the second wife of Prince (then Count) Andreas Razumovsky. Her memoirs are valuable for their contemporary descriptions of Vienna during the Napoleonic Wars. Naturally there is no way of verifying the incredible account which follows, but it is unlikely that the whole thing was fabricated and thus the passage which follows is included on the principle that there is 'no smoke without fire'.

The Princess ... had a remarkable gift of perception, so that she could understand any question, as it were, in flight, and examine it with the greatest clarity. It was not easy to argue with her, since she was mistress of all the fine points of dialectics and of all the sophisms of an imaginative faculty. She would almost always prevail for she had a very open mind, but sometimes her prejudices led her astray. The same was true of her character, in which an excellent heart and a Christian love of her neighbours were combined. These, however, sometimes came into conflict with her preconceptions, since she could not abide certain people and in those cases she would be lacking in any feelings of justice towards them. One could not really say anything derogatory about her because she was far too gentle in her actions. But she could, with a gesture, with a scornful smile, or merely by means of a slightly disparaging remark, destroy someone socially; *elle coulait*, as one says today. This defect was derived, moreover, from the evil spirits of the *coteries* who had dominated Vienna in her youth and whose motto was *nul n'aura de l'esprit hors nous et nos amis* [no one will have wit apart from us and our friends]. Apart from all this, she had another peculiar personal shortcoming which was the cause of the unhappiness of her life ... Her straightforward nature turned into a stiff-necked obstinacy; as soon as she judged some course to be correct and good, she followed it headlong without looking to the right or left and without allowing any kind of reflection.

Her conscience troubled her, for she felt that her coldness had estranged her husband. She did not love him, but she pursued him with advances to such an extent that one day she enticed him into a brothel where, to his great outrage, he recognized his wife who, up to that moment, had worn a mask. Later on, she became determined at any price to bring up a little girl whom she was convinced was the child of her husband. It was perfectly useless for him to declare that he had had nothing, or very little, to do with her origin. She refused to budge from her firmly rooted magnanimity, adopted the child under the name of Lina, gave her the same education as she would have given her own daughter, and left her her entire fortune.

This same obstinacy also resulted in her leaving her only son in the hands of bad people to whom he had been entrusted by his father. She justified this by saying that she had no right to counter the wishes of her husband whom she loved so little ... In her old age she used to give vent to these inconsistencies with a pathetic simplicity. 'When I see', she said to me one day, 'how easily and earnestly so many women fulfil their duties as wives and mothers, I feel quite disconcerted and I, who was so different, am envious of them.' Nevertheless, the poor woman was never unfaithful to her husband who would, in any case, have forgiven her without resentment. He, a cynical rake and a shameless coward, would have deserved to be cuckolded. In my opinion, people of this kind are beyond the pale.[7]

The wording of the court document in the Hofkammer Archives leaves no reason for doubt: the verdict was passed and the affair considered as terminated legally, as witness the court costs which Mozart was ordered to pay. After deduction of taxes, from his salary of 800 gulden, his disposable income amounted to 760 gulden,[8] of which then half was to be withheld. His annual rent in the 'Kleines Kaiserhaus' in the Rauhensteingasse in Vienna was some 330 florins, which left him a mere 50 florins. In simple financial terms, Mozart was to all intents ruined and his goods and chattels were subject to an attachment order. It is of course true that he could expect to earn substantial sums by giving concerts as well as by fulfilling commissions such as that for *La clemenza di Tito* for the coronation ceremonies in Prague or for the Requiem, both in 1791, not to mention smaller works such as chamber music for Johann Tost.[9] But what if – as in the event happened – Mozart fell ill and was unable to work for a shorter or longer period?

Mozart's situation was, of course, well known to Lichnowsky, yet he sued for the debt and won. We may wonder, with Bruce Cooper Clarke, whose lively newsletters began with a translation of and comments on the article by Walther Brauneis (see above), if it was customary for 'members of the nobility in this period routinely [to] use the N. Ö. Landrecht to collect bad debts?'[10] In addition, the mere scandal arising from this lawsuit might have been damaging to Mozart's situation at the Austrian Court: he could have lost his position as *Kammermusikus*, especially given that the Imperial family was not particularly well disposed to his music (this antipathy is dicussed below in the context of *La clemenza di Tito*). And what might have been the effects of the enormously successsful opera *Il matrimonio segreto* by Domenico Cimarosa, produced in Vienna in February 1792, had Mozart's career not been tragically cut short? We can only speculate, but the prospects could hardly have been encouraging for an opera composer who was out of favour at Court.[11]

Until the Lichnowsky Archives now in South America and those housed in the Castle at Hradec (Grätz) in the Czech Republic – the latter badly damaged in 1945 – are opened to scholars, we can only guess at Prince Carl Lichnowsky's motives in bringing this ruinous lawsuit against Mozart.

Equally, we are totally in the dark concerning the aftermath of this lawsuit: how was it possible that the debt is never mentioned again? That Constanze was paid the last part of her late husband's salary? Did someone pay off the debt between 12 November and 5 December, thus avoiding the need for attachment of Mozart's goods and chattels? Was it possible for such a lawsuit to be, as it were, rendered null and void (unlikely, given the structure of the Austrian law courts)? Rather than pursue such speculations, I think it preferable to consider another aspect of this curious situation. How was it that such a man as Lichnowsky could and did put up with Beethoven's impossible behaviour, as recorded in the documents above, as well as in many others not quoted here?

At this point I should like to put forward a hypothesis which I have long entertained: that Viennese society in general, and the Lichnowsky family in particular, must have felt exceedingly guilty about Mozart's death and the miserable financial circumstances of the composer and his family. One can hardly doubt, moreover, that the thought must have occurred to Prince Lichnowsky and his entourage that their actions may have been at least partially responsible for speeding Mozart to an early grave.

When Beethoven arrived in Vienna in the late autumn of 1792 to study with Haydn, the young composer rapidly came under the wing of Prince Carl Lichnowsky, with whom he was soon staying in the Alserstrasse. There he met all Haydn's patrons and all Lichnowsky's friends and relations, so that by 1795, when he published his piano trios, Opus I, Beethoven's subscription list was already very impressive, including as it did the cream of Austrian and Hungarian society.[12]

This society, it seems quite clear, was ready and willing to make amends for their collective guilt about Mozart's decline and fall. They were, in fact, determined not to make the same ghastly mistake with Beethoven, whose situation was economically fragile and who was moreover an orphan in need of a loving family. The Lichnowskys valiantly attempted to be that family; they suffered Beethoven's eccentricities and even rudeness, and they provided moral and economic support in large measure. They provided all the things that they had neglected to do in the case of Mozart, and it must be said that, shabby as was their treatment of the latter, their treatment of Beethoven was magnanimous, as was that of many other members of the nobility. (They were also devoted to the aging Haydn the doyen of Viennese music, and covered him with love and honour, as witness the fervent, ecstatic applause that greeted *The Creation* in 1798 and, in public, in 1799.)

If there is any moral to this rather sinister affair of Lichnowsky's lawsuit against Mozart three weeks before his death, it lies in the history of Beethoven's career in Vienna as the eighteenth century waned: perhaps, if Viennese society had not felt the spectre of Mozart's death at their shoulders, they would not have exerted themselves to the extent they did for the young man from Bonn.

The Empress Maria Luisa and 'Una porcheria tedesca'

After the first performance of *La clemenza di Tito* as the coronation opera in Prague on 6 September 1791, the Empress Maria Luisa is reported to have called the work 'una porcheria tedesca' (a German swinishness). There is no contemporary account of her using these words, nor in fact was any mention of such a criticism made before 1871.[13] To dismiss the remark as apocryphal, however, does not mean that there is no truth at all in the Empress's opinion of the work. In the fourth volume of Otto Jahn's famous biography of Mozart, which appeared in 1859, the author states: 'The Empress is said to have expressed herself very disdainfully concerning the "porcheria" of German music; and it is certain that the first performance of "Titus" was far from being a success.'[14] In *1791, Mozart's Last Year*, I have attempted to cite contemporary documents showing that after the first performance the theatre for *Tito* was half-empty, and also to show that the Court had been against the project from the very beginning ('a *strongly* preconceived aversion to Mozart's composition').[15] On the other hand, there is no doubt that both the Emperor Leopold II and his consort loved Italian opera, and *opera seria* in particular. There is also no doubt that they, although only recently arrived in the Austrian capital, gauged the musical climate of the opera house to perfection: their first major commission was Domenico Cimarosa's comic opera *Il matrimonio segreto*, which was first performed in February 1792, two months after Mozart's death, and thereafter proved to be the greatest success in the history of opera in Vienna to date. It is quite clear that Cimarosa achieved a success far beyond anything that Mozart had ever enjoyed in any opera house. And this was the kind of music that their majesties truly appreciated. It should neither surprise nor shock us.

It is, however, interesting that a recently discovered document confirms that the Empress Maria Luisa did indeed have a jaundiced view of *La clemenza di Tito*. The day after the première, i.e. on 7 September 1791, she wrote to her daughter-in-law Maria Theresa de Bourbon as follows:[16]

> ... au soir au Theatre la grande opera n'est pas grande chose et la musique très mauvaise ainsi nous y avons presque tous dormi. Le Couronnement est allé a merveille. ('... in the evening to the theatre. The grand opera is nothing special and the music is very bad, in fact we almost all fell asleep. The coronation went famously.')

It is astonishing that an authentic document such as this should be rediscovered after two hundred years. Its survival in a Vienna archive shows that, even now, Mozart research is far from exhausted, and its content tends to confirm that, as I have attempted to show above, Mozart's position at Court was perhaps more precarious than he realized. The Lichnowsky lawsuit certainly arrived at a very critical juncture, not only in respect of Mozart's own life but also of his reputation in the eyes of Leopold II and Maria Luisa.

The dating of the Piano Concerto (K.595)

Mozart completed the Piano Concerto (K.595), and entered the work in his thematic catalogue (*Verzeichnüß*) on 5 January 1791, but it has now been suggested that (on the basis of the paper analyses by Alan Tyson) he had begun it several years before, probably in 1788.[17] The reason why Mozart needed the work in January, rather than for his own concert including the work in March, has to do with the arrival of the King and Queen of Naples for a state visit to Vienna. In the course of that visit Mozart's star piano pupil Babette Ployer seems to have played it on 9 January (and perhaps also on 12 or 17 January) before their Neapolitan Majesties. Count Carl von Zinzendorf's diary for 9 January reads: 'Aujourd'hui les Maj. Nap. sont chez le Pce: Adam Auersperg, le roi chantera et Mlle: Ployer jouera du clavessin'. ('Today their Nap. Maj. are invited to the house of Prince Adam Auersperg, the King will sing and Mademoiselle Ployer will play the harpsichord.') A similar concert was given on the 12th at Prince Kinsky's and on the 17th at Prince Auersperg's.[18]

It is pleasant to record that scientific analysis of another contemporary document could be used to help solve a Mozart puzzle which had baffled scholars for some time.

A description of Mozart's apartment in the Rauhensteingasse

The long and detailed report which follows originally appeared in the *Wienerbote*, Beilage zu den Sonntagsblättern, 1848, No. 3. Sonntagsskizze von J. P. Lyser, entitled 'Das Mozart-Haus in Wien'. In translation it reads:

> The house in which Mozart last lived, where he composed *Die Zauberflöte*, *Titus* and the Requiem, and where he died, was bought up in 1847, together with two adjacent houses, by a rich speculator, to make room for a big apartment block. The house, situated in the Rauhensteingasse, could – just like the houses of Shakespeare and Dürer – have outlasted the centuries, and it appears strange indeed that it was just at this moment that the poor little town of Weimar bought Schiller's house for five times its real value, and the whole of England contributed

large sums of money to buy Shakespeare's house in order to preserve it as a national monument.

The last owner of the Mozart house, who also lived in the same flat as Mozart on the first floor at the front wing of the building, was called Mr Dewaldt. Mr Dewaldt was kind enough to allow me to sketch all the rooms; he himself was my guide and he told me many interesting things which he had heard from Mozart's eldest son Karl when he was last in Vienna. The house was nearly in the middle of the Rauhensteingasse – towards the side of the exchange building – in front of the old *Stadthaus* called the *Golden ABC*, the third in the row and with a sharp protruding corner in the direction of the Himmelpfortgasse. J. N. Vogel had mistakenly published in his *Volkskalender* of 1843 the house preceding the one in which Mozart actually lived; Mozart lived neither in that *Marienhaus* nor in the *Golden ABC*, as is often stated.

Entering through the main door, decorated in the rococo style, into the front wing of the house, one found – a few steps to the right – a small winding staircase leading to the first floor; immediately on the first floor to the right was a door which opened into a dark, small entrée; opposite that door was the kitchen and to the left the large, dark bedroom which gained its light through a single window. Opposite this door was another leading to the visitor's room; this room had two windows on the Rauhensteingasse and a third one towards the Himmelpfortgasse. There was the desk at which he wrote the last bars of his Requiem; a few steps away, against the same wall, the bed in which he died; formerly a beautiful pianoforte, a gift of his friend Streicher, had stood there. In the middle of the wall *vis-à-vis* was another door leading to the billiard room – two windows wide – and from there one reached the *Kabinett* (a small room), where Mozart composed *Die Zauberflöte* and *Titus*; this room had light through one window: a papered wall-cabinet, a sofa, Mozart's desk and the little, old and famous *Spinett* (clavichord) which is now in the possession of the Mozarteum in Salzburg. Mozart never used another instrument when he composed, even though he owned several beautiful concert grands. From that study a door opposite the window led into a second anteroom from which one again reached the entrée. Opposite that exit was the staircase to the second floor. The anteroom gained its light, as was also the case with the bedroom, through a window which opened onto the courtyard. The entrée was illuminated by a big, round, curved window. The bedroom had, a few feet away from the window, a glass door, through which one reached a small corridor, used by Mozart as a walk-in closet; from there one arrived in the billiard room through a door opposite the windows. In the corridor Mozart's corpse was laid out until the 6th of December, the day of his funeral.

The apartment was very friendly and cheerful; Mr Dewaldt had kept the colour scheme of the rooms as they had been during Mozart's time; only the billiard table was missing, because in Mozart's last days the billiard room served as a bedroom. At the same spot where Mozart's piano and later his deathbed had been was now Mme Dewaldt's piano; all in all, the distribution of the furniture in the flat looked so suitable that no other arrangement seemed possible, which for someone drawing Mozart's apartment was of great use.

Although this description of Mozart's last apartment was written after the house had been structurally altered (see *1791, Mozart's Last Year*, p. 206), it is nevertheless worthwhile having this report. Some of the details must have corresponded to the structure as Mozart had known it.

Abbreviations of Bibliographical sources

AMZ *Allgemeine Musikalische Zeitung,* Leipzig, 1798 *et seq.*

Deutsch, Dokumente *Mozart: Die Dokumente seines Lebens,* ed. Otto Erich Deutsch, Kassel etc., 1961. Vol II, 'Addenda und Corrigenda', ed. Joseph Heinz Eibl, Kassel etc. 1978

Köchel Ludwig, Ritter von Köchel, *Chronologisch-thematisches Verzeichnis sämtlicher Tonwerke Wolfgang Amadé Mozarts ...,* Leipzig 1862; 8th rev. ed., Wiesbaden 1983. References to works by Mozart occurring in the text and in the notes on the text generally include the original numbers in the Köchel listing and, wherever appropriate, revised numbers (shown in parentheses).

Landon, Beethoven H.C. Robbins Landon, *Beethoven: a documentary study,* London and New York 1970.

Landon, Haydn: Chronicle and Works H.C. Robbins Landon, *Haydn: Chronicle and Works* (5 vols.), London and Bloomington, Ind.: *Haydn: The Early Years, 1732–1765* (1980); *Haydn at Eszterháza, 1766–1790* (1978); *Haydn in England, 1791–1795* (1976); *Haydn: the Years of 'The Creation', 1796–1800* (1977); *Haydn: the Late Years, 1801–1809* (1977)

Landon, Mozart and Vienna H.C. Robbins Landon, *Mozart and Vienna,* London and New York, 1991

Landon, 1791 H.C. Robbins Landon, *1791: Mozart's Last Year,* London and New York, 1988.

Mozart, Briefe *Mozart: Briefe und Aufzeichnungen,* ed.Wilhelm A. Bauer and Otto Eric Deutsch. Letters: 4 vols., Kassel etc., 1962–3. Commentary (ed. Joseph Heinz Eibl): 2 vols., Kassel etc., 1971. Indexes (ed. Eibl): 1 vol., Kassel etc., 1975.

The Mozart Compendium H.C. Robbins Landon (ed.), *The Mozart Compendium,* London and New York, 1990; reprinted 1991.

Nissen Georg Nikolaus Nissen, *Biographie W.A. Mozarts nach Originalbriefen,* Leipzig, 1828; facsimile reprint Hildesheim, 1972.

NMA *Neue Mozart-Ausgabe,* the collected edition of Mozart's works, Internationale Stiftung Mozarteum, Salzburg, Kassel 1955– (in progress).

Novello *A Mozart Pilgrimage, Being the Travel Diaries of Vincent and Mary Novello in the year 1829,* transcribed and compiled by Nerina Medici di Marignano, ed. Rosemary Hughes, London 1955.

Tyson 1987 Alan Tyson, *Mozart: Studies of the Autograph Sources,* Cambridge, Mass., and London 1987

Zaslaw Neal Zaslaw, *Mozart's Symphonies,* Oxford 1989

Notes on the text

IDOMENEO, RÈ DI CRETA (K.366)

1 *The Letters of Mozart and his Family … translated and edited … by Emily Anderson, 2nd ed. (revised by A. Hyatt King and Monica Carolan), London 1966, vol. II, pp. 659f. All other letters quoted from family correspondence are taken from the same source, by kind permission of the publisher, Macmillan Press Ltd.

2 — II, 661.
3 — II, 663.
4 — II, 664.
5 — II, 666f.
6 — II, 672.
7 — II, 674.
8 — II, 676f.
9 — II, 677.
10 — II, 681.
11 — II, 681.
12 — II, 683f.
13 — II, 684.
14 — II, 685.
15 — II, 687f.
16 — II, 692f.
17 — II, 697ff.
18 — II, 699ff.
19 — II, 701f.
20 — II, 704.
21 — II, 708.
22 Robert Münster, 'Mozarts Münchner Aufenthalt 1780/81 und die Uraufführung des "Idomeneo"', in *Wolfgang Amadeus Mozart: Idomeneo*, Munich-Zurich 1981, p. 97.

23 Like the C#″ in bars 11, 12 and 13 of the Aria, which contains more stopped notes of this kind.

24 *A Mozart Pilgrimage* transcribed and compiled by Nerina Medici di Marignano, edited by Rosemary Hughes, London 1955, pp. 76, 115.

25 Extract from notes for a recording of *Idomeneo* issued by Decca International, London, 1988.

MOZART'S INCIDENTAL MUSIC TO *THAMOS, KÖNIG IN ÄGYPTEN* (K.345)

1 [original footnote:] Herodotus in the second book, chapters 33, 34.

2 Wolfgang Plath, 'Beiträge zur Mozart-Autographie II: Schriftchronologie 1770–1780', *Mozart-Jahrbuch 1976/77*, Kassel 1978, esp. p. 173. Tyson 1987, pp. 24f.

3 Mozart *Briefe*, II, pp. 541ff.

4 *Briefe*, III, p. 3.

5 Deutsch, *Dokumente, Addenda & Corrigenda*, p. 64.

6 David Charlton, *Grétry & The Growth of Opéra-Comique*, Cambridge 1986, p. 144.

7 O. Jahn, *W. A. Mozart*, II. Theil, Leipzig 1856, p. 400. English version, vol. II, p. 115.

8 *Briefe*, III, p. 256.

9 For the use of No. 1 as 'Splendete te, Deus' conducted by Salieri during the 1791 Prague coronation ceremonies, see Landon, *1791*, pp. 104, 114. Copies in Mozart's possession: *NMA, Thamos*, p. VIII, also n. 15.

10 DGG Archiv 437556–2 (1993). Alastair Miles (bass), the Monteverdi Choir and the English Baroque Soloists.

MOZART AND PARIS

1 Joseph Haydn, *Thematisch-bibliographisches Werkverzeichnis, zusammengestellt von Anthony van Hoboken*, Band I, Mainz 1957, pp. 361 (quartets), 7 (symphony). Deutsch, *Dokumente*, pp. 30, 33.

2 Baron Grimm's description (letter to Leopold Mozart, 27 July 1778): '… peu actif, trop aisé à attraper, trop peu occupé des moyens, qui peuvent conduire à la fortune. Ici, pour percer, il faut être retors, entre-prenant, audacieux. Je lui voudrais pour sa fortune la moitié moins de talent et le double plus d'entregent, et je n'en serai pas embarassé. Au reste, il ne peut tenter ici deux chemins pour se faire un sort. Le premier c'est de donner des Leçons de Clavecin; mais sans compter qu'on n'a des écoliers qu'avec beaucoup d'activité et même de charlatanerie, je ne sais s'il aurait assez de Santé pour soutenir ce métier, car c'est une chose très fatigante de courir les quatre coins de Paris et de s'épuiser à parler pour montrer. Et puis ce métier ne lui plaira pas, parce qu'il l'empêchera d'écrire, ce qu'il aime par

dessus tout. Il pourrait donc s'y livrer tout à fait; mais en ce pays ci le gros du public ne se connaît pas en musique. On donne par conséquent tout aux noms, et le mérite de l'ouvrage ne peut être jugé que par un très petit nombre. Le public est dans ce moment si ridiculement partagé entre Piccinni et Gluck, et tous les raisonnements, qu'on entend sur la musique font pitié. Il est donc très difficile pour vôtre Fils de réussir entre ces deux partis …'

THE SYMPHONIES: A SURVEY

1 London concert announcements: O.E. Deutsch, *Mozart, a documentary biography*, London 1965, pp. 41, 44f.

2 Concerts in The Hague: Deutsch, op. cit., pp. 49f. (English translation by E. Blom, P. Branscombe and J. Noble).

3 Melchior Grimm, *Paris zündet die Lichter an*, Munich 1977, pp. 257–9.

4 A Latin document; see Deutsch, op. cit., pp. 94f.

5 According to Alan Tyson in Zaslaw, *Mozart's Symphonies*, p. 178.

6 Deutsch, op. cit., p. 139.

7 Ibid., p. 142.

8 For a discussion of this movement, see H.C. Robbins Landon, *Haydn at Eszterháza 1766–1790*, pp. 266, 393; also *Mozart and Vienna*, pp. 48ff.

9 *Neue Mozart-Ausgabe*: Kritische Berichte, Serie IV, Orchesterwerke, Werkgruppe II, Band 4 (Hermann Beck), Kassel 1963, pp. d/44f.

10 Zaslaw, op. cit., p. 293 (information from Alan Tyson).

11 Op. cit., p. 298.

12 *The Letters of Mozart and his Family* (trans. Emily Anderson), 2nd ed. 1966, II, pp. 557f. I believe the passage in the first movement, to which Mozart refers, was at bars 105–18 and in the recapitulation at bars 251–75.

13 Op. cit., p. 565.

14 Zaslaw, op. cit., p. 345.

15 Op. cit., p. 348.

16 This minuet was completed and a trio from another work by Mozart was added in a reconstruction by the present writer; it was first performed in 1981 by the Mozart Orchestra of Philadelphia conducted by Davis Jerome. The proposition that Mozart's Minuet in C (K.409) was added to this Symphony in Vienna is untenable because K.409 includes parts for two flutes, which instruments do not feature in the authentic sources for K.338.

17 Tyson, 1987, p. 140; see also Zaslaw, op. cit., p. 418.

18 Otto Biba, 'Grundzüge des Konzertwesens in Wien zu Mozarts Zeit', *Mozart-Jahrbuch 1978/9*, pp. 132ff. H.C. Robbins Landon, *Neue Mozart-Ausgabe*: Symphonies, vol. 9, Kassel, 1957, and Kritische Berichte, Serie IV, Orchesterwerke, Lieferung 4, Werkgruppe II, Sinfonien, Band 9, Kassel 1963; also *1791*, pp. 31–3. Zaslaw, op. cit., pp. 421ff.

19 The watermarks of these added clarinet and revised oboe parts are, however, partly the same as those of the paper used for the original autograph, which suggests a gap shorter than the period from summer 1788 to April 1791.

20 See *Neue Mozart-Ausgabe*: Kritische Berichte (op. cit.), pp. 267f. The Bärenreiter miniature score (Landon) also contains this revision, pp. 63f. The revision noted, which was evidently the result of external pressure, is not usually performed, but can be heard on the Oiseau Lyre recording conducted by Christopher Hogwood.

MOZART'S MASONIC MUSIC: A SURVEY

1 See *The Mozart Compendium*, p. 270, and, for a divergent account of the work's history by P.A. Autexier, pp. 132ff. Mozart entered the work under date 'July 1785', but the first registered performance was on 17 November. There is also some doubt as to the exact constitution of the added instruments, i.e. the horns might be substitutes for the basset horns. See Hans-Josef Irmen, *Mozart, Mitglied geheimer Gesellschaften*, Neustadt/Aisch, 1988, pp. 158ff. Irmen suggests the date 12 August 1785 for the work's first performance.

2 Not identical with, though similar to, the *Tonus Pellegrinus*. Mozart used that melody in the Requiem and also in the final chorus of *La Betulia liberata* (K.118 [74c]); it also figures in Michael Haydn's Requiem setting of 1771.

JOHANN MICHAEL HAYDN, MOZART AND THE VIOLIN DUOS (DUETS) K.423 AND 424

1 H. Jancik, *Michael Haydn, ein vergessener Meister*, Vienna 1952, pp. 37f. Landon, *Haydn the Early Years 1732–1765*, pp. 350ff., 381.

2 Mozart *Briefe* IV, 35.

3 H. Jancik, op. cit., pp. 134ff. Mozart *Briefe* II, 95ff.

4 *Briefe* II, 209ff., esp. 212.

5 *Briefe* II, 379ff., also II, 48.

6 *Briefe* II, 161.

7 *Briefe* II, 405 and esp. 406.

8 *Briefe* III, 258.

9 Briefe III, 295, 299.

10 For the latest research on the subject of Mozart's copies of Michael Haydn symphonies, see N. Zaslaw, *Mozart's Symphonies*, pp. 391ff.

11 Zaslaw, p. 392 (after information from Tyson).

12 A. Weinmann, *Vollständiges Verlags-verzeichnis Artaria & Comp.*, Vienna 1952, p. 17.

THE PIANO QUARTETS IN G MINOR (K.478) AND E FLAT MAJOR (K.493)

1 Nissen, p. 633.

2 II, 157ff.

3 *Mozart, His Character, His Work*, London 1946, p. 265.

THE HAYDN BROTHERS (MICHAEL AND JOSEPH) AND MOZART'S STRING QUINTETS

1 G.C. Ferrari, *Aneddoti piacevoli e interessanti, Occorsi nella vita di ...* (2 vols., London 1830).

2 H. Abert, *W. A. Mozart*, 7th edition, Leipzig 1955, vol. I, p. 326. It is one of the tragedies of music publishing that the greatest Mozart biography ever written has never been translated into English.

3 *Mozart ...*, p. 191.

4 *A Mozart Companion*, edited by D. Mitchell and H.C. Robbins Landon, New York 1956, p. 74.

5 Einstein, op. cit, p. 206.

6 *A Mozart Pilgrimage* (travel diaries of Vincent Novello and his wife Mary), ed. Rosemary Hughes, London 1955, pp. 170ff., 347.

7 *A Mozart Companion* (op. cit.), p. 132.

8 *The Classical Style*, London and New York 1971, p. 286.

9 The volume consists of:

(1) 'Quintetto / a / 2 Violini / 2 Viole / e / Violoncello / Del Sigre L. van Beethoven' (later: owner's name 'IOS REICH'), which is an arrangement of Beethoven's Septet Op. 20 on 4° paper with 14 lines, watermarks 'AM' and three half moons of declining size.

(2) 'Grand / Quintetto / per / due Violini due Viole / e / Violoncello / Del Sigre Mozart', an arrangement of the Clarinet Quintet K.581. 4° paper, 12 staves, watermarks: 'W' in ornate coat-of-arms, single half moon.

(3) 'Quintetto in D / à / 2 Violini / 2 Viole / e / Violoncello / Di W. A. Mozart' (later: 'N° 4'). 4° paper, 10 staves, letters 'A' over 'REAL', 3 stars in baroque ornament. K. 593.

(4) 'N° 1° / Quintetto in C / á / 2 Violini / 2 Viole / e / Violoncello / Del Sigre W. A. Mozart'. 4° paper, 12 staves, letters 'A' over 'HF' over 'REAL', 3 stars in baroque ornament. K. 515.

10 Rosen, op. cit., p. 286.

11 From the authentic biography of Haydn by A.C. Dies, 1810. See Landon, *Haydn: Chronicle and Works, Haydn at Eszterháza 1766–1790*, p. 754.

12 Rosen, op. cit., p. 287.

SACRED VOCAL WORKS: ORATORIOS AND LATIN CHURCH MUSIC

1 *Briefe* I, 428: 'Fratanto sta componendo il mio figlio un Oratorio di Metastasio per Padua ordinato del Sgr. Don Giuseppe Ximenes de PPi [=Principi] d'Aragona, quest'oratorio mandero, passando per Verona, à Padua per essere copiato, e ritornando da Milano anderemo à Padua per sentirne la Prova'.

2 *Briefe* III, 319.

3 *Briefe* IV, 178.

4 The author formerly owned a score (copied in Rome by the copyist of the Teatro Alla Valle), in which the timpani part was entirely absent. Haydn's drum parts in his Oratorio *Il ritorno di Tobia* were quietly omitted from the score when the work was performed in Rome in the 1780s.

5 *A Mozart Pilgrimage*, p. 158.

6 'Beiträge zur Mozart-Autographie I: Die Handschrift Leopold Mozarts', in *Mozart-Jahrbuch 1960/1*, pp. 82–117; and 'Beiträge zur Mozart-Autographie II: Schriftchronologie 1770–1780', in *Mozart-Jahrbuch 1976/7*.

7 Cliff Eisen, pp. 171ff.

8 'The Mozart Fragments in the Mozarteum, Salzburg: A Preliminary Study of their Chronology and their Significance', in *Journal of the American Musicological Society* 34 (1981), pp. 471–510; and *Mozart: Studies of the Autograph Scores*, 1987.

9 For a résumé, see the author's *Mozart and Vienna*, London 1991, pp. 22ff., esp. pp. 28–32.

10 *Briefe* I, 285.

11 *Briefe* I, 287ff.

12 Tyson 1987 (op. cit.), pp. 100f.

13 The number of this Sony compact disc issued in 1994 is SK 53 368. *Missa* 'Suna bona mixta malis' (XXII:2); Offertorium 'Non nobis, Domine' (XXIIIa:1); *Ave Regina* (XXIIIb:3), *Responsoria de Venerabili* (XXIIIc:4a–d); *Responsoria ad absolutionem* (XXIIb:1); *Salve Regina* (XXIIIb:1); *Missa brevis Sancti Joannis de Deo* (XXII:7). Marie-Claude Vallin (S), Ann Monoyois (S), Tölzer Knabenchor, L'Archibudelli, Tafelmusik, conducted by Bruno Weil. The *Missa* 'Sunt bona mixta malis' is published by Mario Bois, Paris; the other works are published by Doblinger (*Salve Regina* and 'Non nobis, Domine'), Universal Edition ('Libera me') and Henle.

14 *Briefe* I, 532.

15 *Briefe* I, 532f.

16 Deutsch, *Dokumente*, p. 123.

17 'Studien zu W.A. Mozarts kirchenmusikalischen Jugendwerken' in *Zeitschrift für Musikwissenschaft* III (1920), pp. 354f.

18 *Briefe* I, 532.

19 *Mozart, His Character, His Work*, London 1946, p. 327.

20 See Landon, *Haydn: Chronicle and Works: Haydn in England 1791–1795*, pp. 266ff.

21 *Wolfgang Amadeus Mozart, Sa Vie Musicale et Son Œuvre*, vol. I in the Laffont edition, Paris 1986, pp. 734ff.

22 *Briefe* II, 505ff., esp. p. 506.

23 *The Mozart Compendium*, p. 312.

24 'Über Skizzen zu Mozarts "Requiem"', in *Bericht über den Internationalen Musikwissenschaftlichen Kongreß Kassel 1962*, Kassel

1963, pp. 184–7. The sketch-leaf, in the Berlin State Library, is reproduced in facsimile, and transcribed, in the *NMA* edition of the Requiem, pp. 60f.

25 Abbé Stadler reports that 'The widow [Mozart] told me that there were a few scraps of paper [*Zettelchen*] with the music found on Mozart's writing desk, which she gave to Herr Süssmayr. What they contained, and what use Süssmayr made of them, she could not say.' (*NMA* edition, p. IX, n. 13).

26 Plath, op. cit., p. 187.

The Requiem (K.626)

1 Deutsch, *Dokumente*, p. 494.

2 F.X. Niemetschek, *Leben des K.K. Kapellmeisters Wolfgang Gottlieb Mozart*; modern edition in *Staackmanns Almanach 1942*, Leipzig 1942, pp. 45f.

3 Extracts published anonymously in the *Allgemeine Musikalische Zeitung*, Leipzig, 1798-9; the extract quoted is taken from cols. 149–51.

4 O.E. Deutsch, 'Der graue Bote', *Mitteilungen der Internationalen Stiftung Mozarteum*, August 1963, pp. 1–3; complete report first published by Deutsch in *Österreichische Musikzeitschrift* 19 (1964), Heft 2, pp. 49–60.

5 Walther Brauneis, 'Exequien für Mozart: Archivfund über das Seelenamt für W.A. Mozart am 1 0. Dezember 1791 in der Wiener Michaelerkirche', *Singende Kirche* XXXVII/1 (1991), pp. 8ff.

6 L. Nowak, 'Wer hat die Instrumentalstimmen in der Kyrie-Fuge des Requiems von W.A. Mozart geschrieben?', *Mozart-Jahrbuch 1973/4*, Salzburg 1975, pp. 191–201.

7 Facsimile of one page facing p. 151 in I. Kecskeméti, 'Beiträge zur Geschichte von Mozarts Requiem', *Studia Musicologica* I, Facs. 1–2 (1961), pp. 147ff.

8 Mozart, *Briefe*, IV, pp. 491f.

9 J. Dalchow, G. Duda and D. Kerner, *Mozarts Tod 1791–1971*, Pähl 1971, pp. 90f. (with facsimile).

10 Karl Pfannhauser, 'Epilegomena Mozartiana', *Mozart-Jahrbuch 1971/2*, Salzburg 1973, p. 276.

11 *Wolfgang Amadeus Mozart: Requiem KV 626, Vollständige Faksimile-Ausgabe im Originalformat der Originalhandschrift in zwei Teilen nach Mus. Hs. 17.561 der Musiksammlung der Österreichischen Nationalbibliothek, Herausgegeben und Kommentiert von Günter Brosche*, Graz und Kassel, etc., 1990. Foreword and commentary in German and English.

12 *Wolfgang Amadeus Mozart: Neue Ausgabe sämtlicher Werke*, Serie X, Supplement, Werkgruppe 30, Band 2: *Barbara Ployers und Franz Jakob Freystädtlers Theorie- und Kompositionsstudien bei Mozart, vorgelegt von Hellmut Federhofer und Alfred Mann*, Bärenreiter, Kassel, etc., 1989, p. 9 (with facsimile facing).

13 The sketch was first identified by Wolfgang Plath, 'Über Skizzen zu Mozarts "Requiem"', *Bericht über den Internationalen Musikwissenschaftlichen Kongreß Kassel 1962*, Kassel etc., 1963, pp. 184–7. For the redating of the so-called 'Munich' Kyrie, see H.C. Robbins Landon,

1791, pp. 49, 54; for a contrary opinion, see *The Mozart Compendium*, p. 312 (John Arthur). A facsimile of the Amen fugue in question appears in *Wolfgang Amadeus Mozart, Neue Ausgabe Sämtlicher Werke, Serie I, Geistliche Gesangswerke, Werkgruppe I: Messen und Requiem, Abteilung 2, Requiem, Teilband 1, Mozarts Fragment, vorgelegt von Leopold Nowak*, Bärenreiter, Kassel, etc., 1965, p. 60, with transcription on p. 61.

14 Possibly a discarded idea for *Die Zauberflöte*.

15 J.A. André's note: 'Gegenwärtige Abschrift des betreffenden Theiles von Mozarts Requiem, ist Note um Note, und Blatt um Blatt, ganz genau nach dem Mozart'schen Manuscript durch meinen verehrten Freund Herrn Abbé Stadler für mich gefertigt worden. André.'

16 The first editions in print are:

(1) Score, Breitkopf & Härtel, Leipzig, 1800 (with Latin and German text): 'W.A. Mozarti = Missa pro Defunctis / Requiem / W.A. Mozarts / Seelenmesse / mit / unterlegtem deutschem Texte / Im Verlage der Breitkopf & Härtelschen Musikhandlung / in Leipzig.' The publication, dedicated to the Elector of Saxony, was announced in the *AMZ* in December 1799 and published in June 1800. Copy in the Gesellschaft der Musikfreunde, Vienna, I. 1704 (Q 285). In this first edition there are textual changes which are not authentic, i.e. the famous trombone solo in the 'Tuba mirum' is replaced by a bassoon, and there are numerous printers' errors throughout.

(2) Parts, published in 1812 by the Chemische Druckerey, Vienna. The instrumental parts bear the publisher's number 1806 and the vocal parts the number 1812. Copy in the Gesellschaft der Musikfreunde, Vienna. 'Requiem / a / Canto, Alto, Tenore et Basso / II Violini, / II Fagotti, / II Corni di Bassetto o Clarinetti, / III Tromboni, / II Clarini et Timpani, / Viola, Basso e Violoncello / con Organo. / Authore. / W:A: MOZART / Vienna / Nel Magazino C: R: pr: Stamperie chimica sul Graben No 612 / No 1806. 37 bö. Pr: '. 4° format, twenty-one parts comprising a total of 74 sheets.

A DOCUMENT DETAILING MOZART'S INCOME AND EXPENSES (1786 OR 1787?)

1 Mozart *Briefe*, IV, p. 174, No. 1203 (7), also VI, p. 429.

2 Tyson 1987, p. 141.

3 Siegfried Becher, *Das österreichische Münzwesen vom Jahre 1524 bis 1838 in historischer, statistischer und legislativer Hinsicht*. Zweiter Band, Legislativer Theil, Vienna 1838, pp. 333f. and 345 (footnote from the Braunbehrens-Drüner article). Concerning the 'Wiener-Stadt-Banco-Zettel', first introduced in 1762, these had existed in seven denominations ranging from 5 to 1,000 florins since 1 November 1784; see Albert Pick and Rudolf Richter, *Papiergeld – Spezialkatalog Österreich 1759–1986*, Vienna 1986, pp. 16–22, esp. 18 (footnote from Ulrich Konrad's article, see pp. 213f.).

4 Deutsch, *Dokumente*, p. 266.

5 Op. cit., p. 264.

6 See *The Mozart Compendium*, p. 133, 'July' 1785. A similar example of a Masonic setting is 'Zeifließet heut', geliebte Brüder' (K.483); see pp. 118f.

SOME RECENTLY DISCOVERED DOCUMENTS CONCERNING MOZART'S LAST YEAR

1 The court record was located by the director of the Hofkammer-Archiv, Hofrat Dr Gottfried Mraz; Walther Brauneis published it in 1991 in the July issue of *Mitteilungen der Internationalen Stiftung Mozarteum*, Salzburg, and in *Zaubertöne, Mozart in Wien*, Catalogue of the Historisches Museum der Stadt Wien, 6 December 1990–15 September 1991, Vienna 1990, p. 399.

2 Mozart *Briefe*, pp. 88ff., translation from Landon, *Mozart, The Golden Years, 1781–1791*, London and New York, 1989, p. 208.

3 Landon, *Beethoven*, pp. 64f. (after Kerst I, p. 24)

4 Op. cit., p. 65 (after Czerny II); Wenzel Krumpholz (1750–1817), was a violinist at the Court Opera, Vienna, and a composer.

5 Op. cit., p. 66 (after F. G. Wegeler and F. Ries, *Biographische Notizen über Beethoven*, Coblenz 1838.

6 Op. cit., pp. 209f; Max Ring, *Erinnerungen*, Berlin 1898, p. 24; Weiser's account in T. von Frimmel, *Ludwig van Beethoven* (4th ed.), Berlin 1924, p. 44.

7 Landon, *Beethoven*, p. 67.

8 For Mozart's salary, taxes, etc., see Landon, *1791*, p. 221.

9 For Mozart and Tost, see Landon *1791*, pp. 35f.

10 *The Prince Lichnowsky Newsletter* 'Our Motto: All the News that fits the Prince', Hochbruck 1, St Anton/Jessnitz, Austria, starting in August 1991.

11 See Landon *1791*, pp. 90f.

12 For Beethoven's subscription list, see Landon, *Beethoven*, pp. 64f.

13 John A. Rice, *W. A. Mozart. La clemenza di Tito*, Cambridge 1991, p. 64. The quotation comes from Alfred Meissner's *Rococobilder*, Gumbinnen 1871, p. 141. See also J. H. Eibl, "Una porcheria tedesca?" Zur Uraufführung von Mozarts "La clemenza di Tito"', in *Österreichische Musikzeitung* 31 (1976).

14 *Life of Mozart* by Otto Jahn; translation from the German by Pauline D. Townsend (3 vols.), vol. III (Kalmus reprint), p. 289.

15 Landon, *1791*, pp. 116–18.

16 This discovery, made by John A. Rice, is discussed in his above-cited book (note 3), pp. 64, 165. The document is preserved in the Haus-, Hof- und Staatsarchiv, Vienna, Sammelbände, Karton 52.

17 For details see Landon *1791*, p. 34.

18 Dexter Edge in *The Haydn Yearbook* XVII (1992), p. 159.

Acknowledgments

Four of the essays included in this volume are original texts, not previously published. These are: 'Mozart's incidental music to *Thamos, König in Ägypten* (K.345)'; 'Sacred vocal works: oratorios and Latin church music'; 'A document detailing Mozart's income and expenses (1786/1787?)'; and 'Some recently discovered documents concerning Mozart's last year'. The remaining essays, revised as necessary, were originally published in a variety of contexts. The brief details in each case are:

'Salzburg in 1756: the world into which Mozart was born' – *The Sunday Times*, London, 1991

'*Idomeneo, rè di Creta* (K.366)' – The Monteverdi Choir (John Eliot Gardiner), Mozart Festival, London, 1990

'*Die Zauberflöte* (K.620)' – recording by Decca International, 1990

'The Symphonies: a survey' – from Robert Layton (ed.), *A Companion to the Symphony*, Simon and Schuster, New York and London, 1993, by permission

'Mozart's Masonic music: a survey' – recording by Decca International, 1969, expanded 1994; English versions of Masonic texts, translated by Peggy Cochrane, used by kind permission of Decca

'Mozart and Paris' – from exhibition catalogue *Mozart à Paris*, Musée Carnavalet, Paris 1991 (Nicole Salinger, H.C. Robbins Landon)

'Johann Michael Haydn, Mozart and the Duos (Duets) for Violin and Viola (K.423 and 424)' – Time-Life Records 1980; expanded 1994

'The Piano Quartets in G minor (K.478) and in E flat (K.493)' – Time-Life Records, 1980

'The Haydn Brothers (Michael and Joseph) and Mozart's String Quintets' – Time-Life Records, 1980; expanded 1994

'The Requiem: its history and textual problems' – foreword to the new edition (H.C. Robbins Landon) of the Requiem published by Breitkopf & Härtel, Leipzig, 1993

Index